Fool's Gold

A History of British Saffron

Fool's Gold

A History of British Saffron

Sam Bilton

PROSPECT BOOKS
2022

This edition published in 2022 in Great Britain and the USA by Prospect Books at 26 Parke Road, London, SW13 9NG.

Text © 2022 Sam Bilton.
Photographs © 2022 Sam Bilton.

The author, Sam Bilton, asserts her right to be identified as the author of this work in accordance with the Copyright, Designs & Patents Act 1988.

British Library Cataloguing in Publication Data:
A catalogue entry for this book is available from the British Library.

No part of this publication may be reproduced, stored in a retrieval system or transmitted in any form or by any means, electronic, mechanical, photocopying, recording or otherwise, without the prior permission of the copyright holders.

ISBN 978-1-909248-74-8

Set in Adobe Garamond Pro and Cochin by Catheryn Kilgarriff and Brendan King.

Printed by the Gutenberg Press Ltd., Malta.

Contents

Part I: The Story of Saffron

11
Introduction
Why is British Saffron Special?

21
Chapter One
Saffron's Journey to Britain

35
Chapter Two
Saffron Cultivation: The Right Location

53
Chapter Three
Saffron Cultivation: Planting & Harvesting

67
Chapter Four
Saffron as a Medicinal Ingredient

79
Chapter Five
Saffron in the Kitchen

95
Chapter Six
The Decline and Revival of Saffron Production in Britain

Part II: The Recipes

109
Introduction

113
Meat

135
Baking

161
Ango-Indian

181
Fish

201
Poultry & Game

219
Dessert

245
Vegetarian

263
Drinks

273
Miscellaneous

281
Acknowledgements & Picture Credits

283
Notes

293
Bibliography

301
Recipe Index

302
General Index

To Mum and Dad

Freshly dried saffron

Part I

The Story of Saffron

Saffron Corms

Introduction

Whichever Greek myth you subscribe to, the mortal Crocus seems like an unfortunate fellow.

The Greek physician and philosopher Aelius Galenus (better known by his anglicised name Galen) favoured the tale of Crocus' ill-fated relationship with the god Hermes, son of Zeus. Hermes was a deity of many talents. He is probably best known as the messenger of the gods. He was the god of herdsmen and shepherds, favoured by both merchants and thieves (which given that Hermes had stolen a herd of cows from Apollo seems at odds with the former role as god of animal husbandry), as well as being a gifted musician and athlete. Which brings us back to Crocus.[1]

Crocus and Hermes were playing a game of quoits (a ring of iron, rope, or rubber thrown in a game to encircle or land as near as possible to an upright peg). Perhaps the game was not going Hermes' way and in a fit of ire he threw the quoit in a haphazard manner. Maybe Crocus was just in the wrong place at the wrong time. Either way, one of Hermes' quoits accidentally struck Crocus on the head, killing him outright. Crocus' blood seeped into the ground and soon after a beautiful purple flower appeared containing three crimson threads (often referred to in later centuries as 'chives'). Some writers have said the distraught god turned Crocus' actual body into the flower. The flower was given the name Crocus (krokos in Greek) and those threads would become one of the most treasured spices in world – saffron.[2]

A less gruesome story surrounding the legend of the origins of saffron focuses on the love affair (or not, depending on which author you read) between Crocus and the nymph Smilax.

In his book *The Compleat Florist* (1706), Louis Liger recounts the fable of a talented young man with 'a Genius for Gallantry and Amours', and a penchant for the ladies: 'All Company was to him insipid, without the Fair Sex had a Share in it.' He meets Smilax at a festival and is immediately smitten with her. She is equally taken with Crocus. However, so intense are their feelings for each other that 'in a few days their mutual Flame became so violent, that both the Lovers pined to Death'. Liger concludes the fable with this moral:

> When Love has got the Mastery of one's Heart, the Heart knowing no other Felicity but what lies in that Passion, is entirely led by it, and digs its own Grave in what it took to be its sovereign Good. You Lovers, that are passionate to excess, 'tis you that the sense of the Fable points to; with a little more Moderation in your Transports, you would readily avoid this Rock.[3]

Another telling of this myth has an indecisive Smilax prevaricating over whether to take Crocus as a lover much to the irritation of the gods. Sometimes it is Crocus who is indifferent to Smilax's charms.

Whichever account you read, the outcome for both protagonists is the same. As the first century poet Ovid puts it in *Metamorphoses*, Crocus and Smilax are 'turn'd to flow'rs'.[4] Crocus becomes a splendid purple bloom and Smilax is transformed into a thorny climbing plant that bears her name today, more commonly known as a greenbrier (other versions see the nymph transformed into a yew tree). Some varieties of smilax are aromatic and are used to flavour the soft drink sarsaparilla.

So, was it a blessing or a curse to be turned into a flower by the gods?

Introduction

One view is that the lovers were transformed to enable them to remain together for eternity. However, as Peter Bernhardt points out, as plants, crocus and smilax thrive in entirely different situations. The crocus prefers open, dry sunny sites whereas smilax is happiest in the deep, damp shade of a forest. So it seems unlikely that the pair would meet again in the world of flora.[5]

As entertaining as these stories are, the clergyman William Harrison noted in Holinshed's *Chronicles of England, Scotland and Ireland* (1577) that the saffron crocus, or *Crocus sativus* to give it its botanical name, had been growing in the ancient world long before the myths of Hermes and Smilax came to the fore.[6] But however the saffron crocus came into being it has been, and continues to be, prized for the precious spice it produces. If cacao was considered to be the 'food of the gods' by the eighteenth century Swedish botanist, Carl Linnaeus, then saffron is nectar for us mere mortals who covet it for its aroma and vibrancy.

You could say that saffron is in my genes. I was born in Essex, albeit in Harlow, but my parents are both from Thaxted, a village situated a few miles from Saffron Walden. During my lifetime I have been a frequent visitor to this town. That a town in England should carry the name of one of the most alluring spices in the world has always intrigued me. When I discovered later in life that saffron had actually been grown there in centuries gone by, I was filled with questions. Where did this spice originally come from? How did it find its way to the Essex countryside? Why did we grow it, and what exactly did we use it for?

Spices like cinnamon and cloves are grown in far flung destinations like Sri Lanka or Indonesia, but saffron seems to have originated a little closer to home. In 1629-7 BCE the Greek island of Thera, today known as Santorini, was destroyed by a volcanic eruption. Vast plumes of volcanic ash enveloped the island and buried the town of Akrotiri. While clearly devastating for the inhabitants, the ash preserved many fine frescoes. Among these, there is a fresco which shows girls picking flowers that resemble crocuses, in a rocky landscape. One of the girls certainly looks like she is delicately plucking something from within the flower. This has been interpreted as the harvesting of saffron. Baskets of the flowers are depicted being offered to a goddess, illustrating its value in Aegean religion. While this does not categorically point to the plants being cultivated, the number and the uniform way in which the flowers are depicted on the fresco suggests planting by humans rather than the random dispersal one usually sees in nature.[7]

Botanist and saffron grower Dr Sally Francis explains that *Crocus sativus* is closely related to *Crocus cartwrightianus*, which grows wild in Greece, the Cycladic Islands and Crete. Both crocuses produce purple flowers which contain three vivid orange threads. These threads are the female part of the flower and are often referred to as the dried stigmas or style branches. However, the stigmas of *Crocus cartwrightianus* are much smaller than those of *Crocus sativus*, so are too insignificant when dried to be used commercially as true saffron (although some local people still do dry this type for their own use). The meadow crocus (*Colchicum autumnal*) also has purple petals but lacks the bright red stigmas of *Crocus sativus*. This is an entirely different species of plant and is poisonous if consumed. Although it has been used medicinally in the past to treat things like gout or rheumatic pain, herbalist Hilda Leyel says 'though it cures quickly, the disease is apt to recur with greater violence'. The French call the meadow crocus 'mort aux chiens' which really says it all.[8]

It is believed *Crocus sativus* developed from a natural genetic mutation of *Crocus cartwrightianus*. This caused the stigmas in one flower to become much larger than in other crocuses. The longer stamens were spotted by a keen-eyed farmer who purposefully propagated the bulb or corm, effectively forming the foundation stock of the crop. As a result, all of the saffron grown today around the world is thought to have descended from this one exceptional plant.[9]

Crocus sativus is a perennial bulb that flowers each season for a number of years. Unlike many other members of the crocus family which flower in the spring, *Crocus sativus* blooms for a brief period in early autumn (late September to October). The thin, short, grass-like leaves that

Introduction

Colchicum autumnale *or meadow saffron is extremely toxic. It is easily distinguished from* Crocus sativus *as it lacks the bright red stigmas.*

emerge first are an understated herald for what will follow. Six lilac petals appear soon after which open to reveal three pendulous vermilion threads (occasionally more petals and threads are produced). In the Swiss village of Mund, flowers containing more than three threads are known as a 'Princess', 'Queen' or 'Empress' (according to whether they contain four, five or six threads). Although the flowers are scented

Pea Tarts with Saffron

(a rare quality for a member of the crocus family) it is only after the threads have been dried that the characteristic aroma develops. *Crocus sativus* cannot be grown from seed but each year the 'mother' corm produces up to six daughter corms. This process continues each year until the ground becomes overcrowded and flowering declines. This is why saffron growers regularly lift, divide and replant their bulbs.[10]

Saffron has earned itself the reputation of being the world's most expensive spice. Around 150-200 flowers are required to produce just one gram of saffron. Due to the delicate nature of separating the threads from the flower it has to be picked by hand (a process which has remained unchanged for centuries). This has to be done quickly, while the blooms are in their prime, but also skilfully so as to ensure the threads are not damaged. As Francis highlights 'the economical valuable material (in this case, the saffron threads) expressed as a percentage of total plant weight, including the roots…is just 0.5%'. Which begs the question, why does anyone bother to grow saffron as a commercial crop?[11]

Spain and Iran are recognised as being the primary producers of saffron today. But English saffron once rivalled that of Spain or the Near East. How it arrived on our shores is something of a mystery. There are whispers of ancient travellers and pious smugglers, although the truth may forever be obscured by rumour and myth. For several centuries England supported a thriving saffron industry lending its name to Saffron Walden in Essex, a town once renowned for the cultivation of this spice, although the flower has flourished in other areas of the country too. By the nineteenth century, however, this industry had faded to a ghost of its former glory. In culinary terms the only legacy of our saffron obsession is the Cornish Saffron Bun or Cake. Saffron was also used as a dye in the textile industry, although I will leave this story to be told by another writer with the appropriate expertise. What follows is an exploration of why the English fell in love (and for a short time, out of love) with this spice in the kitchen, and how its cultivation is being revived in the twenty-first century.

When you steep a few threads of saffron in a little hot water, some

Introduction

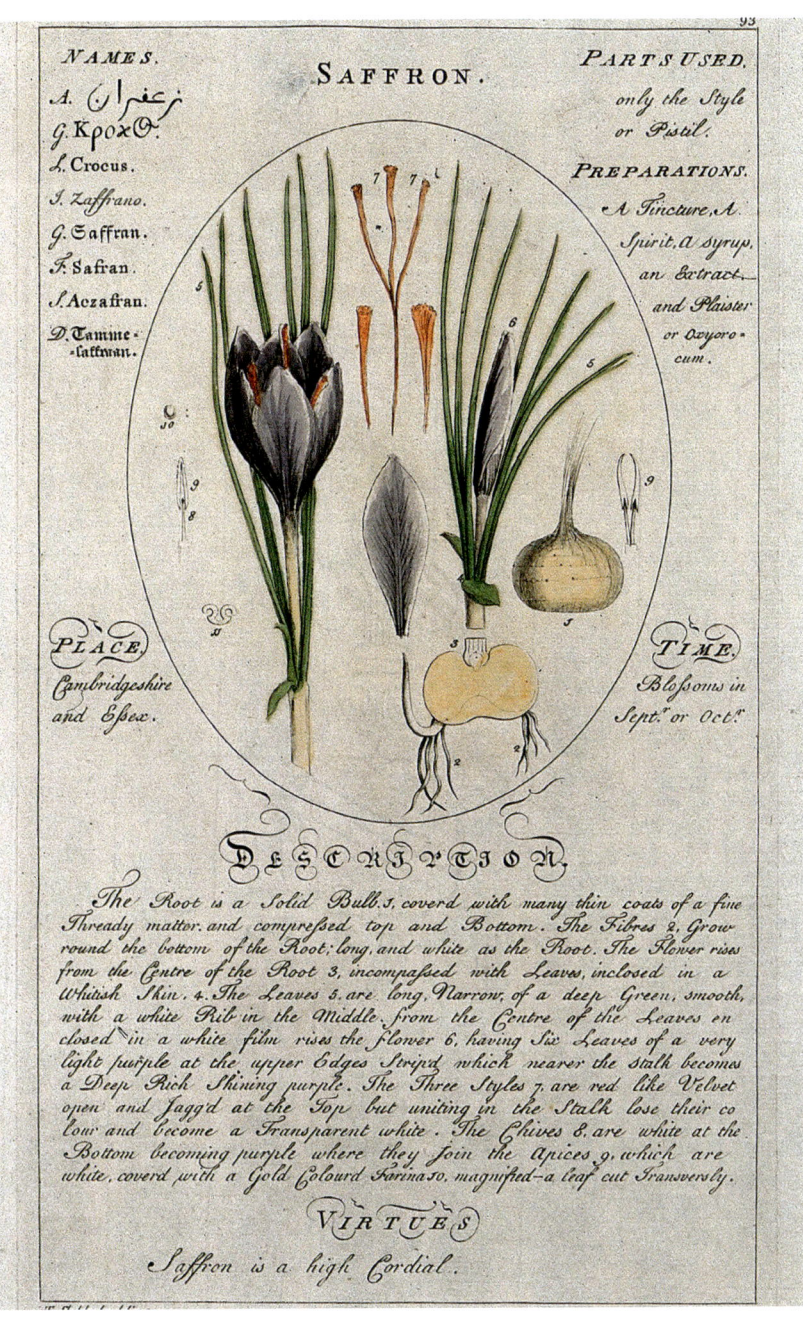

Engraving by C.H. Hemerich of the saffron crocus and its component parts c. 1759.

kind of alchemy takes place. The threads leach a golden pigment which deepens to a vibrant orange the longer you leave it. The Arabic word for yellow is *za'faran* which is where the anglicised name for saffron originates. To my mind, yellow is a joyful colour which, to quote Nicholas Culpeper (1616–1654) on the subject of saffron 'strengthens the heart so exceedingly'.[12] This goes some way to explaining why saffron was prized by the apothecary, and found its way into potions to treat everything from the plague to consumption. I will dip a toe into the medicinal history of saffron but it is the culinary realm that fascinates me most (I find it is hard not to be cheered by food with a golden hue, don't you?). Saffron has a distinct honeyed aroma that exquisitely perfumed the dishes of the medieval and early modern eras, and which seems more befitting of the Persian than the English kitchen. Many of these dishes have found their way into these pages, along with a few more recent additions.

Chef and restaurateur Rick Stein describes the flavour of saffron as being 'almost like perfume in a way. It's so complex that it's almost impossible to describe how it tastes. It's more about how you feel when you eat it and when you smell it, and then you feel cosy, you feel comfort, you feel a sense of the great things in life'.[13]

Saffron really is one of the great things in life. Thanks to the determination of a handful of farmers, this spice is once again being grown on our shores. And as we shall see, there is nothing foolish about the way this spice is produced or used.

Chapter One

Saffron's Journey to England

Have you ever played the Telephone Game?[1] At least three people (although the more, the merrier) line up, then the first player whispers a short sentence to the second who repeats the message to the third player and so forth, until the missive reaches the end of the line. In theory, the object of the game is for the message to arrive at the final player intact. However, invariably (and arguably the real point of the game), the original communication becomes garbled resulting in great hilarity among the participants.

The retelling of stories of how historical events came to pass, particularly when disseminated orally, can have a similar outcome to the Telephone Game. Although these tales may contain a grain or two of truth, they can sprout fantastical creations which are more befitting of the Land of Cockayne[2] than the world as it really was at the time. You only have to look at the legend of King Arthur to see how an Anglo-Roman warrior fighting against Saxon invaders has been transformed over the centuries into a chivalric knight cloaked in magic and romance (if, indeed, he existed at all).

And so it follows that there are a few theories about just how saffron came to be grown in England. Some may well have a basis in fact and others – well let's just say you may need to take them with a large pinch of salt.

Fool's Gold

The Pilgrim Connection

Probably the best place to begin unpicking these accounts is with the legend that surrounds the town of Saffron Walden. The Saxon name for this settlement is recorded in the Domesday Book (1086) as Waledana, which means 'valley of the Britons or serfs' (although eighteenth-century historian Philip Morant claims that Walden is derived from the Saxon 'weald' meaning wood, and 'den' meaning valley). By the middle of the twelfth century the settlement sported a castle, home to Geoffrey de Mandeville, the second Earl of Essex, and a Benedictine monastery. In 1141, the Earl of Essex persuaded the Empress Maud to give him permission to move the local market from Newport in the Cam valley to Walden. This is probably how the town became known as Chipping Walden (derived from the Medieval English word 'chepynge' to denote a market square). From this point forward it is easy to see how the town's fortunes improved, particularly as the wool and cloth trades developed in the area.[3]

The saffron connection would come much later. In 1967, historian Dorothy Cromarty conducted an extensive study of the Chepying Walden Court Rolls from 1381–1420 to see whether she could uncover any further information on how saffron came to be associated with the town. Although dye works are mentioned in the rolls there are no references to saffron being used for this purpose at the time. However, Cromarty suggests that it is entirely logical to make a link between Walden's burgeoning dyeing industry and the growing of saffron in the area. Cromarty concludes: 'It may be that the demand for the yellow dye from the local woollen industry led to the gradual extension of its cultivation so that what began in a small way in the mid-fourteenth century had become important enough to enter land transactions and affect rents in the 1440s.'[4] By the mid-fifteenth century farming was established enough to be mentioned as a tithable commodity in an agreement entered into by the abbot and vicar of Walden. This entitled the vicar to one tenth of the saffron grown in all the gardens and fields outside the precincts of Walden Abbey. Skip forward fifty years or so and the saffron was so intrinsically linked to the town that it became known as Saffron Walden. The saffron crocus featured prominently in the illuminated border of the charter granted to the Guild of Holy Trinity on 24th March 1514 by a young King Henry

VIII. After the dissolution of this Guild, Edward VI granted a new charter of incorporation to the town, complete with a new seal featuring 'walls with four towers, gateway and portcullis enclosing three saffron flowers' stalked and leaved. The flowers being 'walled-in' is thought to be a play on the town's name.[5]

While this may explain why saffron became so closely associated with the town, it throws no light on how the flower arrived there. We have William Harrison (1535–1593) and Richard Hakluyt (1552–1616) to thank for the next pieces in the puzzle.

Harrison was rector of Radwinter from 1559 to 1593, and of Wimbish from 1571 to 1581, two Essex villages situated a few miles from Saffron Walden. As well as being a learned clergyman he was also a historian, and spent much of his life researching and writing the history of the world. It was from this research that he produced the *Description of England* which appears in Holinshed's *Chronicles of England, Scotland and Ireland* in 1577. He writes extensively on the cultivation and uses of saffron, and provides us with this snippet of history regarding saffron's introduction to the area:[6]

> There groweth some saffron in many places of Almain [Germany] and also about Vienna in Austria, which latter is taken for the best that springeth in those quarters. Instead of this some do use the *Carthamus*, called amongst us bastard saffron, but neither is this of any value, nor the other in any wise comparable unto ours. Whereof let this suffice, as of a commodity brought into this island in the time of Edward the Third and not commonly planted till Richard the Second did reign.[7]

Edward III reigned from 1327–1377 and his grandson Richard II from 1377–1400. These dates correspond with Cromarty's theory about the link between cloth dyeing and saffron growing in the area. Unfortunately, Harrison is not clear about how saffron came to England, although he cites Bartolomeo Platina (1421–1481), the Italian Renaissance writer and gastronomist, on the quality of English saffron, which he 'reckoneth among spices, is the most excellent of all other, for it giveth place neither to that of Cilicia, whereof Solinus speaketh, neither to any that cometh from… Aetolia, Sicilia or Licia, in sweetness, tincture, and continuance'.[8] These places relate to modern day Turkey, Greece and Sicily where the saffron crocus is believed to have originated.

Hakluyt was another English clergyman and geographer acquainted with the most important sea captains, merchants, and sailors of Britain. He epitomised the spirit of Elizabethan adventure, particularly when it came to exploring new territories in North America. He is best remembered for his detailed work *The Principall Navigations, Voiages and Discoveries of the English Nation* (1589). The fifth volume of this book focuses on Central and Southern Europe. and it describes how 'this commodity of Saffron groweth fifty miles from Tripoli in Syria, on an high hill called in those parts Garian.' Unlike Harrison, Hakluyt believed the saffron grown in this area to be 'the best of the universal world'. It is from Hakluyt that we learn how saffron came to arrive in Saffron Walden:[9]

> It is reported at Saffron Walden that a Pilgrim purposing to do good to his country, stole a head of saffron, and hid the same in his Palmers staff, which he had made hollow before of purpose, and so he brought this root into this realme, with venture of his life: for if he had been taken, by the law of the country from whence it came, he had died for the fact.[10]

Many people have assumed that the pilgrim in question brought saffron back from the Holy Land, presumably because of Hakluyt's references to the spice growing near Tripoli. The popular and sensational 'travelogue' of Sir John Mandeville, first printed in 1499, describes the knight's journey to Jerusalem in the year 1322 and how he had 'seen and gone through many diverse lands, and many provinces and kingdoms and isles and have passed throughout Turkey, Armenia the little and the great; through Tartary, Persia, Syria, Arabia, Egypt the high and the low; through Lybia, Chaldea, and a great part of Ethiopia'. One of these routes ventures through Tripoli:

> From Tortouse pass men to Tripoli by sea, or else by land through the straits of mountains and fells. And there is a city that is called

Gibilet. From Tripoli go men to Acres; and from thence are two ways to Jerusalem, the one on the left half and the other on the right half.[11]

Mandeville's book, like many pilgrim guides of the medieval era, provides little more than an outline of the routes travelled and the cities and shrines visited. Scant attention is paid to the sights, sounds or tastes experienced along the way. So while it is entirely feasible that the saffron may have come to England with a pilgrim returning from the Holy Land, other overseas pilgrimage destinations should surely be borne in mind, as by the fifteenth century saffron cultivation was spreading across Europe.

To go on pilgrimage in the medieval era was a right of passage for a good number of people, but not one undertaken lightly. The process had long been seen as a 'remedy for sin', a way of doing penance during your lifetime, and hopefully reducing the amount of time spent in purgatory. In theory, anyone could go on pilgrimage providing you had permission from a higher authority to do so. For a peasant, this would come from the lord of the manor. For a member of the clergy it would be his clerical superior, such as an abbot. Nobles, such as Humphrey de Bohun (*c.* 1249–1298), Earl of Hereford and Essex, who lived in Walden castle and went on pilgrimage to Compostela in 1278, got permission from their king. Even monarchs had to get permission from a particular saint or even God himself. Other preparations included settling any outstanding debts both financial and spiritual (in terms of making amends with any person they had previously offended) so that the penitent could make a true confession on arrival at the pilgrimage destination. Pilgrims were also expected to make a will in case they died during the pilgrimage. John Bataill of Hatfield Broad Oak in Essex left instructions for his parents' debts to be paid in his will made on 21 February 1397 in Chelmsford, on the way to a pilgrimage to Jerusalem. The will also made provision for payment to the abbots and convents of both Walden and Waltham, for prayers to be said on his behalf in the event of his death.[12]

Pilgrims therefore came from all walks of life, although arguably overseas pilgrimage was more feasible for those with access to money or funding.

Fool's Gold

Although pilgrims were expected to travel in a state of poverty, they still needed to pay for their passage to mainland Europe or beyond, and often taxes were levied on pilgrims when they arrived at their destination. If you lacked the funds to finance your trip you could offer to undertake a pilgrimage on behalf of another person who was perhaps prevented from pursuing the task themselves due to some physical infirmity. Pilgrims were easy to spot by the unofficial 'uniform' they donned. This consisted of a long, coarse tunic (sclavein) with a soft pouch, usually made of leather, strapped to the pilgrim's waist (the scrip, used to store food and money) and a wooden staff which occasionally had to double as a weapon to defend the pilgrim from attacks by bandits.[13]

There were three major centres of pilgrimage – Rome, Santiago de Compostela and Jerusalem – and the journey to all of these destinations was long, arduous and at times dangerous. Each could be reached via overland routes or by sea. The adage 'all roads lead to Rome' may seem trite but the Romans had left a legacy of highways, and while they may not have been kept in good repair they were at least routes well known to travellers. During the papacy's residency in Avignon between 1309 and 1377, pilgrimage to the holy city was still encouraged. Even if the pilgrim was following a specific route such as the Via Francigena (which travels from Canterbury through France and Switzerland to Rome) they could make detours to visit artefacts like the Volto Santo crucifix in Lucca, which could in turn have exposed them to areas where saffron was grown. As the UNESCO World Heritage Travel website announces, when describing saffron growing around San Gimignano in Tuscany, 'the sight of the shimmering lilac coloured fields astounded the pilgrims who travelled the Via Francigena on the way to Jerusalem,' (although as yet I have been unable to find any contemporary sources to corroborate this statement). Saffron was certainly used by the Romans as a spice and a dye, and frequently appears in Italian recipe manuscripts from the early fifteenth to the eighteenth centuries. However, food historian Gillian Riley notes that it is not clear when saffron came to be cultivated in Italy (the spice may well have been imported, although the UNESCO site states it was introduced after the first crusades in the eleventh century).[14]

Saffron's Journey to England

Cultivation of saffron began in Spain at some point between the eighth and tenth centuries, primarily in La Mancha, Valencia and Aragon, where it arrived with Berber invaders. Saffron is included in Spanish culinary manuscripts from the thirteenth century onwards, and by the sixteenth century it was one of the country's major exports. From Spain, saffron cultivation appears to have spread to southern France by the fourteenth century, gradually wending its way northwards as far as the Gâtinais (a province corresponding roughly to the northeastern part of the department of Loiret, and the south of the present department of Seine-et-Marne). Therefore, it seems likely that anyone travelling overland from England through France to Santiago de Compostela could have encountered saffron in some form on their journey. Although the twelfth century *Codex Calixtinus* does not mention saffron specifically, it did provide pilgrims with plenty of advice on what to look out for at different points on their journey. Gascony gets the thumbs up for 'its white bread and the best and reddest wine'. The author adds the Gascons are 'fast-talking, obnoxious, and sex-crazed, they are overfed, poorly-dressed drunks', but concedes 'they give good hospitality to the poor'.[15]

Prior to the year 1000, most pilgrimages to the Holy Land left from the east coast of Italy by boat, with Venice playing a primary role. By the fourteenth century the Venetian pilgrim travel trade was running like a well-oiled machine. Wealthier pilgrims could pay for 'all inclusive' packages which included food and lodging on and off the ship, overland travel by donkey, and with guided tours of Jerusalem thrown in for good measure. At the height of the pilgrimage era up to two fleets a year sailed from Venice: one in September and another in March. In the late thirteenth century the Genoese and Venetians began regular sailings from Bruges and Southampton to the Holy Land via the straits of Gibraltar. However, for most pilgrims travel by sea meant cramped conditions, with little more sustenance than salt bread and water, assuming, of course, they could even stomach it. 'Our pylgryms haue no lust to ete,' sums up how most fifteenth-century pilgrims overcome by seasickness must have felt.[16] William Wey cautions pilgrims travelling from Venice to take ample supplies of their own, in preparation for the 'febyl bred, wyne, and stynkyng water' likely to be served on the voyage. His advice extends to stocking up on dried fruit and spices, such as pepper, saffron, cloves and mace, which 'schal do yow gret ese by the wey'.[17] What makes the Venetian connection all the more tantalising is that the city was a leading force in the spice trade (hence, perhaps, Wey's suggestion to buy your spices there and not in England). If the pilgrims had failed to come into contact with saffron at their devotional destination perhaps it crossed their path (or even shared their berth) en route?

There is evidence that saffron was being grown and used along many well-trodden pilgrimage routes, so pilgrims may well have encountered it as a spice or the bulbs themselves. This may explain why Hakluyt was so willing to believe the tale he had been told about saffron's appearance in Walden. However, as the Reverend Andrew Clark pointed out in 1910, vast numbers of crocus bulbs would have been required to lay the foundations of a saffron industry in Essex which was firmly established by the beginning of the fifteenth century. To his mind, this 'discounts the romantic story of the pilgrim and his stolen bulb… Importation in some quantity from Kashmir or the Near East, its natural habitat, is a more credible explanation of the arrival of saffron in this country'.[18]

The Roman Connection

If in doubt blame the Romans – the default explanation for cultural developments throughout history from road building to England's love affair with spices. Is it possible that saffron arrived on Britain's shores with Roman invaders in the first century CE?

One piece of 'evidence' proffered to support this theory is the origin of the name Croydon, now part of Greater London. It is thought to be derived from Crogedene, the name given to the settlement in the ninth century as a consequence of the Romans cultivating saffron there during their occupation of Britain. This would later be recorded as 'Croindene' in the Domesday Book of 1086, and has been interpreted as 'valley where wild saffron grows', from the Old English *croh* or *crogen* (saffron) and *denu* (valley). The problem with this theory is that there is very little archeological evidence to suggest that there was a significant Roman settlement in Croydon. Anthony Mills, author of *A Dictionary of English Place Names*, explains that while many towns have old English names which predate the Norman conquest, the Romans themselves left little mark on place names. Of course, it is possible that a variety of crocus once grew wild in this area, but whether it was the species *Crocus sativus* seems to be a matter of conjecture.[19]

The Romans definitely used and prized saffron. In his *Inquiry into Plants* the 'father of botany', Theophrastus (*c.* 371–*c.* 287 BCE) provides a list of aromatic plants which includes the saffron crocus. He adds 'spice plants grow in different places but the most famous and the most fragrant come from Asia and places lying open to the sun'. He is very clear that spices should only be used to enhance the scent or flavour of perfumes or wine, believing spices to be positively deleterious to food.[20]

According to the philosopher and naturalist Pliny the Elder (*c.* 23–79 CE) the best saffron came from the Roman province of Cilicia, located on what is today the southern (Mediterranean) coast of Turkey. This was a view he shared with Theophrastus. Pliny also praised the virtues of the scent of saffron, which was mixed with sweet wine and sprayed in theatres in ancient Rome. David Bird, an archeologist who specialises in Roman sites, notes that saffron may have had medicinal uses in this era, too, such as in salves to treat eye conditions, arguing 'if there was a thriving medical community in London using saffron salves (and surely it would have been a good market) then it might be that local supplies of *Crocus sativus* would be very welcome'.[21]

Despite Theophrastus' reservations about spices in food, the Romans used them extensively in their cooking. Although saffron was not used as widely as pepper or cumin in Roman cookery, it does appear in a number of recipes in the books attributed to Marcus Gavius Apicius. Apicius provides several recipes for spiced wines containing saffron as well as a number of sauces and spiced salts which were 'good for the digestion, for promoting regularity, and for averting all sorts of sicknesses and plague and chills'.[22] Due to the size of the Roman Empire, a considerable number of spices were grown within its realms.

Fool's Gold

'Since Britain is an island it is reasonable to suppose that many of the wide range of exotic plants that appear in the archaeological record for the first time after the Roman invasion of AD 43 were deliberately introduced by the Romans,' writes British archeologist Barry Cunliffe.[23]

Cunliffe lists the plants believed to have been introduced in a domestic form during the Roman occupation. However, he notes that the archeological evidence of seeds does not necessarily mean the plant was grown here. It is even possible the plants arrived in an earlier period. Saffron is conspicuously absent from this list.[24]

The Romans were fond of gardens. Many tombs included a garden which served as a place where remembrance feasts could be held. Trimalchio, the character created by the first century writer Petronius in his work *Satyricon*, wanted an immense tomb garden filled with vines and all kinds of fruit. However, most gardens were more modest affairs perhaps planted with an evergreen shrub and some flowers. Although Virgil's poem 'Culex' ('The Gnat') is rather fanciful (it tells of a shepherd building a tomb for the gnat which saved him from being attacked by a serpent) it does reflect the flowers that were popular with the Romans such as the rose, violet, hyacinth and crocus.[25]

Many private villas and houses in Italy had kitchen gardens where vegetables, herbs and flowers were cultivated for offering to the gods on the household and public shrines. By the late third and early fourth centuries larger country estates and villas were being built by the Romans in Britain, and many of these also included gardens. At Fishbourne Palace near Chichester, West Sussex, it is believed the north-west corner of the land around the building could have served as a kitchen garden. Other areas around the villa are believed to be ornamental gardens.[26]

Given that the Romans did value the aromatic qualities of saffron, both as a perfume and in food, it is conceivable that it could have been grown in gardens like those found at Fishbourne. Unfortunately, it has been impossible to identify what plants were grown at this particular site, as the pollen samples retrieved were too badly preserved. Bird goes on to argue that there must have been many areas in Britain renowned for producing specific commodities which have left no archeological traces. He also points out that the geological location of Croydon is similar to that of Saffron Walden, being on the opposite side of the London Basin, and that the Croydon valley was conveniently situated for road transport. One theory is that the saffron crocus planted by the Romans became naturalised in the English countryside after their departure. However, Pliny noted that it was unprofitable to grow the spice in Italy 'as a whole bed of saffron yields only a scruple of the essence'. It seems unlikely that Britain, with its variable climate, would have provided a more favourable environment for saffron cultivation. The saffron crocus requires a lot of tender loving care to flourish. Many of the modern saffron growers I have spoken to are doubtful that saffron could have survived in the wilds of England for centuries without any human interference.[27]

If saffron were being used by the Anglo-Romans it seems more likely that the spice was imported into the country. The Romans built on trading networks established by the likes of the Phoenicians and Greek Egyptians. This allowed the empire to expand its commercial interests eastwards. Imports from the East were often raw materials, such as coral, gold and silver, which were largely exchanged for manufactured or semi-manufactured goods. *The Periplus of the Erythraean Sea*, an inventory of exports from Egypt thought to date from around 59–62 CE, reveals that the ancient port of Muza (in modern day Yemen on the east coast of the Red Sea) imported 'purple cloths, both fine and coarse; clothing in the Arabian style, with sleeves; plain, ordinary, embroidered, or interwoven with gold; saffron, sweet rush, muslins, cloaks, blankets (not many), some plain and others made in the local fashion; sashes of different colors, fragrant ointments in moderate quantity, wine and wheat, not much'. Wilfred Schoff, who translated the *Periplus* in 1912, notes that it was the saffron spice rather than the corms that were being traded. Its primary use appears to have been for perfumes, although it was also prized as a medicine and used as a dye or in cookery.[28] If the Romans were trading freely with their neighbours in the East, then surely it would have been easy for them to move goods such as spices around the empire to its more distant western outposts like Britain? Olive pips have been found in Roman excavations and these trees certainly did not grow in Britain.

The Phoenician Connection

Cornwall is a county awash with legends. From Arthurian knights to mischievous sprites, you would be hard pressed to find many towns or villages in that part of England which do not have some kind of folklore or tale associated with them.

Cornwall is, I believe, the only county to have preserved its culinary saffron heritage in its famous saffron buns or cakes. While they may not be quite as ubiquitous as that other Cornish 'delicacy', the pasty, saffron buns can be located in the region without too much difficulty. This sits somewhat at odds with the history of saffron in England. Given the importance of the spice in Essex – and particularly Saffron Walden – you would perhaps expect that county to have developed a culinary affinity with this spice. Alas, no recipes containing saffron specifically local to Essex came to light during my investigations. So why should the Cornish cling to their liking for saffron above all other counties?

Perhaps the answer lies in the manner in which it reputedly arrived in the south-west of Britain. The popular belief is that saffron came with Phoenicians, who traded it in exchange for tin. From the eighth century BCE the Phoenicians developed an extensive trading network throughout the Mediterranean, with Carthage and Gades (the ancient name for modern day Cadiz in Spain) serving as important commercial centres. Timber, purple dye (for which the Phoenicians were famous), fine cloths and agricultural products were among the goods they traded. The Phoenicians were particularly renowned for their highly decorative metalwork using materials like bronze, copper and other precious metals. Demand for these metals was high, so Phoenician mariners were encouraged to find new sources for them. It was the quest for tin, required to make bronze, that brought these Mediterranean explorers to Cornwall.[29]

Saffron's Journey to England

According to Avienus in *Ora Maritima* (4 CE) a Phoenician called Himilco ventured further west around 425 BCE to extend Carthage's interests, which were being blocked by the Greeks around the Mediterranean. The aim was to find new sources of tin as the Spanish mines were not yielding enough. It has been suggested that Himilco bypassed Brittany and headed straight to Cornwall.[30]

Victorian scientist Richard Edmonds, a Cornishman by birth, was convinced the Phoenicians had visited the county to trade for tin, and cited the first-century Greek historian Diodorus Siculus as his source. This may well be true but unfortunately Diodorus makes no mention of what the Cornish were given in exchange for their tin.[31]

The Phoenicians did not create their own coinage until the fifth century CE. This meant that trade was conducted by a system of bartering. As well as products from their own country, they may also have traded in goods from other nations such as Egypt and Greece. I have read nothing to suggest that the Phoenicians themselves were particularly associated with saffron. However, if they recognised the commercial value of this spice it is conceivable that they could have used it as a means of payment. Cilicia, the area spoken of so highly in connection with saffron, is in very close proximity to Phoenicia, so the Phoenicians may well have had access to the spice. For many people from Cornwall, the Phoenician connection is still an endearing tale and they remain romantically attached to it, however unlikely it is to be true.

It is of course possible that there are elements of truth in all of the theories above but the most persuasive for me is Harrison's. Pilgrim smugglers aside (one saffron corm does not a saffron harvest make), the timing feels logical. The outbreak of plague known as the Black Death (1348–49) had a profound effect on English society. It is estimated that at least a third, and in some places as much as one half, of the population died at this time. Fewer people meant less labour available to cultivate the land, but also a significantly reduced demand for food. This required farmers to find innovative uses for their land which has been dubbed 'alternative agriculture'.[32]

Fool's Gold

As Joan Thirsk observes 'diversification was the watchword of the age'. Although it was a tragedy for many communities, the Black Death also provided an opportunity for experimentation in which land could be used 'extravagantly rather than sparingly'. Saffron answered this purpose very well. True, it was an incredibly labour intensive crop to farm but as a luxury commodity, highly regarded at noble dining tables, it commanded a great price in the market. It also has the benefit of using relatively small amounts of land, meaning that arable farming could continue alongside it. By the fifteenth century, saffron production was flourishing in eastern England.[33]

The food historian C. Anne Wilson explains that the golden coloured cuisine of the saracens had a huge impact on the crusaders during their on-and-off occupation of the Holy Land over a two hundred year period. They were keen to see saffron adopted into English cookery when they returned home. Therefore, the spice saffron was imported from Spain before eventually being grown in England.[34] Eighteenth-century botanist Richard Bradley credited Sir Walter Raleigh (1552–1618) as being the first to import Spanish saffron corms into England. He believed the Spanish and Portuguese had first received the corms themselves from China. Bradley reasons that China and England have similar climates, which explains why saffron can be grown so successfully here.[35] Over the centuries, England has had a political and commercial relationship with Spain, albeit at times a fractious one. Given how saffron corms multiply, it is not hard to imagine that by the fourteenth century they were being traded alongside the spice itself. And then there is that tantalising link between the Spanish and the Phoenicians, who established a settlement in Gades in the twelfth century BCE. Perhaps the Cornish are not being overly romantic in their notion of how saffron arrived here after all…

Chapter Two

Saffron Cultivation: The Right Location

Sir Hans Sloane's brow creased into a frown as he read the letter in his hand. The urgently dashed off script looked fraught. The words in the missive confirmed that the writer was indeed in a state of desperation. 'Should I miss one day of Publication the whole design will be destroyed,' pleaded Richard Bradley.[1] Bradley, the Professor of Botany at Cambridge University, had done some studies with plants and it concerned Sloane to hear of his present predicament.

The dilemma facing Bradley in September 1727 was lack of money. In order to get his latest pamphlet printed he needed to pay some stamp duty and lacked the funds to pay this tax.[2] So he reached out to the one person he believed would be sympathetic to his plight – the President of the Royal Society, Sir Hans Sloane.

Perhaps Sloane empathised with Bradley because he recognised that they had both come from humble beginnings. Sloane (1660–1753) was born in the North of Ireland, in relatively modest circumstances as the third son of migrants from Ayrshire in Scotland. Born in 1688 close to London, Bradley was also from a middle-class family. Both men were educated but whereas Sloane had gone on to become a physician, serving Queen Anne and Kings George I and II, Bradley never realised his dream of studying medicine in Paris.[3]

Sloane was no doubt aware that the pursuit of science was poorly funded in England at this time. Bradley received no salary from his post at Cambridge. His primary means of income was publishing 'scientific' papers, which he wrote grudgingly. As a professor, he could also raise funds through lectures but again, he seemed reluctant to do this. One of Bradley's harshest critics, John Martyn, who succeeded Bradley to the botany chair at Cambridge, tartly noted in 1730 that, 'It was particularly obliging in our worthy Professor to print these Lectures; seeing not above 3 or 4 of our Students had the pleasure of hearing them read.'[4]

Sloane was a generous man, and on this occasion sent Bradley a guinea to pay for the stamp duty. Five days later Bradley wrote to Sloane again to thank him for his 'great favour' and hoped that the publication of this paper would 'be a means of setting me again into the World'. However, by the end of the communication it is clear that Bradley's woes were far from over. 'I am sure I can discharge all I owe for one hundred pounds,' continued Bradley.[5]

This final revelation would not have come as a surprise to Sloane. Bradley, who became a fellow of the Royal Society in 1712, had been corresponding with Sloane for a number years. Many of Bradley's letters survive in the Sloane Manuscript collection held at the British Library, and some of them include accounts of the botanist's financial straits. Although Bradley lays the blame for his pecuniary dilemmas at the feet of booksellers, it seems more than likely that he was incredibly bad at managing money, even when it was not his own. In 1722, Bradley wrote to Sloane about an 'unfortunate affair at Kensington whereby I lost all my substance, my expectation and my friends,' perhaps alluding to his falling out with a former benefactor, James Brydges, the first Duke of

Saffron Cultivation: The Right Location

Chandos, who accused Bradley of mismanaging the ducal affairs in 1719 to the tune of £460.[6]

Bradley did have the good grace to offer something in return for the remuneration he received from Sloane. He was eager to find 'curiosities' that would appeal to Sloane and that would contribute to Sloane's collections. He also dedicated two books to Sloane. In 1726, one curiosity he offered Sloane was a saffron kiln which he had bought in Cambridgeshire. It is something of a loaded offer as he asked Sloane to reimburse him the eight shillings it cost to buy.[7]

Bradley's biographer, Frank Egerton believes it likely that Sloane would have purchased the kiln as the Royal Society was committed to studying the trades. However, he casts doubt on whether Sloane would have bought any of the manuscripts Bradley mentions at the end of this letter, stating that 'Sloane's assistance to Bradley was usually material rather than intellectual'.[8]

Bradley clearly had a botanical interest in saffron cultivation. In *New Improvements of Planting and Gardening, both Philosophical and Practical* (1718) he wonders 'that this Plant is not, more commonly Cultivated in our Gardens, seeing how valuable a Commodity it produces'.[9] At this point in his career he had little idea about how saffron should be prepared after harvesting. However, by the time Bradley offered the saffron kiln to Sloane he was well versed on the subject of preparing and drying this spice, and as a consequence is often cited as one of the primary historical sources for this process.

Bradley and other fellows of the Royal Society in the eighteenth century, such as James Douglass, were not the first people to write about saffron cultivation. Pliny the Elder had made reference to the corms being transplanted every six or seven years to a 'well dug bed'. A fifteenth century treatise in verse, *The Feate of Gardeninge*, by Master John Gardener provides the following advice on growing saffron:

Fool's Gold

OF THE KIND OF SAFFRON
Of saffron we must tell
He shall be kept fair & well
Saffron will have woust lesyng'
Beds I made well with dung
Forsooth if they shall bear
They would be set in the Month of September (September 8th)
Three days before Saint Mary day Nativity
Other the next woke thereafter so must I the
With a dibble thou shall them set
That the dibble before be blunt & great
Three inches deep they must set be
And thus said Master Ion Gardener to me.[10]

Saffron would feature again in *Five Hundred Points of Good Husbandrie* by Thomas Tusser (1575) and in Gerard's *Herbal* of 1597. However, the observations on the cultivation of saffron by Bradley and his peers provide a good account of how this spice was grown and processed in England, which are examined in this chapter. There are many references to saffron grounds, gardens and plots mentioned in various county archives. The quantity of land is often expressed as a 'rood', 'rod' or 'pole'. A rood is the modern equivalent of a quarter of an acre (10,890 square feet or 1,012 square meters). That's roughly one sixth of a British football pitch.

Many people are surprised to learn that saffron was cultivated on a fairly significant scale in Britain. Nowadays, we associate areas like La Mancha in Spain, or Iran, with their arid climates, as saffron growing hubs. But the temperate climate we have in Britain has never been a barrier to growing this spice.

The type of soil saffron corms were planted in was a critical factor. Clay or 'stiff ground' was universally reviled. Free-draining sandy or chalky soil was the best according to Charles Howard and James Douglass, writing in the Royal Society's *Philosophical Transactions* in 1678 and 1728 respectively. This would explain why saffron has

Saffron Cultivation: The Right Location

thrived in some areas of the country over others.[11]

The land surrounding the Essex town of Saffron Walden is a prime example. Dorothy Cromarty has observed that although heavy clay soil is prevalent in parts of Essex, the land around the town of Saffron Walden contains a good degree of chalk, making it perfect for cultivation of arable crops. The same can be said of land just over the county border in Cambridgeshire, where a number of towns were historically associated with saffron production.[12]

Climate is also a factor. Howard was of the opinion that extreme cold or high rainfall would be detrimental to saffron. East Anglia (an area of Eastern England that includes Norfolk, Cambridgeshire and Suffolk) is renowned for its relatively mild, dry climate. Coupled with the fact that much of the land was suited to arable farming, it is hardly surprising that saffron production thrived in eastern England.

Essex

When researching the history of English saffron the obvious place to start is Essex, home to Saffron Walden. The Elizabethan antiquarian, topographer and historian, William Camden, describes the county as 'abounding in Saffron'. Essex was also renowned for its caraway, coriander and teasel crops. Caraway and coriander were used in medicine, condiments, distilling and brewing, while teasel was used in the textile industry. In an early twentieth-century study of field names in Essex, local historian William Chapman Waller identified at least twenty-eight parishes in the county where saffron had been grown. Twenty-one of these are situated in north-west Essex and most are within ten miles of Walden (as Kenneth Neale notes the local population did – and still do – refer to the town simply as Walden, only using the 'Saffron' prefix when formally referring to the place). The diarist John Evelyn remarked that the saffron of this district was 'esteemed the best of any foreign country'.[13]

Fool's Gold

One of the best indicators of just how widespread the cultivation of saffron was in this and other areas are the wills left by the county's residents. In 1542, Robert Newman of Wendons Ambo left a bequest to his sister of 'a bedd of my saffron grounde'. John Turnour of Littlebury made a similar bequest in 1565. There are even references to saffron fields in my ancestral hometown of Thaxted. Saffron cultivation was not restricted to the area directly surrounding Walden. In 1568, a grocer and alderman from Colchester, Robert Brown, left £10 to the 'poor people' of his home town, which sum was to be 'levied out of the yearly rent of my saffron garden in the parish of St Leonard in Colchester.'[14]

Joan Thirsk refers to saffron as a multipurpose crop, not only in demand in the kitchen but also used as a yellow dye and as a medicine. It was this latter usage which prompted a spread in cultivation in the sixteenth century. The value of the spice was certainly acknowledged. In 1548 a pound of saffron cost twelve shillings, and it steadily increased in price over the next fifty years or so before selling for over £3 per pound by 1614. Such a valuable commodity could prompt criminal behaviour. Dorothy Daye, a widow from Littlebury, was a victim of such a crime in 1587. A gang of six malefactors, led by John Wybroughe and Henry Mott of Greenwich, broke into Dorothy's house and stole three ounces of saffron worth five shillings and a towel worth 12d before evicting her from the premises. It is not clear why six men were required to expel one woman (perhaps she had a number of burley children in tow?) but Mott was later bound to keep the peace towards Dorothy.[15]

Monarchs visiting the grand Audley End House on the outskirts of the town were given gifts of this spice by the Corporation of Saffron Walden. When Charles II visited Audley End in 1665 he was presented with 1 lb 4 oz of saffron at a cost of £4 1s 10d along with some plate which cost over £16. The historian of the Rowntree family, C. Brightwen Rowntree, suggests that the town gave this generous gift as an act of contrition. Walden had been the headquarters for the parliamentary army during the English Civil

Saffron Cultivation: The Right Location

War (1642–1651), and it was from the Sun Inn in Church Street that Cromwell despatched his soldiers to seize Charles I on the Isle of Wight. The town authorities hoped that by making this generous donation to the royal coffers they would keep the charter to hold a market, granted by Henry VIII in 1514. By contrast, William III and Queen Mary only received 14 oz saffron costing £3 11s 8d and silver plate to the value of £4 6s 6d when they visited Audley End in 1689.[16]

The saffron industry helped Walden thrive, and along with it ancillary industries such as malting, brewhouses and hostelries also prospered. It seems it is possible to have too much of a good thing. During the mid-sixteenth century there was a glut of saffron causing the price of the spice to fall, much to the dismay of the 'crokers', the appellation given to men who farmed saffron. Many crokers grumbled that 'God did now shite saffron', and had consequently choked the market, causing their revenue to plummet. Harrison seems convinced that this blasphemy resulted in a sharp decline in saffron production in subsequent years, to the degree that the plant 'was almost lost & perished in England'. Fortunately for the crokers in Essex, by the time Harrison was writing his *Description of England* (around 1577), the crokers had been forgiven and the saffron industry was being revived.[17]

When James Brome sojourned in Essex, 'a Country of as great Variety as Delight' at the turn of the eighteenth century, saffron continued to be an important crop. The cultivation and processing of this spice was still taking place around Walden in 1701 when John Percival visited the area with William Byrd. However, production in Essex began to decline during the eighteenth century. When George I visited Audley End in 1717 the Saffron Walden corporation spent just £6 on a gift for the king. Although it included traditional saffron, it had to be purchased from Stortford as it was no longer being grown in the town. By 1726, Littlebury was one of the last places where saffron could be found growing in the county. The spice was available to purchase at events like the Newport 'Cold'

Fair, but by November 1770 the saffron sold there was being sourced from Cambridgeshire.[18]

Cambridgeshire

Few of us can hope to leave a mark on history. Those that do have usually accomplished some feat, on the battlefield, for example, or in government, or in the sporting arena. Others, like Mistress Anne Turner, gained notoriety through nefarious acts.

Anne Turner, née Norton, was born around 1576 in Hinxton, Cambridgeshire. The village is situated nine miles south-east of Cambridge and five miles north-west of Saffron Walden. The land in the southern reaches of Cambridgeshire on the border of Essex was relatively flat, with rich and fertile soil. This made it ideal for growing barley (used to make beer) and saffron. Hinxton supported a small but thriving saffron industry. During the sixteenth and seventeenth centuries the spice was grown in small plots and gardens. In 1539, John Paycke of that parish left his wife Alyce '3 roods of Saffron Ground' (a substantial and valuable plot). Saffron was also tithed in the parish at 2 s. a rood in 1692, and in 1772 a saffron dealer is reported to have lived there. It was evidently cultivated in the area early into the nineteenth century.[19]

Anne had married a respectable London doctor called George Turner but when he died in 1610, Anne had to find another means to support herself. She soon became famous for her starched fabrics, coloured yellow with saffron, which were then fashioned into ruffs and cuffs, or yellow bands, popular at the Jacobean court. Some contemporary commentators even credited her with inventing yellow starch. Yellow bands were at the height of fashion in the early seventeenth century. Whether Anne had always been involved in the textile industry or began this sideline following her husband's death is unclear. Given where she grew up she certainly would have been familiar with (and presumably had access to) the saffron used in the creation of yellow starch.[20]

Saffron Cultivation: The Right Location

As with most fashions at any point in history, yellow starch accessories attracted criticism. Historian James Howell (c. 1594–1666) believed yellow starch 'so much disfigured our Nation, and rendered them so ridiculous'. To some sixteenth- and seventeenth-century citizens there was something decidedly unsavoury about clothing dyed with saffron. Travel writer Fynes Moryson (1566–1630) was of the opinion the Irish coloured their linen with saffron to 'auoid lowsinesse, incident to the wearing of foule linnen'. To ensure the fastness and depth of colour of the yellow dye, Camden explains that the Irish would soak their shirts in cold urine for a few days. The saffron was most likely imported into Ireland from Spain or possibly the Middle East. This foreign, and largely Catholic, connection did not help yellow starch's cause in the eyes of its Protestant detractors.[21]

Anne was either oblivious or dismissive of these staid views. Whether the likes of Howell approved of yellow starch or not was immaterial, the upper echelons of society were huge fans. As Mistress Turner's renown grew, so she attracted a more esteemed clientele, including Frances Howard, the reluctant wife of Robert Devereux, third Earl of Essex, with whom she developed a close but dangerous friendship.[22]

Anne soon became embroiled in the Countess's romantic intrigues. Frances, whose first marriage had been annulled on the grounds of not being consummated, wanted to marry her lover Robert Carr, the Earl of Somerset. However, his friend, Thomas Overbury (1581-1613) was vehemently opposed to the match and counselled his friend against it. (Overbury referred to Frances as 'that base women' and thought she was little better than a whore). The Countess decided to remove her arch rival Overbury, initially by contriving to get him thrown in gaol, then seeking a more permanent solution through poison. Having purchased some white arsenic from an apothecary, Frances persuaded Anne to pass the poison to his gaoler. Although earlier attempts to poison Overbury, in the form of doctored jellies and tarts, had been uncovered, nobody appeared unduly suspicious when Overbury died in 1613. However, when the apothecary's assistant confessed to supplying the Countess with the lethal enema that eventually killed him the game was up. Overbury's death was ruled as murder in 1615, but it was Anne who went to the gallows at Tyburn, not the Countess.[23]

Ann Jones and Peter Stallybrass, in their history of Renaissance cothing, have argued that it was not merely Anne Turner who was on trial but also yellow starch. It was a sensational case, and Lord Chief Justice Edward Coke (1552–1634) concluded that Anne was 'a whore, a bawd, a sorcerer, a witch, a papist, a felon, and a murderer'.[24] Nevertheless, accounts from the time appear to be fascinated with the accused's link to yellow starch. Howell believed yellow starch would 'receive its funeral' as a result of its connection to the murderess.[25] Politician and antiquarian Simonds d'Ewes (1602–1650) wrote:

> Mrs Turner had first brought up that vain and foolish use of yellow starch, coming herself to her trial in a yellow band and cuffs; and therefore, when she was afterwards executed at Tyburn, the hangman had his band and cuffs of the same colour, which made many after that day of either sex to forbear the use of that coloured starch, til it at last grew generally to be detested and disused.[26]

William Larkin's portrait of Lady Anne Clifford, the Countess of Pembroke (1590–1676), painted around 1618 somewhat puts the kibosh on this theory. It depicts a demure young woman wearing a delicate golden ruff made from fine lace which appears tasteful rather than louche. It seems the fashion for these accessories had faded by 1630, but more as a result of changing tastes than the scandal surrounding Mistress Turner. Suffice to say, the Overbury Affair had a negligible impact, if any at all, on the English saffron industry, which continued to flourish into the eighteenth century.

Hinxton is just one of a myriad of settlements in southern Cambridgeshire which was renowned for growing this 'very rich

Saffron Cultivation: The Right Location

spice'.[27] Writing in the early eighteenth century, clergyman and travel writer James Brome was extremely complimentary about his home county:

> This is an extream pleasant open Country, and a place of such Variety and Plenty, that fruitful *Ceres* with a smiling Countenance, invites the Industrious Peasant to behold with Joy the Fruits of his Labour, whilst she crowns his Industry with a plentiful Harvest; and as if the Earth strove not to be behind-hand with him in conferring other Largesses, she in divers places makes some Annual Additions of another Crop, by adorning the Fields with large Productions of Saffron, by which great Profits do continually arise.[28]

There are numerous references to saffron in villages dotted around this part of the county in wills. Saffron cultivation was well established in Sawston by the middle of the sixteenth century (one study has found at least ten references to saffron bequests in this village alone during this century). One Sawston resident, William Hocheson, was evidently a generous man. He left a rood of saffron to his wife Johan and his maid Margery in 1531, while his son John received half an acre.[29]

Ickleton's position on the west bank of the river Cam or Granta, eleven miles south of Cambridge, has made it ideal as a settlement from at least Roman times, if not earlier. The southern branch of the pre-Roman Icknield Way ran through the parish, and the village evolved close to the point at which the road crossed the river. Much of the soil in and around the village is chalky, although there are some areas of clay. The fields near the river were historically prone to flooding and therefore not so good for cultivating crops.[30]

From the late fifteenth century saffron was grown in Ickleton. As in other areas of the country, it was grown in small plots, some of which were leased from the Priory Manor (the Benedictine priory had been dissolved in 1536 as part of Henry VIII's Reformation). An Ickleton parish church register notes that in the year 1607 there 'was a great frost of long continuance which stayed ye plowes thirteen weeks and more and presently after all the corn was deare and all saffron heades rotten and wheate greatly hurt at ye froste'. The Vicar of Ickleton, Augustus Rolph, who died in 1678, was a saffron grower – and a reasonably wealthy one at that. He left an acre and a half of saffron ground valued at over £11, and 12 lbs saffron worth £22. He also kept a still for drying saffron in the hall. When he died, he bequeathed money to the parish paupers to be paid in the church porch at his funeral. However, there is no record of saffron being grown here after the seventeenth century.[31]

Linton, just under ten miles north of Saffron Walden, had been granted the right to hold weekly markets in 1246. It began life as a provisions market selling meat, fish and bread, but by the seventeenth century all manner of goods could be found there, including gloves and shoes – and saffron. In 1727, Richard Bradley believed Linton's market to be better than Saffron Walden's for procuring saffron.

The spice had been grown in the parish from at least the fifteenth century. A dispute over the tithe of saffron between the vicar and Pembroke College occurred in 1470. Presumably the vicar felt he was not receiving his fair share of the proceeds generated from saffron cultivation in his parish. In 1473 the college acquiesced, granting the vicar a tithe of the saffron grown in five acres of named 'closes' (small fields created by partitioning formerly common land), with a further annual tithe of 3s 4d for saffron grown elsewhere. By 1592, twenty-four acres of fallow field were kept inclosed primarily for the cultivation of saffron.[32]

Saffron cultivation continued to thrive in Cambridgeshire into the eighteenth century. But like its neighbour Essex, the attraction of growing saffron began to wane towards the end of the century. In 1808, Daniel Lysons observed: 'In the parishes of Fulbourn and [Cherry] Hinton, a considerable quantity of saffron was formerly cultivated, but its culture has been wholly disused more than thirty years.'[33]

Saffron Cultivation: The Right Location

Cornwall

Despite its attachment to saffron buns, Cornwall is not a county immediately associated with the growing of saffron. Several people have tried to uncover the mystery of Cornwall's saffron-growing past. Cookery writer Vida Heard, who retired to Cornwall in the late twentieth century after spending 'half a lifetime' in Southern Africa, concluded 'the Cornish might call anything saffron that is bright yellow: fields of rape, mustard, buttercups, or whatever. And when you ask old farmers if they have seen or heard of anyone growing saffron, the reply can be 'the climate baint no good – don't ee know?'[34]

It is fair to say that Cornwall does have a tendency towards a damp, temperate aspect. George Worgan cited the Cornish adage 'it will bear a shower every week-day, and two upon Sunday,' when describing the county's climate.[35] However, it is not all doom and gloom. Antiquarian Richard Carew, who wrote his *Survey of Cornwall* in 1602, believed its particular meteorological atmosphere could provide health benefits:

> …the air thereof is cleansed, as with bellows, by the billows, and flowing and ebbing of the Sea, and therethrough becommeth pure, and subtle, and by consequence, healthful; so as the Inhabitants do seldom take a ruthful and reaving experience of those harms, which infectious diseases use to carry with them. But yet I have noted, that this so piercing an air, is apter to preserve than recover health, especially in any languishing sickness which hath possessed strangers…
>
> The Spring visiteth not these quarters so timely as Eastern parts. Summer imparteth a verie temperate heat, recompensing his slow fostering of the fruits with their kindly ripening. Autumn bringeth a somewhat late Harvest, especially to the middle of the Shire, where they seldom inn their corn before Michaelmas. Winter, by reason of the South's near neighbourhood, and Sea's warm breath, favoureth it with a milder cold then elsewhere, so as, upon both coasts, the Frost and Snow come very seldom, and make a speedy departure.[36]

Fool's Gold

When I visited Brian and Margaret Eyers at the Cornish Saffron Company on the Roseland Peninsula, in October 2021, it was mizzly sort of day – perhaps the kind of weather the Scots would describe as 'dreich'. Nevertheless, they still manage to grow saffron successfully. The weather was indeed a shame, as I was assured that on a fine day you can see the sea from their saffron grounds.

Much of the soil in Cornwall is derived from granite. Worgan describes three types. The first is a shallow black earth known locally as 'growan' (gravelly) which was used for grazing. Other areas had slaty soil or loam, which if manured produced good crops. Wheat, barley and oats were grown but Worgan also notes that growan was 'particularly suited to potatoes'. While neither Carew nor Worgan mention saffron growing directly, the fact that much of the top soil was free-draining would surely have made it conducive to growing these flowers? Some farmers operated a crop rotation system whereby a few years of growing corn would be followed by a year of turnips (on well fertilised ground). The land would then be laid to dressed grass for some four years before returning the refreshed soil to corn. Again, it is easy to imagine that *Crocus sativus* corms could replace grass (assuming the latter was not required for cattle) in a rotation system.[37]

Imagination is one thing, but is there any evidence to suggest that saffron was grown in Cornwall? Vida Heard talks of being 'led up many a garden path with rumours of saffron parks and gardens'.[38] Charlotte Hawkey's nineteenth-century family memoir provides a brief mention of saffron being grown in the vicarage garden in Launcells (on the north coast of Cornwall, close to Bude). 'For culinary purposes,' she wrote, 'there were to be found the angelica and caraway plants, and

Saffron Cultivation: The Right Location

the saffron crocus, within whose blue petals was stored a supply of genuine colouring for the manifold cakes and Revel-buns for which Launcells was celebrated.' However, this was clearly not a commercial enterprise. It appears from Hawkey's description that the garden was home to a number of horticultural curiosities, of which saffron was just one: 'Some shrubs and plants flourished in this garden which I have rarely seen elsewhere.'[39]

More concrete evidence of saffron growing in Cornwall can be found in the archives at Kresen Kernow. A saffron meadow belonging to the Treffry family of Place House in Fowey was leased on at least two occasions during the mid to late seventeenth century. John Treffry (1595–1658) briefly sat in the House of Commons from 1621 to 1622. Although his family could trace their Cornish roots back to the thirteenth century and were significant landowners in the area (his father, William, owned six manors when he died at the beginning of the seventeenth century), John found himself in financial difficulties in the two decades leading up to the English Civil War. Much of the estate he had inherited from his father was set aside to generate dowries for Treffry's sisters, or was tied up in jointure arrangements[40] for his mother and grandmother. In 1636 he incurred at least twenty-five writs of outlawry for debt, although few of these seem to have been executed.

Treffry remained loyal to the Crown when war broke out in 1642. He was involved in defending Fowey on behalf of Charles I when the town was attacked by parliamentary troops in 1644. Despite his royalist affiliation, Treffry (and Place House) managed to escape the conflict relatively unscathed. This was most likely due to his parliamentary connections. His brother-in-law, John Trefusis (1586-1647), was a prominent parliamentarian (it is he who, Treffry family tradition states, prevented Place House from being pillaged). Although he was unsympathetic to other royalists, Trefusis protected his Treffry relatives from having their assets seized by the government.[41]

In 1654, John Treffry's estate was cleared of any claims upon it.

Nevertheless, in December 1653, he was still able to lease a saffron meadow for 99 years to William Major, a merchant from Fowey. When Treffry died in 1658, his estate passed on to his cousin, Thomas Treffry, as he had no children. Thomas's son John entered into another 99-year lease for a saffron meadow in December 1697. On this occasion, the lessee was a Fowey merchant called John Pomeroy. As both lessees are listed in the agreements as 'merchants' it seems unlikely that they were working the land themselves. However, saffron growing must have been a profitable sideline for them both, particularly given Fowey's shipping connections.[42]

Another notable Cornish family with links to saffron meadows were the Enys's. The family appears to have fallen on hard times during the early seventeenth century (not unlike the Treffrys) forcing them to sell a lot of their land. However, when Samuel Enys (1611–97) returned from Spain after the Civil War, having made his fortune as a merchant, he proceeded to purchase some of the remaining familial lands. His grandson, also called Samuel (1681–1744), married well and continued to consolidate and increase the family's estates in Cornwall. This included the purchase of the manors of Pettigrew and Nampity, situated in Gerrans on the Roseland Peninsula, in the early eighteenth century.

On 29 September 1711 Samuel Enys let two fields called 'the Saffron Meadows' which were part of the Nampity tenement. The lessee was a yeoman called John Quintrell and the duration of the agreement was 99 years or three lives. Hilary Thompson's book *A History of Gerrans and Portscatho 1700–1830* contains a map of the manors of Pettigrew, Nampity and Tregaswick dating from 1793 and the saffron meadows were still known as such. The purpose, past or present, of other fields such as Mustard Meadow, Sow's Meadow, a hop garden and orchards is also detailed on the map.[43]

Of course there is no guarantee at this stage that the Enys fields were being used to grow saffron specifically. Another lease signed in 1793 between John Carthew, gentleman, and Joseph Gawler, an innkeeper,

Saffron Cultivation: The Right Location

both of St Austell, for five fields in Tregorrick, refers to the land as 'commonly known by the name of Saffron parks'. The annual rent for this land was £17 10s 6d. The fact that the fields have retained the name of Saffron Parks implies that the spice was grown there at some point, although it is unknown exactly what Gawler intended to do with the land.[44]

County archives record that saffron was grown to some extent across many southern and eastern counties in England, from the sixteenth to eighteenth centuries. Harrison heard that saffron was being grown as far west as Gloucestershire, and thought cultivation would thrive around the Chiltern Hills and the Vale of the White Horse (he even goes as far to say that some people thought saffron from this area was superior to that of Walden, fetching 6d to 12d more per pound as a consequence). There is some evidence to support this theory in references to saffron gardens around Tewkesbury, dating from the seventeenth century. In High Wycombe, Buckinghamshire, on 1 February 1692, John Archdale leased three roods of meadow called Saffron Plot and five acres called Pardon Croft to George Bradshaw for a period of fourteen years. The annual rent for these lands was £6 16s. A saffron garden in 'Apuldram' (or Appledram, a small parish on the north-eastern upper reach of Chichester Harbour in West Sussex) was leased to William Ryman in 1656.[45]

Further eastwards, Reginald Grey of Wrest included two saffron closes in the twenty-one year lease for 112 acres on the site of Norwood Manor in Silsoe, Bedfordshire, to a yeoman called Robert Cheilde in 1567. Throughout the seventeenth century there are records of saffron 'pens', 'land' and 'panes' leased or sold in Suffolk. Norfolk with its 'healthful, serene and mild' climate was also home to saffron cultivation. In the seventeenth century, Camden recorded that the 'little town' of Walsingham 'is noted at present for producing the best Saffron'. In 1461, 20d was paid for planting saffron in the infirmary garden attached to Norwich Cathedral priory.

As well as its popular pilgrimage site, by the sixteenth century

Fool's Gold

Walsingham in Norfolk had also become famous for its saffron. During this period, townsfolk such as Margaret Grey and Edmund Heyward left bequests of saffron grounds in their wills. *Pigot's Directory of Norfolk* (1839) lists saffron as a one of the county's agricultural crops. However, Sally Francis notes that by 1847 this crop had not been grown in Walsingham for many years.[46]

These are just a few examples to illustrate the breadth of saffron cultivation in the country, albeit on a small scale. The legacy of this micro industry can be found in surviving street names such as Saffron Lane in Leicester, and Saffron Hill in London.[47]

Chapter Three

Saffron Cultivation:
Planting & Harvesting

'Lockers on board a ship are nothing to the cupboards of an old house,' wrote the Reverend Henry John Wale (1827–1892). The Reverend Wale's ancestral home had been full of them. When the house in Little Shelford, Cambridgeshire, was eventually pulled down, one of these cupboards was found to contain a number of household account books that had been kept by Thomas Wale (1701–1796), the reverend's grandfather. Reverend Wale published extracts from these books in 1883 which provide a fascinating insight into the life of an eighteenth-century gentleman farmer.[1]

Thomas Wale returned to his Cambridgeshire estate in the summer of 1764 after a successful career in Latvia as a factor, spanning some forty years (primarily trading in ships' masts, hemp and flax). Once back on his home turf, he devoted his energies to farming. As well as a record of household expenditure, his pocketbooks contain a variety of recipes (culinary and medicinal), and a series of domestic and agricultural observations, including detailed notes on growing saffron, which he obtained from William Clarke Senior, in 1771. It is unclear whether Mr Clarke was leasing his 'saffron gardens' direct from Wale or cultivating saffron on Wale's behalf, but Wale obviously felt Clarke's observations were pertinent enough to record in his pocket book. Records show that saffron was grown in Shelford (there is barely a mile between Little Shelford and neighbouring Great Shelford) during Wale's lifetime. A wheelwright called Richard Tunwell of Great Shelford left 'one moiety of my stock of Saffron heads… to be planted in the Saffron Grounds of Shelford' to his son Thomas in his will in 1711.[2]

Saffron was often planted on fallow ground which had born barley the previous year. It was grown on a rotation system as noted by Clarke:[3]

> We have always three plantations, whereof we plough up one every year, gather out the heads or roots and clean them one by one throwing away all the are rotten or infested, they plant them again in another plot of land which has not born saffron for years before.
>
> They doe not bear the first year they are planted, except for a few flowers, which we call our dorts.
>
> The next year it bears and then we call it our new ground – and the summer after we plough up, so we have always two bearing grounds, and one that does not bear.[4]

Clarke adds that the ground was much improved after a period of saffron cultivation. William Harrison claimed that barley could be successfully grown on a former saffron plot for eighteen to twenty years without the need for any further fertiliser. Preparation for planting a new plot of saffron begins in the spring by ploughing the ground. In 1558 Robert Barker of Hinxton left his wife, Margery, among other things, saffron crops with instructions that 'Anthony and Richard, my sons, plough the saffron grounds for his wife and carry the saffron heads and corn to Harvest for her life'.[5] According to James Douglass, a doctor and a member of the Royal Society, the best time is around Lady Day (25 March) or early April. He explains that saffron grounds typically range from one to three acres in size. Charles Howard and Douglass, in their respective papers to the Royal Society, both recommend digging in plenty of well-rotted manure three or four weeks later. Richard Bradley (being Bradley) has different views on the subject of dung. Although he acknowledges that it is widely used in areas renowned for growing saffron, he claims dung 'is of bad consequence to the Roots, which are

Saffron Cultivation: Planting & Harvesting

bulbous, by breeding a Canker in them'. He adds 'my Experience teaches me a fresh Earth; a little light, if it has about five or six inches Surface or Staple, with a tolerable Bottom, will do much better than all the forced Earth by Dungs.' Bradley appears to be in the minority here, with other eighteenth-century commentators following Howard's lead.[6]

At midsummer the grounds would be ploughed again. Trenches were dug with a spit shovel (made of thin iron it should measure ten inches (25 cm) in length and be five inches (12.5 cm) in width and have a means for attaching a long handle). The depth of the trenches was three inches (7.5 cm). They were spaced three inches apart. Every two to three metres a path would be left to facilitate the picking of the saffron later in the season. This also served as an area where weeds could be thrown. The trenches were dug in blocks of a pole or a rod (sixteen and a half feet, or a little over five metres). Sometimes a broad trench was left between each parcel of land to act as a boundary if there were more than one 'croker' farming in an inclosure.

The planting of the saffron corms, which generally occurred between July and early September, was a joint effort. As the man (and this manual element appears to have been men's work) dug the trench his partner, often a woman, would set the bulbs or corms (which Harrison describes as resembling a medium-sized chestnut) in the furrow leaving roughly three inches (7.5 cm) between each corm. The earth from the second trench was used to cover these bulbs. And so the pair would continue until the whole rood had been planted. According to Howard, sixteen quarters of saffron heads were sufficient to plant one acre. In his day (1677) a quarter (about 2 stone or 12.7 kg) of saffron heads cost 10 s which meant an acre would cost £8 to plant. Kenneth Neale estimates that an acre could contain as many as 400,000 heads of saffron.[7]

Pests, such as cattle, sheep, pigs or hares, were a perennial problem. The croker could circumvent this by fencing in his plot. When William Ellis visited a grower near Saffron Walden, he found a two-acre plot enclosed with rodded hurdles to 'entirely secure it from the Damage of Hares, who would certainly destroy it [the saffron], if they had Liberty to come at it'. Evidently,[8] hares loved the leaves, but in eating them they could weaken the corms for the following season. Johann Ferdinand Hertodt (1647–1714), a German physician best known for his book devoted to saffron, *Crocologia,* of 1671, warns that mice and moles attack saffron bulbs because they are sweet. He recommends a mixture of white hellebore, rind of dog's mercury, pearl barley, eggs, wine and milk. Small balls of this paste were put into the holes made by moles to act as a deterrent. Cattle and sheep also needed to be kept away from the plots, as they could trample the tender shoots. Any person who allowed their livestock to trespass onto and damage a saffron ground could face a hefty fine. Hog owners were presented at a manorial court in 1518 for allowing their animals to trespass in some saffron beds. Weeds too had to be removed and raked into the furrows 'otherwise,' Douglass informs the reader, 'they would hinder the Growth of the Plants'. Clarke speaks of making the grounds 'as fine as a garden,'[9] in preparation for the harvest.

In England, the saffron crocus begins blooming around mid-September (about two weeks before Michaelmas on 29 September). The shoot appears like 'a small white spire about as big as the small end off a tobacco pype, which contains sometimes two or three flowers besides the grass'.[10] There could be no delay in the harvest and the flowers had to be picked 'before they are full blown, whether wet or dry. This was done early in the morning before the sun was so powerful that it would cause the flowers to 'welk or flitter' (dry up or wither), as Harrison puts it. This work was often carried out by women and children, who would delicately but swiftly remove the flowers and place them in a basket. Ellis speaks of being surprised at the 'considerable number of Women and Girls gathering the Blue Flowers of the Saffron, at the Break of the Day'. Only the blooms were picked. The long spiky leaves would be left until they 'withered away'. Any further leaves produced between May and September could be mown (if they had not yet died back) and fed to livestock until the harvesting commenced. The saffron pickers were usually done with the morning harvest by ten or eleven o'clock. They were expected to return to the grounds every day, including Sunday, during the blooming season whatever the weather, until all the crop had been gathered. The length of the season varied according to the climatic conditions, but in England

SAFFRON CULTIVATION: PLANTING & HARVESTING

Peasant depicted picking saffron in the fifteenth century Tacuinum Sanitatis.

it was generally around four to six weeks (although it could stretch into November on a good year or if the flowers appeared later than usual).

Douglass notes that warm summers with 'gentle showers from time to time' provide the most optimal weather for saffron production. Clarke also observes that the grounds should not be overhung by trees to give the plants the full advantage of the sun. 'If the weather be warm, sometimes an acre will employ 10 people when there is a great crop,' explained Clarke, 'but that does not often happen.' In years such as this, itinerant labourers were hired. In 1580, Elizabeth Cole travelled to Walden from her home of Mildenhall in Suffolk to pick saffron. Unfortunately, she appears to have fallen in with the wrong crowd. She was arrested by the constables of Bocking, Essex, and charged with being a vagabond. One of Elizabeth's companions, Mary Watson, was also accused of stealing a number of items including a petticoat and a cheesecloth during their acquaintance.[11]

Drying

For those working in the saffron industry, the day was far from over when the harvest had been gathered. The pickers would return to their homes or place of work, and the flowers were spread on a large table. Sitting around the table, they would begin carefully removing the 'chives' (the red stigmas). Clarke notes that the flowers were always thrown away 'into ye street'. The best saffron is, 'that which consists of the thickest and shortest chives, of a high-red and shining colour, both without and within alike'. This labour intensive, hands-on approach is one of the reasons why saffron was, and continues to be, the world's most expensive spice. The fresh or wet chives could be left to dry a little in the sun (assuming there was some). Bradley warned that wet weather bruised and spoilt the stigmas, causing the saffron to be 'small and weak'.[12]

Then came the crucial business of drying the chives. This is where it could all go horribly wrong. 'Considering how many Accidents the Saffron is subject to,' notes Bradley in the *The Country Housewife* and *Lady's Director* (1727), 'that is dry'd upon the common Kilns, by the scorching of it by too hot a Fire, and the unskillfulness of the dryers; I do not wonder that there is so much Saffron spoiled.' Bradley had studied several methods for drying saffron. He makes particular mention of his 'Ingenious Friend, Samuel Trowell,' who would go on to write *A New Treatise of Husbandry, Gardening, and other Curious Matters relating to Country Affairs* in 1739. Trowell grew saffron in his garden in Poplar, Essex. After harvesting the chives Trowell would dry the saffron 'by putting it into a Bladder, and keeping it for some time in a warm Pocket'. Another method for drying saffron was to put the chives 'between two thick Glasses, letting them lie in the sun for some time'. However, Bradley notes that both methods are only suitable for small quantities of saffron. He adds that 'there is only this Rule we ought to have before us; and that is, to dry it in such a manner, that only the watry parts may be exhaled, and none of the fine parts: for which reason, if the Glass will bear the Fire of the Kilns I have mention'd, I judge that it will be much the best way'. According to Clarke, saffron could also be dried between two sheets of coarse white paper placed on the brass face of a warming pan, particularly when the yield was low.[13]

Bradley goes to great lengths to describe how a kiln should be constructed. The kilns were relatively small and were designed to be portable (although given the oak frame and thickness of mortar I daresay they would still have been cumbersome to move):

> The Kiln is much narrower at the bottom than at the top; that is, about a foot square at the bottom, and two foot at the top, and about two foot high. This is made of Oak, framed together, and cover'd with Laths on the outside, as well as lined with them. Upon these Laths within-side, is spread a strong Mortar two Inches thick, and the outside is cover'd with Lime and Hair; but the bottom on the inside must be cover'd four or five Inches thick with the strong Mortar, to serve as an Hearth to lay the Fire on, leaving a hole on one side to put in the Charcoal Fire, and give it Air.[14]

Modern methods for drying saffron result in individual threads known as 'hay'. At the time Howard, Bradley and Douglass were writing, it was more common for the saffron to be dried in 'cakes':

> Upon the top of this Kiln must be strain'd a Hair-Cloth as tight as possible, and nail'd very fast; because when we put on our Saffron between the Papers to dry, we must press it with a Weight of twenty-five or thirty Pounds in the drying of it. Keep the Fire as constant and gentle as possible, and as soon as it begins to smell pretty strong, turn the Papers, and set on the Weight again, till the other side of the Cake is well dry'd.[15]

Initially, the fire was kept 'pretty strong' to encourage the chives to sweat – as they did so steam would escape from the papers. At the end of the saffron harvest, Douglass recommends sprinkling the cake with a little small beer (Bradley recommends brushing the cake with a solution of beer mixed with saffron before it is turned, perhaps to prevent burning the exterior of the cake). A close eye had to be kept on the saffron in case it scorched. After an hour. the saffron 'sandwich' would be carefully flipped over and cooked for another hour. These first two hours were crucial. So long as the saffron did not catch, most crokers reckoned that the remainder of the drying process would be plain sailing. From this point onwards the fire was kept low (charcoal was the best fuel as it smoked less) and the cake was turned every half hour for twenty-four hours.[16]

The papers used to protect the cake were valuable in themselves and could be sold after the process was complete. As the saffron began to sweat (aided with a little beer) the papers would absorb the moisture. Although the tincture contained within the sheets was far less potent than cake saffron, it could still be extracted and used as a saffron solution. This, Bradley explains was one of the dryer's perks:

> The Paper you dry it in, must be white Paper; and in many places they will lay the Paper under and over six or seven sheets thick, especially on the top, on purpose to get the Tincture of the Saffron, but this must be guarded against: and likewise they will put the outside Papers to fresh Saffron, on purpose to make them full partake of its Tincture; but this weakens the Strength of the Saffron, as I have observ'd before, and the Papers sell well, which are the Dryers Perquisites.[17]

A year later, Bradley said he had contrived a kiln to efficiently dry saffron without any fear of it being scorched. Whether this was the kiln that he had offered to Sloane is unknown. Bradley planned to publish details of the kiln in his next book, a proposed natural history of Cambridgeshire and Essex, but unfortunately he died before it saw the light of day, so any changes he proposed to make to the method outlined above are unknown. Once the cakes were 'nicely dryed', they would be wrapped in paper, then dry flannels before being kept in a trunk or chest to protect them from moisture.[18]

Saffron Cultivation: Planting & Harvesting

Yields

The drying process significantly reduced the weight of the harvested saffron. Five pounds of wet chives when dried usually yielded one pound of dry saffron. The quantity of wet chives harvested each season varied considerably, depending on the age of the corms, environmental factors, and interference by pests. The first season was always a little uncertain. For a good first year, Douglass claimed a rood could produce five or six pounds of wet chives. However, some saffron plots produced as little as one or two pounds 'and sometimes not enough to make it worth while to gather and dry it'. As a conservative estimate, Douglass suggests that in the first year an acre would yield two pounds of dried saffron. However, once the plants were established the croker could anticipate twenty-four pounds of dried saffron per acre in the second and third years, with the last year being considerably larger than the second. Bradley was more conservative still, putting the common yield at fifteen pounds per acre.[19]

In Essex and Cambridgeshire the corms were raised in the middle of the summer following the third year's harvest (according to Harrison, the crokers of Norfolk and Suffolk left their corms *in situ* for seven years, which is more in line with Pliny's advice). When Samuel Dale (1659–1739), a naturalist and apothecary, returned to his home in Braintree, Essex from Cambridge, he observed the crokers of Great Chesterford at work:

> [T]hey were now very busy in taking up of their Saffron roots, that they might plant them again in fresh ground about Michaelmas. When they have taken them up they bring them home and there take off their outward skin which they call Ross.[20]

The lifting of the corms, which occurred around July, could be as labour intensive as planting them. Like many bulbs, saffron corms are not terribly big and are a nutty brown colour which means they are well camouflaged when in the soil. This presumably meant a bit of rooting around to locate them. Plus the ground had to be ploughed or dug over after the corms were removed to prepare it for future cultivation. This could provide enough work for fifteen people. Dirt was removed from the saffron corms which were stored for planting a little later in the year and old, spent corms were discarded. The best thing for the croker about raising the bulbs was that they were said to 'child' (i.e. multiply) in the ground. Twenty-four quarters of re-plantable corms could be realised from an acre of ground at the end of a saffron rotation. The croker kept the 'largest, plumpest and fattest' roots for himself. The smaller roots or those that were long and pointed (called spickets or spickards) were rejected or sold on. Harrison felt that minimal profit could be made from the sale of these 'children', unless a particularly harsh winter had caused the corms to rot (as occurred in 1607 in Ickleton). Douglass calculated the costings to cultivate an acre of saffron ground over a three-year period:[21]

Rent for three years	£3 0s 0d
Ploughing three times	£0 18s 0d
Dunging	£3 12s 0d
Hedging	£1 16s 0d
Planting the heads	£1 12s 0d
Weeding	£1 4s 0d
Picking the flowers	£6 10s 0d
Drying the flowers	£1 6s 0d
Instruments of labour for three years with the kiln	£0 10s 0d
Ploughing the ground once and harrowing twice	£0 12s 0d
Gathering saffron heads	£1 0s 0d
Cleaning and sorting the heads	£1 12s 0d
Total	**£23 12s 0d**

Based on the assumption that an acre of saffron ground would yield twenty-six pounds of neat saffron over three years, and fixing the price per pound at thirty shillings, the croker could make £39 for his saffron harvest. The selling price was as unpredictable as the yield. When saffron was plentiful it sold for as little as twenty shillings per pound, but in poor cropping years it had been known to fetch between £3 and £4 a pound. This was still the case in Clarke's day. This equated to an annual profit of £5 4s. Douglass had assumed that the crokers would employ labour,

Saffron Cultivation: Planting & Harvesting

but concedes this cost could be saved if the work were carried out by themselves and their families.[22]

Saffron adulteration

It stands to reason that something as valuable as saffron would attract attempts to increase profits made from the sale of it through adulteration. It is an age-old temptation across Europe and further afield. In Pliny's opinion 'nothing is adulterated as much as saffron.'[23]

Henry II of France attempted to stamp out this fraud by issuing an edict in 1550:

> For some time past a certain quantity of the said saffron has been found altered, disguised and sophisticated by being mixed with oil, honey and other mixtures, in order that the said saffron, which is sold by weight, may be rendered heavier; and some add to it other herbs similar in colour and substance to beef over-boiled, and reduced to threads, which saffron, thus mixed and adulterated cannot be long kept and is highly prejudicial to the human body; which, besides the said injury, may prevent the above said foreign merchants from purchasing it, to the great diminution of our revenues, and to the great detriment of foreign nations against which we ought to provide.[24]

Harrison referred to these fraudsters as 'crafty jacks' who would combine genuine saffron with other plants, such as Sonchus (sow thistle – a small, dandelion like flower), petals from plants such as safflower (*Carthamus tinctorius* – known as bastard saffron because it can resemble the true spice but lacks its flavour), and pot marigold (*Calendula officinalis* – which seventeenth-century herbalist Robert Turner regarded as being 'not much inferiour to Saffron'[25]). Slices of pomegranate flowers were also used as adulterants. Sometimes, saffron from which the colour had already been extracted was added, and even fibres of dried smoked beef were utilised to doctor batches of of the spice. Another trick was to grease the papers used in the drying process with a little candle grease, as this would improve the

Fool's Gold

The dried petals of Carthamus tinctorius known as bastard or false saffron have been passed off as the true spice in the past.

colour of inferior saffron. Bradley admits that dryers would sometimes not dry the saffron as much as they ought to out of a 'willingness to get money'. Butter or oil could also be sprinkled over the cake to increase the weight. Clarke was convinced that 'the saffron produced and brought from Spain is greatly inferior to ye English on account of ye Oylls the

Saffron Cultivation: Planting & Harvesting

Spaniards use in drying loose and not pressed cakes as the English doe'.[26]

Various tests could be employed to ascertain whether saffron was genuine or not. Pliny believed that pure saffron should be so brittle that it crackled when rubbed between the fingers. He also said it that if you touched your face or eyes after doing this test they would sting. Harrison claimed adulteration with a fatty substance could be detected by holding some fibres over a fire in a silver spoon. Colour was also an indicator – if the chives were too dark they were likely to be inferior saffron (e.g. scorched), or something else entirely. In the case of meat fibres, these could be exposed by submerging some of the saffron in hot water, which would cause them to expand and soften, thereby exposing their true nature.[27]

It would be easy to assume that the adulteration of saffron no longer takes place. However, as a valuable commodity, the temptation to doctor this most precious of spices still occurs in the twenty-first century. The Iranian saffron industry, which produces some ninety per cent of the world's supply, is 'beset by smuggling, counterfeiting and adulteration'.[28] In the introduction to their translation of Hertodt's *Crocologia,* Sally Francis and Maria Teresa Ramandi note that safflower florets or ground turmeric are still passed off as real saffron to unsuspecting tourists in markets. Other adulterants include maize silks, dyed willow, grass roots, annatto, honey, artificial colours like tartrazine (E102), nylon fibres, gypsum, and chalk (to name but a few).[29] After the Second World War, annatto was used to replace saffron in the traditional saffron buns popular in the West Country. Elizabeth David remarks 'it was soon appreciated by those familiar with the originals that saffron was a very great deal more than just a colouring agent'.[30]

David Smale of English Saffron keeps an eye out for counterfeit saffron on his travels, and has accumulated a bit of a rogues gallery of fake samples over the years: 'The worse example I found was in an Indian market. This guy was insisting it was genuine saffron which I knew it wasn't. I bought some anyway and later, on closer inspection, it turned out to be little bits of paper shredded up and dyed red.'[31]

Fool's Gold

Today, there are more stringent tests available to weed out fraud in saffron, by detecting certain bioactive compounds that are found in the spice. The three major compounds are crocins (powerful colourants which have strong antioxidant properties), picrocrocin (which give saffron its flavour and bitterness); and saffranal (the volatile oil responsible for the spice's hay like aroma stimulated by the proper drying of saffron). Much of the saffron trade now uses the International Standards Organisation's Specification (ISO 3632-1: 2011) and test methods (ISO 3632-2: 2010). These detect the colour giving strength, the safranal content and picrocrocin level. Three grades can be awarded with level one being the highest, reserved for the best quality saffron. However, despite the advances in science and technology, some synthetic chemicals can be used to mimic the appearance of powdered saffron and can escape detection even by these stringent standards.[32]

CHAPTER FOUR

Saffron as a Medicinal Ingredient

Since classical times, saffron has been imbued with a number of beneficial qualities, particularly in the sphere of medicine where it could be combined with other ingredients to remedy a variety of disorders. Pliny and Dioscorides provide a long list of complaints that saffron could treat, such as inflammation or discharge from the eyes (particularly when applied with woman's breast milk) and skin rashes like erysipelas. 'Those who take saffron first will not feel the after effects of wine and will become intoxicated with difficulty,' Pliny assured his readers. Saffron was a diuretic; was good for all manner of inflammations but especially chest infections, and could help with gynaecological issues such as suffocation of the womb.[1] It also aided digestion (when mixed with passum, a raisin wine, it could counteract the affects of over indulgence), could induce sleep (although later authors like John Gerard would beg to differ on this point) and was an aphrodisiac. But it was not without its dangers. Dioscorides believed three spoonfuls taken in water could be fatal.[2]

From ancient times, medicine had been governed by the theory of the four humors or humours – blood, yellow bile, black bile and phlegm – first mentioned by Hippocrates in his treatise *The Nature of Man* in 5 BCE. Galen would expand on this theory in 2 CE.[3] It was a cocktail of these natural elements in the body that dictated a person's temperament or complexion. The humors were used to explain different characteristics between personalities, genders, age and even race. They were also used to explain the cause of disease. All functions could be condensed into four qualities: hot, cold, dry and wet. An individual's complexion, acquired at the moment of conception, could be described with a mixture of these qualities. Blood was present in all people (acting as the mixer if you like) and was combined with different degrees of the other humors. If yellow bile predominated you were hot headed (choleric); people with a high level of black bile were melancholic (the 'cup is half empty' personality); apathy and lethargy ruled people of phlegmatic disposition; when blood was at the fore people were pleasant and warm.[4]

Your complexion could also be affected by other factors that were deemed to be non-naturals, such as the air that we breathe; exercise (which included sex); sleep and waking; secretions, like sweat, and excretions, like urine; emotions (anger, grief and envy) and ingested substances like food, drink and medicine. The non-naturals were carefully managed to ensure good health through an appropriate regimen or treatment prescribed by a physician. A good physician was able to determine how long a disease or ailment would run to its final conclusion i.e. recovery or death. The treatments they prescribed were designed to restore the individual back to health. These prophylactics were made from herbs and minerals known as *materia medica*. Each *materia medica* had its own qualities (hot, dry, wet, cold) in different degrees ranging from the first (imperceptible) to the fourth (fatal). Saffron, notes Nicholas Culpeper, was hot in the second degree and dry in the first degree. It 'powerfully concocts, and sends out whatever humour offends the body, drives back inflammations; applied outwardly, encreases venery, and provokes urine'.[5]

In order to re-establish humoral balance within a patient, a medicine of an opposing quality would be prescribed. Excessive heat caused by illness would be treated with a medicine containing ingredients possessing cold qualities. If just one ingredient were used it was referred to as a 'simple'. However, often several ingredients were mixed together to produce more complex medicines.

Of the non-natural factors, the food and drink consumed by an individual was one of the most influential. 'When we make proper use of foods in recipes, the attendant humours follow,' explained Galen.[6] In his *Physick for the Sicknesse, Commonly called the Plague* (1636), Stephen Bradwell devotes over ten pages to explaining what foods are good to prevent or treat sufferers of plague. 'Let your meate be always good and sweet, temperate betwixt hot and cold, and not too moyst or fleshie: easie of digestion, and such as makes the best Bloud,' he asserts. For the very sick and weak, who were unable to eat solid food, he recommends a rich meaty broth spiced with cinnamon, cloves, saffron, red coral and sugar (unless you were female, he advised women to avoid saffron and to use a powder of harts horn, red and yellow sanders, cloves and cinnamon instead).[7]

Women were chiefly responsible for the health and well-being of the household. Some of those from wealthy backgrounds were actively involved in preparing their own medicines and tonics, such as Lady Grace Mildmay (1552–1620), who recorded her medicinal remedies in her private journals.[8] The raw materials for these remedies could be purchased from apothecaries, who themselves provided a multitude of ready-made potions. Apothecary John Clerk counted Edward IV (1442–1483) and a number of noble families and high-ranking ladies among his clientele, such as Katherine Neville, Duchess of Norfolk. Over a period of eight years Clerk had supplied the Duchess with 'simples' (the collective name for individual 'pharmaceutical' ingredients), like saffron, galingale, liquorice, cinnamon and sandalwood.[9]

Individual herbs and spices, like those purchased by the Duchess, were revered for their health-giving benefits. In later eras some, like saffron, would even prompt entire books to be written about them. Seventeenth century physician and naturalist Johann Ferdinand Hertodt's *Crocologia* (1671) provides a plethora of pharmaceutical preparations including saffron (and other ingredients) to treat everything from headaches to the plague. 'Saffron is a restorative medicine, which deservedly must be mixed with drugs both for internal and external use; in fact it fortifies and enriches,' declared Hertodt. However, he also warned that 'saffron causes laughing and it should not be difficult to believe that men die of immoderate laughing because of the excessive saffron eaten'.[10]

Medical treatises published during the seventeenth century, such as the compendium of treatments known as *Natura exenterata* published under the pseudonym Philiatros in 1655, were aimed at both lay and professional practitioners.[11] These 'physic' books, which largely concerned the art of distilling, were a valuable source of home-made remedies. Between the years 1735–38, Rebecca Tallamy made her own notes in the margins of a 1651 edition of John French's *The Art of Distillation* (such as a cure for yellow jaundice that includes saffron and turmeric written at the bottom of a 'contents' page at the beginning of the book). On some blank pages at the back of the book she has recorded her own culinary, household and medicinal recipes.[12] Aristocratic women, and some men too, wrote down medical recipes in notebooks. It is also not unusual to find domestic notebooks that record both culinary and medical recipes, albeit in different sections (harking back to Galen's advice on food's relation to health). Ann Blencow (b. 1656) includes a section devoted to 'Physical Receipts' in her Receipt Book of 1694.[13]

Medicinal waters and cordials were often quite complex concoctions that required distilling, the action of purifying a liquid by a process of heating and cooling. They were valuable remedies to have on standby, both to treat family ailments and to be distributed to the poor in the surrounding area. Aqua vitae ('water of life'), which in the medieval era had been touted as an essential elixir said to cure a multitude of

Saffron as a Medicinal Ingredient

complaints and illnesses, was frequently recommended as a base for these medications.

Elizabeth Freke (1641–1714), an elderly widow from Bilney in Norfolk, was clearly a skilled distiller of cordial waters. She owned all the equipment required to make medicines such as an alembic, a cold still and a bain marie. She also kept a meticulous record of the cordial waters she stored in her closet for her own use.[14] Her stocktake on 27 May 1712 records around fifty quarts of cordial waters and the year in which they were distilled, and includes one quart of saffron syrup. There was another little cupboard above this which contained a further sixteen pints of various tinctures and cordials, including '2 pints of hungary water for my wretched head, 1709' and a little vial of saffron water.[15]

Like many noble women of the era Elizabeth kept a book of handwritten recipes which included extracts from popular physic and herbals books, like that of John Gerard. Of the virtues of saffron, transcribed from Gerard's *Herbal*, she writes that it 'strengthens and opens the chest, removes obstructions, and is useful in remedies for the lungs; it is also good for surfeits, stopping the liver, and yellow jaundice; and finally it will provoke urine.' Elaine Leong has observed that over seventy per cent of the recipes in Elizabeth's notebook concern specific ailments. As few of these prescriptions are logged by Elizabeth as being ready made and stored in her closet it suggests they were made on a needs be basis.[16]

Simple distilled waters, like rose or aniseed water, could be purchased direct from the apothecary or distiller. These were used as the basis for more complex waters. Elizabeth's recipe for syrup of saffron requires the saffron to be steeped in aniseed water for twenty days, shaking the stopped bottle once a day. After this time further ingredients were added and then the mixture was boiled down to a syrup. The syrup was then strained, simmered for a little while longer before being left to cool in a silver basin and then finally bottled.[17] The syrup of saffron would have been ready to use on its own (saffron cordial was good for small pox or the ague)[18] or to add to other preparations.

'Gold in physic is a cordial,' wrote Chaucer in the prologue to the *Canterbury Tales*. Saffron had been used to give aqua vitae a golden hue since the fifteenth century. It is easy to understand why – gold was believed to prolong life and strengthen the heart. However, most physicians knew that small particles of gold leaf simply passed through the patient's digestive system so sought of find a way to make a digestible liquid gold. Several recipes appeared during the Tudor period for drinkable gold, some of which involved complex processes of heating and numerous distillings to extract the beneficial qualities of the metal (a goldsmith's son called Francis Anthony (1550–1623) made a fortune from selling *aurum potabile* or 'drinkable gold'). Lady Grace includes a recipe in her notebook that she notes is 'wonderful good to stay all manner of bloody flux and subtle humours'.[19] A simpler solution was to take a golden cordial which usually comprised brandy, coloured with alkermes (a forerunner of cochineal) and saffron, flavoured with oil of cloves, and sweetened with sugar. Eliza Smith's 'Golden Cordial' in *The Compleat Housewife* (1727) included small pieces of gold leaf just to emphasise how beneficial it was to health.[20]

Medicinal recipe collections like Elizabeth Freke's usually contain at least one polycrest or universal 'cure-all' medicine. Elizabeth had three such formulas in her cupboards like the ten pints of *aquamirabolus* distilled in 1710. The chief use seems to be treat consumption but it was 'excellent for all weak people' and considered a 'great cordiall water'.[21] They were often attributed to a particular physician, such as Anthony Duffy, whose *Elixir Salutis* (often referred to as Duffy's Elixir) promised to be the 'most Excellent Preservative of Man-kind' suitable for 'all Ages, Sexes, Complexions and Constitutions'. It claimed to cure everything from gout to rickets, and anything in between.[22] Perhaps one of the most famous recipes for an all-purpose cordial was that created by Sir Walter Raleigh. While incarcerated in the Tower of London from between 1603 and 1616, Raleigh passed the hours by distilling waters and cordials in a hen house within the grounds. His Great Cordial contained forty ingredients (various herbs, spices, like saffron, seeds and roots as well as pearls, coral, amber and musk) steeped in spirits of wine before being distilled. James I's wife, Anne of Denmark, was convinced the cordial had saved her life when she fell ill so asked Raleigh to send some to her son Prince Henry when he contracted typhoid fever in 1612. Unfortunately, it failed to save the young prince's life. Henry had contrived to get his father to agree to the release of Raleigh at the end of the year. However, on his son's death the king forgot his promise and Raleigh remained in prison for a further four years.[23]

The reputation of Raleigh's Great Cordial outlived the man himself. Charles II was keen to revive the cordial and ordered a French chemist and alchemist Nicolas le Fèvre (1615–1669) to review its benefits. Le Fèvre concluded that it was 'sufficient to maintain that beautiful and admirable Harmony that causes Health.' Of the many ingredients within the formula he has this to say about saffron:

> Saffron is one of the richest and most necessary morsels of our dish; and that is absolutely necessary to our Great Cordial, by reason of those admirable virtues that this Flower hides in it self. For it must needs be that Saffron has something above the other Drugs, since that after it hath been dried by Art, it seems as if it had some inward magnetick virtue, which recalls to it self the Balsam of the Air, which gives it again the same weight, the same vivacity of colour, and the same activity of odour; which is a thing worthy enough consideration. It is a sovereign Cordial, and esteemed to be the soul of the Lungs, by whose action the virtue of this Flower is carried unto the last Digestions by the Circulation and Respiration. It appeases pains, and gently procures Sleep; it cleanses the Womb, helps Child-birth, and purges the Woman: in fine, it is a little Panacea against the Plague, and against all other malignant diseases; it is also most happily used against the Jaundise.[24]

Raleigh was not the only gentleman to have a keen interest in distilling medical remedies. Sir Kenelm Digby (1603–1665), a nobleman with many strings to his bow (from diplomat to privateer and reputedly a generous lover), wrote a number of medicinal recipes which were later published by his steward George Hartman. Hartman had served Digby both at home and abroad and was given permission by Digby's only surviving son, John, to publish his 'Excellent Curiosites and Receipts' in memory of his father, whom he clearly admired. There are a number of recipes calling for saffron which are designed to treat a range of ailments from small pox; labour pains (which was also good for bringing on the afterbirth); palsy; an ointment to treat all manner of aches, bruises and redness of the face and a remedy to procure conception.[25] The recipe for 'A great Cordial made out of English Saffron' calls for four pounds of fresh saffron (i.e. that which has not been dried) to be shredded then placed in a pitcher which was buried in the ground for six weeks after which time the mixture was distilled in a bain marie over a low to moderate fire (to avoid scorching the saffron). Only a little of this tincture (two or three drops) was required in each dose. It was considered 'exceeding good in all Diseases' but was particularly adept at expelling poison and reviving the spirits.[26]

Saffron was included in many remedies for specific complaints like yellow jaundice, melancholy and a number of female reproductive health issues. These more complex recipes are the kinds of waters and cordials that Lady Grace and Elizabeth Freke would have made. I have included a few formulas containing saffron as examples below. Hopefully, it goes without saying that these are included for illustrative purposes only and have not been tried and tested by myself (and nor do I recommend that should you attempt these at home).

Plague was a constant threat hovering over the population in Britain during the early modern period so cordials to help prevent or treat the disease are frequently found in the domestic medicinal armoury. The Westminster law courts were suspended in 1464 due to an outbreak of

Saffron as a Medicinal Ingredient

plague and there were further outbreaks in 1467 and 1471. Preventatives against the pestilence were consumed in considerable quantities at the court of Edward IV. The Duchess of Norfolk bought a pomander from John Clerk as protection from the miasmic air thought to carry the plague as well as 8 lb of cordial powder and over 6lb of water explicitly against the disease. On 20 July 1665 the diarist Samuel Pepys reported that 1089 people had died from plague in the past week alone. He must have been quite reassured to receive a bottle of plague water from Lady Cateret. Like Elizabeth Freke, the Countess of Kent is of the opinion that this remedy improves with age although I am not entirely sure where she sourced the unicorn horn.[27]

> **The Countess of Kent's approved Medicine for the Plague, called the Philosophers Egge, it is a most excellent Preservative against all Poysons, or dangerous Diseases that draw towards the Heart. (1653)**
>
> Take a new laid Egg, and break a hole so broad as you may, take out the white clean from the yolk, then take one ounce of Saffron and mingle it with the yolk, but be careful you break not the shell, then cover it with another piece of shell so close as is possible, then take an earthen pot with a close cover, with warm embers, so that the shell be not burned, and as those embers do cool, so put in more hot, and doe so for the space of two dayes until you think it be dry, for proof whereof you shall put in a Pen, and if it come out dry it is well, then take the Egge and wipe it very clean, then pare the shell from the Saffron, and set it before the fire, and let it be warm, then beat it in a Morter very fine, and put it in by it self, then take as much white Mustard seed as the Egge and Saffron, and grind it as small as meal, then searse it trough a fine Boulter, that you may save the quantity of the Egge so searced, then take a quarter of an ounce of Dittany roots, as much of Turmentil, of Nuces Vomicae one drachm, let them be dryed by the fire as aforesaid, then stamp these three last severally very fine in a Morter, then mix them three well together, after that take, as a thing most needful, the root of Angelica, and Pimpernel, of each the weight of sixpence, make them to pouder, and mix them with the rest,

then compound therewith five or six simples of Unicorns horn, or for want thereof of Hartshorn, and take as much weight, as all these fine pouders come to, of fine Triacle, and stamp it with the pouders in a Morter until all be well mixed and hang to the Pestle, and then it is perfectly made, then put the Electuary in a stone pot well nealed, and so it will continue twenty or thirty yeares, and the longer the better.[28]

The medicinal benefits of snails have been revered since ancient times. Pliny recommended crushed, boiled snails in raisin wine as a cure for running colds and sore throats. Lady Grace Mildmay suggests a distilled Snail Water consisting of the molluscs, rosemary, celandine, angelica, cloves and hartshorn as a cure for jaundice. They were also used in remedies to cure consumption which often included saffron. Sometimes the remedy came in the form of snail water, like the one suggested by 'W. M.' in *The Queen's Closet Opened*. On other occasions snails were incorporated into a pottage, as in a recipe provided by Robert May in *The Accomplisht Cook* (1660). Charles Elmé Francatelli was still espousing the benefits of this type of broth for sufferers of inveterate coughs in 1846. His version includes saffron, frogs and snails (but, you will be relieved to hear, no puppy dog tails) and possesses 'soothing qualities'.[29]

Laudanum was a remedy used to treat all manner of emotional and physical disorders. Lady Grace's recipe contains sixteen ingredients claiming that 'it helpeth against madness [and] against all fluxes of blood or wasting of nature'. She warns that laudanum was not suitable for those suffering from the falling sickness (epilepsy) but adds 'it taketh away all pains of grief of whatsoever it proceeds and in what part of the body soever if lieth'.[30] Judith Austen shared Lady Powell's recipe (which is considerably simpler than Lady Grace's) with her sister Elizabeth Freke, primarily to relieve the latter's colic (in this case colic appears to mean general pain rather than something particularly digestive. Elizabeth suffered with headaches and chronic back pain). Judith had taken laudanum for eighteen months, beginning with twenty drops a day and increasing to twenty-five drops in a spoonful of wine, beer or coffee. She does not say what affliction Lady Powell was suffering from but she was administering fifty drops a day, convinced that laudanum was keeping her alive. Judith provides other examples of women who have benefitted from this cordial adding 'itt is butt a small penance to purchas to our selves a little ease whilst we live in this world'.[31]

> **Lady Powell's Recipe for Laudanum (1700s)**
> Take two ounces of the best opium and one ounce of fine saffron. Cutt the opium very thinn and small, and pull the saffron into small pieces; then infuse them in a quarte if the best sack in a deep earthen pott covered with a blader pricked full of pin holles. And then sett itt in a kettle or skillit of boyleing watter till the quantitye in the pott bee halfe wasted. Lett itt infuse, still keeping the vessell conveniently filldup as itt wasts; and when itt is done enough (which will be a great while first), iff you please, deer Madam, to strain itt and squeeze itt hard out and keep itt close stoopt for your use.[32]

Laudanum was not without its dangers. The Member of Parliament for Lewes in Sussex was found dead in April 1712 after taking a large dose of liquid laudanum.[33] As Lady Grace counsels, 'it is [a] dangerous thing to wear and distract the humours in the body by extreme purges or extreme cordials'.[34]

By the eighteenth century it became fashionable to offer cordial waters to guests or visitors as a refreshment. Around the same time, the manufacture of cordials moved away from the lady of the house and was picked up by a servant, usually the housekeeper. Unfortunately, the servant did not always have the experience of heating the stills which could result in disaster for the final product. If the still were overheated, the organic elements could burn thereby tainting the distillate, leaving a taste like burnt tobacco. Other factors like a greater reliance on medicines based on inorganic materials that could be sourced through apothecaries and improved access to those businesses thanks to new toll roads reduced the dependency on household remedies. Where was the need to make these medicinal waters when alternatives were readily available? Cordials did not entirely disappear but their importance from a health perspective had diminished considerably by the turn of the nineteenth century.[35]

CHAPTER FIVE

SAFFRON IN THE KITCHEN

The hardships of the First World War have been well documented by the men who wrote home to their loved ones from the 'beastly trenches'.[1] Although a lot of the correspondence was edited by the censor, it is still possible to get a sense of the privations suffered by the troops.

It was a constant battle for the allied forces to meet the challenge of feeding the troops, which numbered over 1.8 million on the Western Front alone in March 1918. Soldiers were officially allowed 4200 calories per day. However, the men did not necessarily receive the prescribed ration, indicating that food was not as freely available as officially stated. Their diet consisted largely of bully beef and hard tack biscuits. Potatoes were served sporadically, and there was scant fresh fruit and vegetables available, so their diets were lacking in vitamin C (there was limited knowledge of nutritional requirements at this point in the twentieth century).[2]

It is perhaps no wonder, then, that food was a major preoccupation for the soldiers, and is often mentioned in their correspondence. 'It is really extraordinary the part played by the stomach in life. It simply rules the world, and affects all our outlook on life. We are paralysed, absorbed, hypnotised by it. The chief topic of conversation is rations with the men, and food and wine with the officers,' wrote Reverend Oswin Creighton from France in early 1917.³ The official ration was monotonous, prompting the soldiers to seek additions or alternatives to army food. 'We have any amount of food,' wrote Captain Phillips of the Royal Horse Guards in November 1914, 'but occasional small packets of chocolate, tinned tongue, potted meat, etc. – not sardines or anything messy – are welcome.'⁴

Pleas from the Front for food from home were duly answered. By 1915, 4000 mail bags crossed the Channel daily, a number that rose to over 50,000 a day in the period before Christmas 1917. Between August 1914 and March 1920, 320,409 tonnes of mail and parcels were shipped to the British Expeditionary Forces. Home-made treats like cakes were particularly welcome. Among those sent such gifts was Private F. H. Passmore, who received a parcel in Christmas 1917 courtesy of Newquay Urban District Council. He praised the usefulness of the parcel contents, but especially 'the good Cornish cake, for it was a real pleasure to taste a piece of saffron cake once more'.⁵

Newquay, like many towns around Britain, organised committees to prepare these Christmas parcels for their men on the front in December 1917. The packages included cocoa, 'cafe au lait', biscuits, soap and 'over 200 lbs of real old saffron cake – the sort that mother used to make.' The contents of each packet varied with the exception of the cake, 'so all the boys will have some Christmas cake.' The cakes had been made by Mrs Small and baked by Mrs Richardson of the Dorothy Cafe in Newquay, prior to being weighed (to ensure everyone received the same amount) and wrapped in greaseproof paper. The committee's only regret was that they had not begun the initiative sooner, so that the boys further afield could enjoy them too.⁶

Many of the recipients wrote to the council in Newquay to thank them for the parcels. George Hubert Ennor, a Quartermaster Sergeant with the Durham Light Infantry, replied 'I must here mention a few words about the cake. My friends being north countrymen were a bit doubtful about it, owing to its rich yellow colour, the first of its kind, I am sure, they had seen. After a little persuasion however they consented to give it a trial and the verdict was that it was "Tre Bon".' [sic]7

It was common for soldiers to share the contents of these packages with their comrades. It helped develop friendships, but also meant that the chances of hunger or starvation were reduced.8 Private Hunt shared his 'real old Cornish cake' with some of his 'Irish chums' who 'unanimously passed it as unbeatable'. The last word is even underlined in the original letter to emphasise just how well the saffron cake was received.9

In Cornwall, saffron cakes were a staple food on feast days, of which Christmas was just one. Yeast leavened currant cakes coloured with saffron were traditionally baked on Christmas Eve (it was considered bad luck to start preparing for Christmas too soon). These festive saffron cakes had a particular form. A portion of dough was fashioned into a small cake and positioned on top of the larger cake (presumably this would have made it look something like a traditional cottage loaf). The smaller cake was called 'The Christmas'. To ensure good luck for the year ahead, the cake was not to be cut until Christmas Day itself. It is unknown whether those saffron cakes sent to the men on the front included a festive adornment, but clearly there was a fond association between saffron cakes and celebrations.10

It is said 'there are more saints in Cornwall than there are in heaven'. Each parish has its own particular saints to which its church is dedicated. Feasts held in their honour took place on the nearest Sunday or Monday to the dedication day, and were known as 'feasten' Sundays or Mondays. The celebration would call for a special dinner. Saffron buns or cakes often featured too, and were sometimes called Revel Buns.11 This perhaps explains why Cornwall, above all other counties in England, has retained its affinity with this special kind of spiced bread. Edith Martin includes eight recipes in her book *Cornish Recipes: Ancient and Modern* (1930), one of which dates back to 1805, gathered from various chapters of the county's Women's Institute. Martin writes 'the method of making these is similar in each recipe given. The ingredients vary, according to the quality and quantity desired'.12 However, only one of these includes an actual method for how to make the buns, perhaps the assumption being that all Cornish housewives were *au fait* with making saffron buns? Cornish writer Arthur Quiller Couch (1863-1944) mentions saffron cakes on several occasions in his novels. One of the most memorable is in *The Astonishing History of Troy Town*, when Master Sam Buzza wins a wheelbarrow full of saffron cakes for drinking the most beer at the Man O'War public house:

> High on the barrow, and symmetrically piled, rested five-and-twenty huge cakes – yellow cakes such as all Trojans love – each large as a mill-stone, tinctured with saffron, plentifully stowed with currants, and crisp with brown crust, steaming to heaven, and wooing the nostrils of the gods.[13]

During the mid-eighteenth century, Methodism began to gain a foothold in Cornwall. John Wesley's message, that God's love was omnipotent and available to all, appealed to the poor in the industrial areas of the North and the South West. As Maldwyn Edwards notes 'the tin-miners of Cornwall learnt to their astonishment and joy of a God who cared for the least and who could work His miracles in the lives of the most unlovely. It was an irresistible invitation to fullness of living'.[14] By 1851, Cornwall was the only county outside of North Wales where attendees at Methodist chapels were in the majority.[15]

One of Wesley's greatest achievements was his encouragement of Sunday schools. As well as Bible lessons, children received elementary education in reading and writing, providing a foundation for popular education.[16] It would eventually become common practice for the Sunday schools to organise an annual tea, often over the Whitsun weekend (the Christian holiday of Pentecost, which is celebrated fifty days after Easter Sunday). It is evident from the reminiscences of people who grew up in Cornwall how fondly these events were remembered:

> Children eagerly anticipated the annual tea treats, organised by both church and chapel. Allegiances were put aside and most joined in every one. Farm wagons took the children to Pendower

or Towan beaches, where games were organised followed by a tea with saffron buns and heavy cake. All were dressed in their Sunday best – no swimming, but perhaps a decorous paddle. The headmaster of Gerrans School noted in June 1876 the small attendance one day 'as most children were desiring to attend the Wesleyan Sunday School Tea meeting'.[17]

On Good Friday, some Cornish housewives, like Hettie Merrick's mother, would mark their saffron buns with a cross (her Aunt Hartie always did this, whatever the time of year). The original purpose of the cross was to ward off evil. Some Good Friday buns were merely glazed with a saffron wash with a few currants stuck on it. Penzance was famed for its large currant buns measuring 4 inches (about 10 cm) in diameter, marked with a large cross that divided it into four equal pieces. There was a belief that buns made on this day would never become mouldy. Some households would keep a Good Friday bun hanging from a string on their bacon rack. A little of the lucky bun grated into the food of an invalid was thought to cure all manner of illnesses in humans and animals.[18]

Of course, Cornwall did not have the monopoly on saffron buns or cakes. Saffron was frequently included in recipes for celebratory spice cakes like this seventeenth-century recipe from Nottinghamshire-born Gervase Markham:

To make Spice Cakes
To make excellent spice Cakes, take half a peck of very fine Wheat-flower, take almost one pound of sweet butter, and some good milk and cream mixt together, set it on the fire, & put in your butter, and a good deal of sugar, & let it melt together, then strain Saffron into your milk a good quantity, then take seven or eight spoonfuls of good Ale-barm, and eight eggs with two yolks, and mix them together, then put your milk to it when it is somewhat cold, and into your flower put salt, aniseeds bruised, Cloves and Mace, and a good deal of Cinnamon: then work all together good and stiff, that you need not work in any flower after, then put in

a little rose-water cold, then rub it well in the thing you knead it in, and work it thoroughly: if it be not sweet enough, scrape in a little more sugar, and put it all in pieces, and hurle in a good quantity of Currants, and so work al together againe, and bake your cake as you see cause, in a gentle warme Oven.[19]

Saffron is just one of the spices recommended as banqueting stuff by Thomas Dawson in *The Good Housewife's Jewell*, published at the close of the sixteenth century (in the Tudor and Stuart eras a 'banquet' was a sweet course served in a private room). Dawson's small book calls for saffron in a number of recipes, including 'Peascods for Lent' (spiced fruit paste shaped like a pea pod before being dipped in a saffron batter and fried – there were no restrictions on eating spices during this period of fasting) and 'Fine Cakes' which appear to be a type of spiced biscuit. There is also a rather alluring recipe for inkhorn-shaped sweet spiced bread rolls drenched in clarified butter:

To make good Resbones.
Take a quart of fine flower, lay it vpon a faire board and make a hoale in the middest of the flower with your hand, and put a spoonefull of Ale yeast thereon, and ten yolkes of egges, & two spoonefuls of sinamom & one of ginger, and one of cloues and mace, and a quartern of suger finely beaten, and a litle saffron, & halfe a spoonefull of salt, then take a dish full of butter, melt it and put it into your flower, and therewithal make your paste as it were for mancheat, and mould it a good while, & cut it in péeces of the bignes of Ducks egges, and so mould euerie peece as a mancheat, & make them after the fashion of an inckhorn broad aboue and narrow beneath, then set them in the Ouen, and let them bake thrée quarters of an houre, then take two dishes of butter and clarifie it vpon a soft fire, then draw it out of the Ouen, and scrape the bottom of them faire and cleane, and cut them ouerthwart [crossways] in foure péeces, and put them in a faire charger, and put your clarified butter vpon them, and haue sinamom and ginger readie by you, and suger beaten verie small, and mingle altogether, and euer as you set your péeces together,

cast some of your suger, sinamom & ginger vpon them, when you haue set them all vp, lay them in a faire platter, & put a litle butter vpō them, & cast a litle-suger on them, & so serue them.[20]

In later recipes, rather than dried fruit, some saffron cakes contain seeds such as coriander (Sarah Harrison, *The Housekeeper's Pocket Book and Compleat Family Cook*, 1739) or caraway (Hannah Glasse, *The Art of Cookery Made Plain & Easy*, 1746). Sometimes it was just the outer coating of the cake that included the saffron. That popular Easter treat, the Simnel cake, originally took this form. In Shropshire and Herefordshire, and particularly in Shrewsbury, a rich fruit cake enclosed in a saffron-coloured crust would be made in mid-Lent for Mothering Sunday (although they were also made for Easter and Christmas).

I'll to thee a simnel bring,
'Gainst thou go'st a-mothering:
So that when she blesseth thee,
Half that blessing thou'lt give me.[21]

Given the expense of the ingredients contained in the Simnel, the cakes were available in a variety of sizes. In the nineteenth century prices ranged from a guinea for an extra large cake to half a crown for a smaller cake. The cake would be boiled prior to baking, resulting in a crust 'as hard as if made of wood'. Some people receiving Simnels as presents were confused as to their purpose. One lady even mistook hers for a footstool.[22] Like so many cakes the Simnel began life as a type of bread in the Medieval era, gradually picking up spices and currants through the centuries. The sixteenth century physician Andrew Boorde was resolutely against any 'bread' that had been pre-boiled or that contained saffron:

Sodden breade, as symnels and crackenels, and breade baken upon a stone, or upon yron, and breade that saffron is in, is not laudable.[23]

Boorde appears to have believed that eating any manner of 'crust', including that of saffron bread and Simnels, could cause kidney stones to form, and he refrained from eating all types of bread unless it was at least twenty-four hours old. These days, Simnel cakes are simply baked and the pastry outer has been dropped in favour of a golden marzipan topping, complete with eleven almond paste balls representing Christ's faithful apostles (the 'missing' marzipan apostle being Judas).[24]

It is easy to scoff at Boorde's dietary theories. However, centuries before Jean Anthelme Brillat-Savarin wrote: 'Tell me what you eat: I will tell you what you are.'[25] The idea that food could have an impact on your physical and mental well-being had long been established. Dietary theory from the ancient world through to the nineteenth century was closely allied with humoral theory. Given that each humor possessed its own hue, it is easy to see why the colour of food would be considered so important for earlier generations (and arguably remains so today albeit for different reasons).[26]

The use of colour in food to convey the particular characteristics or benefits was at its apogee in the medieval era. Colour provided meaning to a dish and rarely related to flavour. What it did provide is an indication of the nature of the object not only from a humoral perspective but it also could also carry moral and spiritual connotations. At a very basic level it could be as simple as white (good) versus black (evil), but it was not always as straightforward as this. For example, in the thirteenth century the colour yellow could denote falsehood, but anything golden was considered to be good.[27]

The colour of food mattered a great deal across medieval Europe, but owes a debt to the cuisine of the Arabic nations. The Normans had experienced Arab cooking in Sicily, and maintained close links with their kinsfolk who had settled there. Influence also came from Arabic southern Spain, and from the Crusader states like Jerusalem and Antioch at the eastern end of the Mediterranean. Returning crusaders encouraged the adoption of Saracen style cuisine in French and English cookery. The thirteenth-century scribe al-Baghdādī's *Book of Dishes* (*Kitāb al-Tabīkh*) contains many golden-hued recipes, coloured with saffron, which appear to have particularly struck a chord with the Normans. Gold was thought by Arab physicians to lengthen human life. Therefore, by eating saffron coloured food you were metaphorically consuming the life-enhancing quality of gold.[28]

Qualities like the lustre and shine that could be imparted by ingredients such as saffron were also important in medieval food. Professor Chris Woolgar notes that 'objects that shine reflect light, but medieval people saw these objects as the source of light, and the divine qualities of light made them virtuous in their own right – or the close association that came from touch transferred those benefits from or to immediately adjacent objects or beings. Eating anything that shone, or was close to shining, such as foods with a strong yellow colour, or indeed, eating from shiny objects such as gold or silver plate, would bring the beneficence of light'.[29]

Colours therefore gave food both a divine and a luxurious aspect. 'I must have saffron, to colour the warden pies,' declares Clown in Shakespeare's *The Winter's Tale,* for the sheep-shearing feast his adopted sister, Perdita, is presiding over.[30] For such dishes were reserved for special occasions in elite Medieval households, like a feast to celebrate a marriage or to commemorate important people at a funeral. Colourants like saffron, sanders and parsley even became a popular addition to the bread sliced for 'trenchers' at feasts (trenchers are edible platters on which food would be placed). At the coronation feast for Richard III in July 1483, attended by around 1000 guests, 3 lbs of English saffron were bought for the saucery (the department responsible for preparing the sauces for a feast), with more being purchased for the wafery (responsible for sweetmeats and confectionary). Along with saffron and spices, such as cinnamon and anise, other decorative ingredients required for this feast were 14 lbs sanders; 16 lbs red and white comfits (usually sugar-coated seeds like caraway); 12 lbs turnsole (which was used to create a shade of blue) and 100 sheets of pure gold leaf.[31]

A feast held in January 1337 by Dame Katherine de Norwich to mark the anniversary of the death of her second husband, an Exchequer official, required 4 oz of sanders costing 12d and 2 oz saffron, which came from a bulk purchase of 2 lb bought for 11s 8d as part of her spice allowance for the year. Katherine was not alone in buying her spices in volume. Lady Margaret Marshall, Countess of Norfolk, bought a whopping 24 lbs of saffron in the year 1385–6 (no price given). Expensive spices were usually bought at a market or fair, away from the vicinity of the household. Markets could be regular events but fairs, like the Stourbridge Fair in Cambridge, were only held on specific dates so provided infrequent opportunities to purchase such luxuries. The Lord (or Lady) would employ their most trusted officials to purchase these goods. The cellarer (the person in a monastery who is responsible for provisioning and catering) for Battle Abbey in East Sussex bought saffron in 1 lb and 5 lb quantities from markets in London and Canterbury. In 1319–20 he managed to secure 13 lb for the bargain price of 39s 11d (which was relatively cheap for saffron by medieval standards).[32]

We can get a feel for just how precious these ingredients were to noble medieval households by examining their accounts.[33] Valuable commodities like cloth, wax, jewellery and spices were detailed in the wardrobe accounts. Dame Alice de Bryene purchased the following goods at Steresbreg Fair (the old name for Stourbridge in Cambridge) in 1412–13:[34]

Item	Cost
20 lb almonds	4s 2d
4 lb rice	4d
1 lb pepper	3s 3d
2 lb ginger	3s 4d
1 lb cinnamon	4s 5d
1 lb cloves	3s 4d
1 lb mace	3s 8d
1 lb saffron	13s

Stourbridge is around 40 miles from Dame Alice's Suffolk home in Acton. A charter to hold a fair at Stourbridge was granted to the Cambridge leper hospital in the thirteenth century (the leper hospital had closed by 1279 although the fair continued). Its proximity to the River Cam and the main roads linking Cambridge to East Anglia, the Midlands and North London meant it was very accessible to merchants. The Stourbridge Fair attracted people from near and far, including representatives of religious houses, royalty and King's Hall (a forerunner of Trinity College at Cambridge University) buying everything from spices and honey to cloth and timber.[35]

On occasion, when nobles had to travel, say to a coronation or royal wedding, the accounts represented cash purchases for immediate consumption, the household not wishing to carry excessive stocks. When Sir John de Dynham (sometimes written as Dinham) junior, a noble with extensive lands in Devon, Somerset and Cornwall, travelled to London for the marriage of Richard II and Anne of Bohemia in 1381-2, his food purchases included 1 lb of dates, almonds, ginger, and saffron.[36] By all accounts Dynham junior was a bit of a rogue with a fierce temper. When his father's murderers escaped from Ilchester gaol in 1382-3, Dynham killed one of the assailants, Robert Tuwyng, and pursued the other, John Broun, to the Cathedral Church of Exeter where he had sought sanctuary. Dynham smashed down the door and captured Broun after a fierce struggle in which Broun was injured. Dynham was pardoned by Richard II in March of that year (probably around the same time he had travelled to London to pledge his homage and fealty to the king). We also know from records kept by Dynham's steward that he purchased various items for Lady Dynham (his first wife, Ellen) during this visit, which included food items such as saffron.[37]

In book 1 of Harlian MS 279 devoted to 'Potage Dyvers', dating from around 1420, some 68 of the 153 recipes contain a reference to colour either in the name of the dish or the cooking instructions.[38] In many cases saffron is mentioned specifically, as in this dish of chicken cooked with garlic and milk:

>.lxxxx. **Hennys in Gauncely**e
> Take Hennys, an roste hem; take Mylke an Garleke, an grind it,

an do it in a panne, an hewe thin hennys there-on with yolkys of eyron, and colour it with Safroun an Mylke, an serve forth.³⁹

Saffron could be employed to enhance other natural colours such as green in sauces. By the sixteenth century this method would also be employed to boost the colour of pea tarts. It was known as 'gaudy green' in English, or 'vert gay' in French.⁴⁰

Verde Sawse. xx.vii.
Take parsel. mynt. garlek. a litul serpell and sawge, a litul canel. gyngur. piper. wyne. brede. vynegur & salt grynde it smal with safroun & messe it forth.⁴¹

Sanders (a colourant from the red sandalwood tree) frequently partnered saffron in recipes such as a beef stew and an early gingerbread recipe in *Two Fifteenth Century Cookery Books*:

.iiij . Gyngerbrede . – Take a quart of hony, & sethe it, & skeme it clene ; take Safroun, pouder Pepir, & throw there-on; take gratyd Brede, & make it so chargeaunt that it wol be y-lechyd; then take pouder Canelle , & straw there-on y-now; then make yt: square, lyke as þou wolt leche yt; take when thou lechyst hyt, an caste Box leves a-bouyn, y - stykyd thereon, on clowys. And if thou wolt have it Red, coloure it with Saunderys y-now.⁴²

Although colour was important, saffron must also have been valued for the flavour it lent to a dish. A number of medieval recipes containing saffron also include a melange of spices, such as cinnamon, pepper and cloves, which would interfere with the shade produced by the saffron. Other ingredients, such as a preponderance of dried fruits, could also mute the colour, as in Risshewes, a type of medieval fried fruit pasty:

Risshewes
Take figges, and grinde hem aƚ rawe in a morter, and cast a little fraied oyle there-to; And then take hem vppe yn a vessell, and caste

there-to pynes, reysyns of corañce, myced dates, sugur, Saffron, pouder ginger, and salt: And theñ make Cakes of floure, Sugur, salt, and rolle the stuff in thi honde, and couche it in the Cakes, and folde hem togidur as risshewes, And fry hem in oyle, and serue hem forth.[43]

On occasion, saffron would be sprinkled over a dish right at the end, instead of being stirred in (rather like we would sprinkle something with sugar now). C. Anne Wilson explains that in the fourteenth century guide to household management, *Le Ménagier de Paris* (translated in 1928 by Eileen Power as *The Goodman of Paris*), this is described in French as 'frangé' (literally 'fringed' – there is no English equivalent for this term, which has led to the word being mistranslated in some English versions of the text as 'coloured'). Some noblemen, like Thomas Morton who was a canon residential of York around 1449, kept boxes of powdered spices (often described as 'good powder') in the dining room which were sprinkled on dishes just before serving.[44]

Sometimes the coloured element was only present in the exterior of the dish, particularly when it came to pies or special roasts. Recipes frequently end with the instruction 'endore with yolkys of Eryroun & Safroun' (gild with egg yolks and saffron). The fantastical Cokyntryce, which consisted of the front part of a pig with the rear of a capon (a castrated or neutered cockerel), was finished with a basting of egg yolks, saffron and ground ginger before being served as a 'ryal mete' (i.e. something that was fit for a lord).[45]

> **Chike endored.** Take a chike, and drawe him, and roste him, And lete the fete be on, and take awey the hede; then make batur of yolkes of eyron and floure, and caste there – to pouder of ginger, and peper, saffron and salt, and pouder hit faire til hit be rosted ynogh.[46]

The very best medieval cooks were artists in their own right. Their ability to transform the mundane into something astounding or even to deceive the diners into believing they were eating entirely different ingredients, was highly prized. 'Gold was the colour into which much dross food was transmuted,' observes Madeleine Pelner Cosman. 'Like the alchemists working over their cauldrons and brews, the kitchen colourists made gold semblances since they could not create the perfect "immortal" metal. Since aurifaction was impossible, they practiced aurifiction.'[47] Glazed meat 'apples', like those that were served at the coronation feast of Henry IV in 1399, are a good example of this spectacle:

> **For to make pomme dorryle and other thinges. xx.viii. xiiii.**
> Take þe lire of Pork rawe. and grynde it smale. medle it up wiþ powdre fort, safroun, and salt, and do þerto Raisouns of Coraunce, make balles þerof. and wete it wele in white of ayrenn. & do it to seeþ in boillyng water. take hem up and put hem on a spyt. rost hem wel and take parsel ygronde and wryng it up with ayren & a party of flour. and lat erne aboute þe spyt. And if þou wilt, take for parsel safroun, and serue it forth.[48]

Illusion foods, such as the Cokyntryce, were a kind of food entertainment. Known as entremets or entremesses, these dishes were served between banqueting courses. They were designed to be eaten, unlike the more elaborate decorative subtleties which acted as signifiers that a course had ended. Entremets were still the preserve of the wealthy, but were more accessible than the 'subtlety', which was only to be found in the most noble of households. Nevertheless, the author of *Le Ménagier de Paris* councils his young wife not to worry too much about them 'it is not work for a citizen's cook, nor even for a simple knight's'. Imitation hedgehogs, he explains 'can be made out of mutton tripe and it is a great expense and a great labour and little honour and profit, wherefor *nichil hic*'. In other words, why bother?[49]

Saffron continued to be used throughout the sixteenth and seventeenth centuries, but by the eighteenth century its use in the kitchen begins to wane, particularly in savoury recipes. Where saffron is used for savoury dishes, the recipe is often linked to a foreign cuisine:

Saffron in the Kitchen

Young Turkies with Saffron after the Polish Way
Get a young Turky, draw it, toss it, and spit it with Slices of Bacon and Paper round it; then put in a Stew-pan Slices of Onions, and boil them with some broth; being done, strain them off, and if they are too thick, pick some, more Broth to them; and these Onions must be as thick as an Essence of Ham; then put a very little pounded and dryed Saffron in a Cup, mix it with a little Broth, and pour it by Degrees into your Cullis, til it begins to have a fine Colour, but not too deep: Your Turkies being taken off, cut off the Wings and the Legs and put them in your Cullis: Serve them up for the first Course.[50]

By the nineteenth century, the use of saffron in English savoury cookery had all but disappeared. However, the British love for curry was blossoming, thanks to our presence on the Indian subcontinent. Our interpretation of Indian cuisine under the all-encompassing term 'curry' helped preserve the use of saffron in British kitchens (although turmeric was also employed to produce a shade of yellow). There are some 82 references to saffron in Robert Flower Riddell's *Indian Domestic Economy and Receipt Book* (1852). While Riddell's recipes are undoubtedly far from being truly authentic, they do at least use whole spices such as cardamom and cumin, and fresh ginger rather than the bog standard curry powder used by many Victorian authors to create curries.

Baked goods and sweet treats fared better. Saffron cakes (akin to modern day saffron buns) regularly appear in eighteenth-century cookbooks, although this tails off somewhat by the Victorian era. That said, May Byron felt compelled to include a number of recipes for saffron cakes, including a yeast leavened and fruited 'sponge' version, in her *Cake Book* (1915).[51] The fact that saffron buns are still commercially available today in Cornwall shows they have not disappeared from our culinary repertoire.

Coloured jellies have also remained popular. In the sixteenth and seventeenth centuries, milk jellies known as 'leaches' (made with diary or almond milk) were common. Hannah Woolley delicately scents hers with sliced ginger, a cinnamon stick and one spoonful of rosewater, adding 'you may colour it with Saffron, and some with Turnsole, and lay the White and that one upon another, and cut it, and it will look like Bacon; it is good for weak people, and Children which have the Rickets'.[52] From the mid-nineteenth century, cookbook authors began to advocate the use of commercially produced food colourings. The entrepreneurial Agnes B. Marshall has a full page advertisement in the back of her book *Fancy Ices* for 'Marshall's Harmless Vegetable Colours.' One of the colours listed is 'SAFFRON. To produce beautiful Yellow and rich Creamy shades'. Eight drops of this was required to colour just over a litre of lemon jelly. Whether it contained genuine saffron or curcumin (found in the rhizomes of turmeric to produce the modern food colouring E100) is, I feel, open to question though.[53]

CHAPTER SIX

THE DECLINE AND REVIVAL OF SAFFRON PRODUCTION IN BRITAIN

'Would to God that my countrymen had been heretofore (or were now) more careful of this commodity! Then would it no doubt have proved more beneficial to our island than our cloth or wool. But alas! So idle are we and heretofore so much given to ease, by reason of the smallness of our rents, that few men regard to search out which are their best commodities.'[1]

This lamentation was uttered by William Harrison in 1577, arguably at a time when saffron production had recovered from the blip it had experienced twenty years earlier, when the price of the spice fell due to the market being flooded with it. But from Harrison's observations it appears that the desire to grow this product was beginning to wane somewhat, even at this early date. Growing saffron was hard work, and while the profits could be good, they were by no means guaranteed. According to some, the laborious nature of saffron cultivation made the crokers prone to grumpiness.[2] It 'bindeth the labourer to greate travaile and diligence; and yet at length yealdeth no small advantage to recomforte him agayne'.[3] However, despite the arduous nature of saffron production, Joan Thirsk notes that it could 'make all the difference in hard times between solvency and bankruptcy' to small farmers.4

John Knott of Duxford in Cambridgeshire could be described as the final croker standing (at least he appears to be the last documented saffron grower who is commonly talked about). Little is known about this gentleman who died in 1827 at the age of 89. The snippets of history relating to his saffron cultivation come from Joseph Clarke, a naturalist and archeologist who died at his ancestral home near Saffron Walden on 14 July 1895. Like Knott, Clarke lived a long life (he was born in 1802) and had close links to Saffron Walden Museum. He was an authority on the natural history of the district. In 1884, he presented a paper to the Essex Field Club entitled 'Notes on the Saffron Plant (*Crocus Sativus, L.*) and in Connection with the Name of the Town Saffron Walden'. 'Probably,' he announced, 'I am almost the only man who has ever seen a field of saffron in bloom – that is, in this vicinity.'5

The Knotts were a farming family. Clarke describes himself as being well acquainted with John Knott as a child – perhaps he was a friend of his grandson (also called John Knott), to whom he makes a passing mention in the paper. According to Clarke, Knott grew half an acre (two roods) of saffron in Duxford up to the year 1816. He makes no mention of any other crops, if any, that he grew. Clarke remembers the kiln and papers used to dry the chives, showing that little had changed since Bradley and Douglass had described the process almost a century before. Knott's grandson laughed at the notion that saffron flowers should be gathered in the morning. I suspect this was because his grandfather employed others to perform this task rather than picking the blooms himself later in the day. Once a year, Knott would travel to dispose of his harvest (again, Clarke does not enlighten us as to where Knott went to do so). When this journey became too arduous for him, he called on his friend and fellow farmer, William Thurnal, to take the harvest to market.6

By the early nineteenth century, domestic saffron production had all but died out. Lord Braybrooke claimed it had disappeared entirely

The Decline and Revival of Saffron Production

from Walden by 1790. He attributed its decline to competition from imported saffron, plus a reduction in its use in medicinal remedies such as cordials. In 1678, Gideon Harvey had noted that druggists in London were selling English saffron at over fifty shillings per pound, whereas the same quantity of Spanish saffron was retailing at twenty-four shillings, less than half the price.[7] While these issues may have played a role in the dwindling cultivation of saffron during the eighteenth century, there are certain social and economic factors during this period that also had an impact. The population of England and Wales steadily increased in the second half of the eighteenth century, from 6.2 million in 1751 to 7.6 million in 1781, and it continued to accelerate until it reached 17.9 million in 1851. More people meant a higher demand for grain, and farmers were therefore encouraged to grow mainstream crops such as wheat. More arable land was required to meet the needs of a growing population and even grassland and heaths were turned into fields. Larger, more efficient farms were created by merging small farms. 'The retreat of alternative produce from the farming scene was the negative impact of the agricultural revolution,' writes Thirsk.[8]

The medicinal benefits of saffron were being called into question even before the eighteenth century drew to a close. In 1770, Edinburgh physician Dr William Alexander wrote a series of essays on experiments he had conducted with various substances, including saffron, 'with a view to selecting the valuable from the useless'. Alexander administered four doses of saffron beginning with ten grains (a little over half a gram), gradually increasing the dosage over four days, culminating in a scruple of saffron (just over five grams). His temperature and pulse remained normal, and even his urine was unaffected (he seemed to think that the consumption of such a quantity of saffron would have at least tinged his urine orange). 'I cannot help thinking that it is a medicine (if it deserves that name),' he concluded, 'just as innocent and as useless in any in all the *materia medica*.'[9] At least he did not succumb to a fit of hysterics.

If professional attitudes were cooling towards saffron as cure for various diseases, it remained in use in the sphere of domestic medicine. In the late nineteenth century, Clarke mentions that saffron was still used in the treatment of measles, as highlighted by Mrs Beeton in 1861:[10]

> **Saline Mixture** – Take of mint-water, 6 ounces; powdered nitre, 20 grains; antimonial wine, 3 drachms; spirits of nitre, 2 drachms; syrup of saffron, 2 drachms. Mix. To children under three years, give a teaspoonful every two hours; from that age to six, a dessertspoonful at the same times; and a tablespoon every three or four hours to children between six and twelve.[11]

In her book *Herbal Delights* (1938), Hilda Leyel also makes reference to saffron tea as a remedy for measles (she also notes that saffron could be added to the drinking water of canaries when they are moulting). She provides a recipe for 'An Excellent Medicine For Dry Convulsive Asthma' ('Give at bedtime 8 or 10 grains of choice Saffron; pulverised grossly in a little syrup or conserve of violets to embody it with') and the recipe below to counter the effects of alcohol, recalling Pliny's advice on one of the benefits of saffron:

> **Lohoch of Coleworts**
> Take a pound of the juice of Coleworts, clarified; Saffron, 3 drachms; clarified sugar and honey, of each, ½ pound. Make into a lohoch. This we recommend to be eaten off the end of a stick of liquorice. Prescribed for the after effects of a drunken orgy.[12]

By 1950, saffron was regarded as being 'pharmacologically inert' by a correspondent for the *British Medical Journal*, and of a historical interest only. However, towards the end of twentieth century medicinal plants started to gain favour again. Thirsk notes that for some medical conditions there is a preference for herbal over chemical remedies, as well as the acknowledgement that plants could make medicines more affordable in poorer areas of the world. Although further investigation is required, recent clinical trials have indicated that saffron (or crocin) can have a beneficial impact on cardiovascular diseases such as diastolic blood pressure; depression and anxiety; ocular disease such as age-related macular degeneration; fibromyalgia; Alzheimer's disease; diabetes and ADHD (Attention Deficit Hyperactivity Disorder), as well as some

The Decline and Revival of Saffron Production

cancers. Dr Himadri Panda has termed the scientific exploration of the benefits of saffron as 'saffronology'.[13]

Saffron continues to have role in the British food scene, even though it is largely associated with savoury Mediterranean, Middle Eastern or Anglo Indian cuisines. The Cornish remain resolutely attached to their saffron buns and have taken their passion with them wherever they have settled in the world. Daphne du Maurier estimated that a third of the mining population in Cornwall had emigrated to America, South Africa or Australia by the end of the nineteenth century. Vida Heard recounts how postal workers in Johannesburg were initially deeply suspicious of fragrant parcels arriving from Cornwall, fearing the 'bright yellow contents must be rank poison'. Despite what she describes as vast numbers of Cornish people swarming to the country, saffron has never found a place in South African cookery.[14]

Spain is believed to satisfy seventy per cent of the world's demand for saffron. Spanish saffron from La Mancha received protected designation of origin (PDO) status in 2001 and commands the highest prices. However, Iran actually produces ninety per cent of the world's saffron and half of that is exported to Spain, which is then repackaged and sold as a Spanish product. An article in the Spanish newspaper *El Pais* in January 2011 stated that 190,000 kilos of saffron were exported from Spain, despite only 1,500 kilos being produced on domestic soil in 2010. By exporting their saffron to Spain, Iranian producers can achieve higher prices for their product and minimise the effects of boycotts and sanctions.[15] With such levels of competition is there space in the saffron market for a product grown in England?

'The successful commercialisation of a new venture,' writes Thirsk, 'depended on the stimulus being given at exactly the right moment, allowing the pioneers sufficient time to experiment, make mistakes, overcome them, and finally launch a serious enterprise while the economic conditions were still favourable.'[16]

Although Thirsk's words were written in reference to historical alternative agriculturalists, they still feel pertinent today. At the end of the twentieth century new crokers began to appear. In 1997, Sally Francis, a botanist from Norfolk who now specialises in alternative agriculture, was given twenty saffron corms as a birthday present by her mother. 'It was wonderful to harvest our first, very small crop of saffron,' she says. After several years of lifting, dividing and re-planting the corms, it became apparent that Sally and her family had more saffron than they could use themselves. In 2009, they established Norfolk Saffron.[17]

Around the same time that Sally received her first saffron corms, David Smale was wondering why saffron was no longer grown in Saffron Walden. David was looking for a new project and set about experimenting with growing saffron. However, finding anyone (in this country at least) who could advise him on how to proceed was far from straightforward. Even agricultural colleges were somewhat stumped by his enquiries about what they considered to be a defunct horticultural curiosity. After various trials the English Saffron company was born in 2004, and now has grounds in Essex and Devon. David has been actively involved in organising the town's first saffron harvest festival, planned for October 2022 (close to the date of the original Ursula's Fair held on 21 October), which the festival committee hopes will be an annual event.

Sally and David have contributed to the revival of an industry which had once thrived in their home counties. Saffron has always been grown in pockets in England. Modern saffron growing is no different, and it is now cultivated in small areas around the country, from Cornwall to Cheshire. While English saffron still needs a fair amount of tender loving care to thrive, it is possible to cultivate it in areas not traditionally associated with the spice. I spoke to growers in Kent and Sussex where the soil errs on the heavy side. By creating raised beds and incorporating plenty of organic matter to condition the earth, they manage to successfully grow saffron. Plant biologist Peter Gould has been growing saffron with his brother Douglas in Cheshire since 2014. Their particular site is on a sandstone ridge, so it benefits from free-draining soil, even if the weather is less that optimum. The size of the

The Decline and Revival of Saffron Production

saffron grounds themselves appear to be similar to those farmed by the crokers of old. Typically, they range from a half to one acre, although there are growers who maintain more than one ground. Some growers have ready access to land, like Sophie Tod who began experimenting with growing saffron on her sheep farm in Mayfield, Sussex, in 2019. Others lead a more nomadic existence in the search for suitable grounds. In the south and east of England, small pockets of arable land are increasingly hard to come by. They are also in demand from horse owners and rental prices can be high. This is not a new problem. Thirsk points out that those farmers involved in alternative agriculture initiatives, like saffron growers, 'often have to choose fringe areas of land and disadvantageous sites simply because their resources are limited'.[18] Saffron remains subject to molestation by a variety of pests, although hares no longer top the list.[19] Rabbits, badgers, rats, voles and slugs (mulching with wood chip, and wild birds like pheasants can help with the latter) are persistent offenders. Fencing is still the obvious solution. Some crokers did mention the possibility of planting the corms in cages buried in the earth to prevent pests from digging them up, though this is quite a costly measure. The British climate presents as many challenges today as it did several hundred years ago, with rain posing the biggest threat during the picking season.

One of the striking things about twenty-first century saffron cultivation is how little has changed. It remains incredibly labour-intensive to plant and harvest, and much of the work is still done by hand. The initial preparation of a new plot can certainly be made easier with a rotivator or tractor. Mechanical bulb planters (popular with horticulturalists in the Netherlands) can be used, but are expensive to hire, particularly if only required for a small plot. At first glance, many saffron grounds seem rather small and, dare I say it, eminently manageable. Now consider that half an acre can accommodate thousands of corms, all of which have to be planted manually if the expense of hiring a bulb planter is to be spared. Suddenly the task at hand seems all the more daunting. Several of the crokers I spoke to operate on a three-year rotation system, lifting the corms and dividing after this time (as described in Thomas Wale's pocket-book). Due to their size, there appears to be no easy way to get the corms out of the ground. Some have trialled potato harvesters, but the corms tend to fall through the sorting mechanism. The only other option is to dig them up by hand. If you are running a saffron growing business, there is a good chance that you are removing corms from previously cultivated areas and planting up new grounds on an annual basis.

Due to the delicate nature of the flowers, there are no mechanical shortcuts available when it comes to harvesting. The flowers are still picked in the morning before they are fully open. Andrew Bodey enlists the help of his wife Nan (and his daughters during the school holidays), to gather the saffron on their grounds near Whitstable in Kent. Nan's family manages a jasmine farm in Thailand, so flower processing runs in the family. In Cornwall, Brian and Margaret call on family and friends to help with the harvest. As it is hard to predict exactly when the flowers will come or how numerous they will be, it is difficult to hire seasonal staff. Plus, the physical effort required to do this job cannot be downplayed. It can be back-breaking work, and needs to be done come rain or shine (and in an English autumn the former is often likely). Tales of people signing up for the harvest but failing to return after one day's work are not uncommon.

Getting the flowers in is only the start. The day's harvest is spread on a table and then the painstaking process of removing the stigmas by hand begins. Having read historical accounts of people suffering from headaches from overexposure to saffron, I had expected the floral scent to be overpowering in the processing room (which is frequently situated in the croker's house), something akin to hyacinths. In actual fact, the honied aroma is rather delicate, even when one is presented with a whole jar of fresh stigmas. The characteristic scent that we associate with saffron actually develops after the saffron has been dried and left to mature for a number of weeks. One croker told me he can pick around one thousand flowers in an hour, but it can take three hours or more to process the blooms.

The biggest innovations in saffron cultivation are evident in the way it is dried. Kiln drying is no longer used (at least I have not come across any modern crokers using this method commercially). The saffron produced in England today is what is known as hay saffron (i.e. individual threads or strands) as opposed to the saffron 'cakes' produced during Richard Bradley's time. Commercial dehydrators seem to be the preferred method, although some growers have experimented with drying saffron in low ovens, microwaves, or by freeze-drying. A Chinese study on the optimal method for drying saffron found freeze-drying to be the most effective in terms of the colour of the final product, but it also took the longest amount of time. Infra-red drying and microwave drying (which was the fastest method) preserved the greatest quantity of aroma compounds. As freeze-drying and infra-red drying were the most costly and energy hungry methods for processing this spice, the researchers concluded that microwave drying was the most cost effective way to preserve the crocins and aroma components of the saffron.[20]

Today's crokers are keen to preserve an ancient industry, but are mindful of modern techniques which can help improve the way saffron is produced. Saffron is a truly seasonal plant and has a very short window of productivity. A challenge facing crokers all over the world is how to extend this season while maintaining the integrity of the product. One potential solution is hydroponics. Trials have been conducted where the saffron corms are placed in a static nutrient solution that is continually oxygenated. Some systems can be placed outside to ensure the plants receive direct sunlight. One of the benefits of a hydroponic system is that corms are not having to vie with other plants for nutrients or light, as they do when they are grown in the ground. It is also believed that hydroponic cultivation can circumvent any fungal infections that saffron corms could pick up in the soil. It is also hoped that hydroponics could result in higher yields, with ultimately a better quality product. One early study indicated that soilless cultivation resulted in fewer flowers and lower levels of the flavour compound picrocrocin in the dried product than traditionally cultivated saffron, although there was no difference between the two varieties in terms of pigment. Nevertheless, the authors concluded with further study there could be benefits in using hydroponics or similar systems to grow saffron in the future.[21]

Fool's Gold

The Gould brothers, who run the Cheshire Saffron Company, initially began growing saffron on a small scale in a shed, using a hydroponic system with a good degree of success. However, from a commercial perspective this method was not cost effective, so they have been growing saffron in fields since 2015. However, they are looking at ways to combine both methods in order to extend the growing season.

In the sixteenth century, the historian William Harrison thought the saffron produced in England to be 'the most excellent of all other… In sweetness, tincture and continuance'.[22] Today, British growers are a long way from being able to compete with Spanish or Iranian producers in quantity, but how does our modern saffron compare to that available from other nations? Domestic producers like Sally Francis have their saffron graded each year to ISO 3632 standards and consistently achieve category 1, the highest international grade. Will we ever see a time where English saffron achieves Protected Designation of Origin status, like that of La Mancha? There is now a separate protected designation of origin status for Krokos Kozanis in Greece and saffron from Mund in Switzerland, although they had to demonstrate that there was something unique about their product.[23] Some saffron growers in England are definitely convinced that you can taste the difference between the saffron grown here and that grown overseas, so perhaps their time will come.

As well as growing the spice we use in our kitchens, our home grown crokers produce a variety of ancillary goods. Saffron flour, gin, tea blends and sea salt are just some of the products available. Some are even finding a use for the petals that are usually discarded. If the crokers act quickly, it is possible to dehydrate the petals (evidently the petals quickly become slimy after they have been picked) and they can be used in organic confetti. They can also be used as a dye, and have been included in cosmetics such as the soaps produced by Sandlings Saffron in Suffolk. However, the problem with processing the petals is the time it takes, as time is something that is in short supply during harvests, according to most of the crokers I spoke to. A number of these crokers are either planning to cultivate, or already grow, other 'alternative' crops

The Decline and Revival of Saffron Production

like liquorice, fennel (for the pollen) and coriander (which was once widely cultivated for its seeds in Essex).

Call me biased, but I believe there is something special about the saffron grown here in Britain. All of the English saffron I have sampled (and I have used a lot during the course of this project) has looked, smelled and tasted fantastic. So can English saffron hold its own in the global spice market? Absolutely.

In the mid-seventeenth century, Walter Blith, who wrote books on agriculture and animal husbandry, expressed surprise at the number of people who were not aware that saffron could be grown in England. 'Now Saffron is a very soveraign and wholsom thing & if it take right it is a very great advantage for price;' he advises readers of his book, *The English Improver Improved*, 'it hath its ebbings & its flowings, as almost all things have, yet I would fain give encouragement to this Improvement also.' Blith was keen to encourage his fellow countrymen to undertake new farming initiatives in order to improve the productivity of the land.[24] I think he would be heartened to discover that over three hundred years later, saffron is still being grown in England.

Part II

The Recipes

Introduction

A man who is stingy with saffron is capable of seducing his own grandmother.

Norman Douglas

How much is a pinch of saffron? So many modern recipes call for just that, but what one person considers to be generous another could deem wholly inadequate.

In the course of researching this book I have come across many different measurements for saffron. In older recipes the cook is instructed to use 'a little' or 'some' saffron (it is rare to find a culinary recipe from the medieval era that contains specific measurements for things like spices). As vague as this is, in some ways it is easier to deal with, as the confident cook can use their judgement and adjust the quantities according to taste. The confusion arises because saffron was historically sold in different measurements such as grains, drams and drachms (and over the years recipes have accordingly adopted these measurements). A grain, not to be confused with a strand, is approximately 0.065 g (this was based on the weight of a grain of wheat). About 27 grains make up a dram (1.77 g). One drachm is 3.88 g. That is a lot of saffron when you consider many supermarkets sell it in weights of 0.4 g.

Vida Heard recalls how her 'cousin Nancy remembers her mother telling her of how, as a child, she was sent to the village shop on her bicycle with a threepenny bit which was weighed against a dram of saffron, sufficient for a week's baking'. Hettie Merrick, who was brought up in Porthleven during the 1930s and 1940s, explains that a shilling's worth of saffron, weighed by the grocer using a special set of scales, was sufficient to colour 1.5 kg / 3 lb 5 oz of flour 'to a glorious yellow'. Her memoir was first published in the 1980s and she bemoans the fact that 'ten grains of saffron now costs nearly £2 and scarcely colours the same quantity darker than a primrose'.

'There are few spices or aromatics which possess and impart scent, taste and colour in such a high degree as saffron,' explains food writer Elizabeth David. 'Properly administered, it can make a rice dish, a soup, a sauce, most wonderfully attractive; incautiously used, that penetrating smell, that pungent, bitterish taste can turn the same dish into something quite repellent.'

How much saffron is too much? This is very much a matter of taste. Several of the English saffron growers I interviewed said they count out the strands they put in each recipe. So, for example, Sally Francis of Norfolk Saffron uses thirty threads in her saffron risotto recipe. This may sound like a bit of a palaver but with good quality English saffron it is reasonably easy to pick out individual threads, and is nowhere near as time consuming as you may think. However, saffron is very brittle and therefore the strands are liable to break. This means you have to use your judgement and perhaps count two or three broken segments as one single thread (yes, I know, this is beginning to sound increasingly complicated).

The saffron you are able to purchase in a supermarket is likely to be more crumbly than that sold by domestic producers, making it very hard to count out individual strands. Based on the many historical recipes I have tried, which are far more numerous than those contained in this book, I have come to the following conclusion: one 'Bilton pinch' is about twenty to thirty threads, which is approximately one eighth of a teaspoon (it is virtually impossible to measure one eighth of a teaspoon

Recipes: Introduction

of saffron accurately, so I provide this measurement as a guide only). Two pinches is equal to forty to sixty strands, or quarter of a teaspoon. Once you get beyond this measurement you can use half teaspoon measures and upwards.

Taste is a very personal thing. Taking the herb coriander as an example, some people (like my husband) describe the flavour as being soapy and therefore unpleasant. I find the taste of coriander leaf fresh and zesty, although I agree that it can be overpowering if used extensively in a dish. I do wonder whether saffron is the same. I have heard people describe the flavour as being bitter and metallic. This has never been the case for myself, although in the course of my research I may have become inured against the repellent effects described by Mrs David. Therefore, I have probably been quite generous with my measurements so if you are concerned that there is too much saffron in a recipe feel free to use slightly less the first time you make it. I'm sure your grandmother will be perfectly safe.

You can add the threads directly to a recipe, of course, but there are a few things you can do to maximise the flavour and intensity of colour that saffron lends to a dish. A Mrs Bath from Stithians in Cornwall used to dry her saffron in the oven between two sheets of baking paper before rolling the papers with a rolling pin to crush the strands to a powder. However, this additional desiccation process is redundant now given the very effective methods of drying saffron today. Crushing the saffron strands in a small pestle and mortar is definitely worthwhile, particularly if you do not have much time to infuse the saffron. Food writer Orlando Murrin told me that his Iranian friend grinds 5 g of saffron with a sugar cube to improve the density of the powder. However, any saffron grower you speak to will tell you that the key to getting the most flavour and best colour out of this spice is a long infusion. I would suggest at least an hour before you make a recipe is a good amount of time, but preparing the saffron infusion the night before, if you can, is even better. There are one or two exceptions to this suggestion in the following recipes but generally the longer you can leave the crushed strands to infuse the better.

Fool's Gold

Here are a few further notes about the recipes:

- Most of the recipes serve four unless otherwise stated.

- Eggs were historically smaller so I always use medium eggs (if you need to use an alternative size I will say so). Medium eggs are better from a hen welfare perspective too. That said, if you only ever buy large eggs you should be able to use them instead of medium eggs in most recipes without anything disastrous occurring.

- I work in a metric kitchen so these are the weights and measurements I have tested in the recipes. Imperial and cup measurements are provided as a guide and may have been rounded up or down slightly to fit in with the metric system.

- The cooking times and temperatures in the recipes have been tested in my conventional domestic oven (i.e. not fan-assisted). However, if you know that your oven is particularly fierce or mild then please use your judgement to adjust the cooking times or temperatures accordingly. This is particularly important if you use a fan-assisted oven. The general consensus appears to be that the oven temperature should be reduced by 20°C / 40°F for fan-assisted ovens but check your oven's instruction manual for specific guidance, as ovens can vary.

- Clearly, these recipes will work with genuine saffron from all over the world but please consider using English saffron. It really is lovely stuff and it is always wonderful to support our local producers.

Happy cooking!

Meat Dishes

Aloes of Lamb with Verde Sawse

Adapted from the recipe for 'Allowes de Mutton' in *Two Fifteenth Century Cookery Books* (Harl MS 4016).

Ingredients (serves 4 as a starter or light lunch)
2 tbsp double cream or milk
1 pinch / 20-30 saffron strands, crushed
2 tbsp vegetable oil
1 small onion, peeled and finely chopped
2 eggs, beaten
¼ tsp ground ginger
2 tbsp chopped parsley
4 lamb boneless leg steaks (500 g / 1 lb 2 oz in total)
salt and ground white pepper to season
8 x cocktail sticks
verde sawse to serve (see page 251-2)

Method
1. Heat the cream or the milk in the microwave for around 10 seconds then pour over the saffron and leave to infuse.
2. Heat a tablespoon of the oil. Fry the onion in the oil until softened and golden.
3. While the onion is cooking combine the saffron cream and beaten eggs together.
4. Mix the ground ginger into the onions followed by the egg and cream mixture. Stir over a lowish heat until the egg starts to set (a bit like

Fool's Gold

   scrambled eggs). Continue to cook until set but still soft. Stir in the parsley and season with salt and pepper. You can allow the mixture to cool now if you want to make this in advance.
5. Remove any excess fat from the steaks then cut each one in two horizontally. Place the steaks between two pieces of cling film then beat with a rolling pin until thin. Season both sides well with salt and pepper.
6. Place around 1 heaped teaspoon of the egg mix at one end of each thin piece of meat. Roll the meat up into a little parcel ensuring the egg mixture is fully enclosed. Secure with a cocktail stick.
7. Heat a griddle over a medium to high heat (or cook on a BBQ). Brush the lamb rolls with the remaining vegetable oil. Cook them for 2 to 3 minutes on each side depending on how well done you like your meat. Serve with some salad and plenty of verde sawse.

Herby Veal (or Chicken) Stew with Almond milk

Adapted from the recipe for 'Buknade' in *Two Fifteenth Century Cookbooks* (Harl. MS 4016).

Ingredients
750 g / 1 lb 10 oz / 5 cups diced veal or diced chicken thigh meat
1 onion, peeled and halved
1 carrot, peeled and halved
1 clove garlic, peeled and crushed
2 sprigs thyme
1 bay leaf
2 blades mace
2 cloves
300 ml / ½ pint / 1 ¼ cups water
300 ml / ½ pint / 1 ¼ cups white wine
1-2 pinches / 20-60 saffron strands, crushed (to taste)

Recipes: Meat Dishes

100 g / 4 oz / ¾ cup whole blanched almonds
1 tsp cornflour
2 egg yolks
½ tsp ground ginger
1 tbsp verjuice or lemon juice, plus more if required
salt and ground white pepper, to season
1 tbsp each chopped parsley, sage and thyme (or hyssop)

Method

1. Place the veal, vegetables, thyme, bay leaf, mace, cloves, water and wine in a large, lidded casserole. Bring to the boil, cover and simmer for 30 to 45 minutes, or until tender.
2. Strain the stew through a sieve into a jug, removing the meat and reserving until required. If you are making this ahead of time, refrigerate the meat when cool.
3. Take two tablespoons of the hot stock and mix with the saffron threads. Pour the remaining hot stock over the blanched almonds. Leave for at least one hour for both to infuse.
4. After the hour (or more) has passed, place the almonds and stock into a blender. Process until smooth then pass the almond milk through a sieve lined with muslin, squeezing the muslin to extract as much of the milk as possible.
5. Mix the saffron infusion with the cornflour to create a smooth paste then stir in the egg yolks, ginger and verjuice or lemon juice.
6. Place the veal and almond milk in a large lidded casserole. Bring up to a gentle simmer for a little while (10 to 15 minutes) to ensure the veal is heated through. Just before you are ready to serve add one to two tablespoons of the cooking liquor to the saffron and egg mixture before returning this to the pan. Stir constantly until the liquor begins to thicken. Adjust the seasoning then add the chopped fresh herbs just before serving.

Fool's Gold

Golden 'Apples' with Apple & Almond Sauce

This is an example of the illusion foods that were popular at grand feasts during the medieval era. It is adapted from the recipes for 'Pomme Dorryle' in *Forme of Cury* (1390), and 'Apple Muse' in *Two Fifteenth Century Cookbooks* (Harl MS 279).

Ingredients (serves 4)

For the golden 'apples':
2 pinches / 40-60 saffron strands, crushed
2 tbsp hot water
600 g / 1 lb 5 oz / 3 cups good quality sausage meat
1 tsp powder fort (see page 275-6)
1 large clove garlic, peeled and crushed
2 tbsp chopped fresh parsley
1 tbsp verjuice or white wine vinegar
50 g / 2 oz / ⅓ cup currants
2 eggs, separated (you only need 1 of the whites)
1 tbsp plain flour
salt to season
2 litres water for cooking the meatballs
2 chicken stock cubes
4 bay leaves and edible gold spray (optional) to decorate

For the apple and almond sauce:
1 pinch / 20-30 saffron strands, crushed
75 ml / 2 ½ fl oz / ⅓ cup warmed almond milk (see page 275)
1 large cooking apple (225 g / 8 oz)
1-2 tbsp honey
3-4 tbsp fresh white breadcrumbs
pinch salt

Method
For the 'apples':
1. Infuse the saffron in two tablespoons of hot water for at least an hour.
2. Mix the sausage meat, powder fort, garlic, parsley, verjuice or vinegar

and currants in a bowl. Add one of the egg whites and a tablespoon of the saffron infusion. Mix well and fry a little of the mixture to test the seasoning adding more salt if required.
3. Divide the mixture equally into four then form into apple shaped balls.
4. Bring a deep pan of water to the boil, add the stock cubes, then reduce to a vigorous simmer. Using a slotted spoon carefully lower the meatballs into the simmering stock. Simmer the meatballs for 15 to 20 minutes or until cooked through. Remove with a slotted spoon and drain on absorbent kitchen paper.
5. Preheat the oven to 200°C / 400°F / Gas 6.
6. Blend the egg yolks, flour, remaining saffron infusion and a small pinch of salt together to create a thick batter.
7. Pat the meatballs dry with more kitchen paper then place on a baking sheet lined with baking paper or a silicone liner. Brush each meat ball with the batter then bake for 3 to 5 minutes or until the batter is set. One coat should be enough but you can reapply it if you have enough.
8. Insert a bay leaf into the top of each meatball to resemble apple leaves. You can add to the gilded effect by spraying with edible gold dust. Serve with the apple and almond sauce.

For the apple and almond sauce
1 Add the saffron to the almond milk. Leave to infuse for a while.
2 Peel, core and roughly chop the apple. Place in a pan with 2-3 tablespoons of water then cook until pulpy. Pass the purée through a sieve into another pan.
3 Add the saffron infused almond milk, 1 tablespoon of the honey, the breadcrumbs and the salt. Cook over a gentle heat, stirring constantly, for around five minutes or until the purée is thick. Add more honey if you think it is needed although remember this is a condiment rather than a dessert so it shouldn't be too sweet.

Recipes: Meat Dishes

Ham Hock Terrine with Pickled Pears

Whole joints of meat, like joints of gammon, were often baked in a pie, as Thomas Dawson did in the recipe 'To bake a Gammon of Baken' which appeared in *Good Huswife's Jewell* (1587) and which inspired this dish. Dawson's seasoning also fares well in a classic ham terrine like the one suggested by Raymond Blanc in *Kitchen Secrets* (2011). This does need to be made a least a day ahead to ensure it has time to set. The recipe for Pickled Pears takes its inspiration from a medieval 'chutney' called compost (which contains pears and a variety of vegetables) found in the *Forme of Cury*.

Ingredients (serves 8)

For the ham hock terrine:
2 onions
4 cloves
25 g / 1 oz / 1 cup fresh parsley, leaves picked and stalks reserved for the bouquet garni
1- 2 ham hocks, weighing a total of 1.5 kg / 3.3 lb
2 litres / 3.5 pints / 2.1 quarts cold water
Bouquet garni (2 bay leaves, 2 sprigs of thyme and parsley stalks from above, tied together)
8 black peppercorns
2 pinches / 40-60 saffron strands, crushed
¾-1 tsp coarse ground pepper
4 leaves / 12 g gelatine
1-3 tbsp verjuice or white wine vinegar
12-16 cornichons or small gherkins

For the pickled pears:
1 tsp mustard seeds
1 tsp aniseeds
1 tsp fennel seeds
2 cloves
5-7.5 cm / 2-3 in piece cinnamon stick, broken into smaller pieces
2 pinches / 40-60 saffron strands, crushed

Recipes: Meat Dishes

240 ml / 8 ½ fl oz / 1 cup cider vinegar
240 ml / 8 ½ fl oz / 1 cup white wine
170 g / 6 oz / ½ cup runny honey
50 g / 2 oz / ⅓ cup raisins
2 slices fresh ginger
1 tsp salt
4 firm small-medium pears

Method
For the ham hock terrine:
1. Peel the onions and cut each one in half. Stick a clove in each half of onion.
2. Blanch the parsley leaves in boiling water for 15 seconds. Refresh under cold water, drain well then roughly chop.
3. Place the ham hock in a large sauce pan. Cover with water then bring to the boil, skimming off any impurities. Reduce to a simmer then add the onions stuck with cloves, bouquet garni and peppercorns. Cook for 3 to 4 hours or until the meat is literally falling off the bone.
4. While the hocks are cooking line a large loaf tin with cling film leaving around 10cm hanging over the edge.
5. Remove the meat from the water and place on a board to cool a little. Strain the liquor reserving 400 ml / 13 ½ fl oz / 1 ⅔ cup for the terrine. Put the saffron into a saucepan and pour over the reserved liquor.
6. Remove the rind and fat from the ham hocks. Flake the meat ensuring you keep some large chunks. Place in a bowl and mix with the chopped parsley and coarsely ground pepper.
7. Soak the gelatine in cold water for five minutes. Bring the saffron infused liquor to a simmer. Add the soaked gelatine and verjuice or vinegar to taste then stir until the gelatine has dissolved.
8. Pack half of the shredded ham into the lined loaf tin. Arrange the whole cornichons or small gherkins on top of this layer then top with the remaining shredded ham. Pour over the saffron liquor ensuring the meat is completely covered (press the meat down if necessary). Tap terrine firmly on a hard surface to knock out air pockets, then cover with cling film. Refrigerate overnight.
9. To serve, uncover the terrine. Place a board on top of the tin then

Fool's Gold

flip it over to remove the terrine. Remove the cling film then cut into chunky slices. Serve with plenty of crusty bread and some pickled pear on the side.

For the pickled pears:
1. Lightly crush the mustard, aniseed and fennel seeds for the spice mix. Place on a small piece of muslin with the cloves and cinnamon stick pieces. Gather the up the edges of the muslin to make a little bundle then tie the top with a neutral coloured piece of string.
2. Place the crushed saffron in a shallow pan large enough to hold the pears in one layer. Add the vinegar, wine, honey, raisins, ginger, spice bag and salt. Bring to the boil.
3. While the pickling liquor is heating up peel the pears leaving the stalks on. If the pears are particularly large you may want to cut them in half and remove the core. Once the liquid has come to the boil lower the pears into the poaching liquor and reduce to a simmer.
4. Cook for around 25-40 minutes (depending on the size and ripeness), turning every ten minutes or so or until the pears are tender. Allow to cool in the pickling liquor then remove the spice bag and sliced ginger before serving at room temperature.

Lamb Shanks in Spiced Ale

Adapted from the recipe 'To make stewed steaks' in *The Good Huswifes Handmaide for the Kitchen* (1594).

Ingredients
2 pinches / 40-60 saffron strands, crushed
2 tbsp boiling water
½ tsp salt
½ tsp ground mace
½ tsp ground cinnamon
½ tsp ground black pepper

Recipes: Meat Dishes

½ tsp ginger
2 tbsp vegetable oil
4 lamb shanks
salt and pepper to season
2 onions, peeled and chopped
1 tbsp plain flour
360 ml / 12 fl oz / 1 ½ cups golden ale (if you are using a 330 ml / 11 fl oz can just add a little more stock)
240 ml / 8 fl oz / 1 cup chicken or lamb stock
bouquet garni (2 sprigs thyme, 2 sprigs parsley and 1 sprig rosemary, tied together)
100 g / 4 oz / ¾ cup raisins
1 tbsp date syrup (or dark brown sugar)
1 tbsp red wine vinegar or verjuice
2 tbsp chopped fresh parsley

Method
1. Before you start cooking the lamb shanks infuse the saffron in boiling water.
2. In a separate bowl mix the salt and ground spices.
3. Heat the oil in a large, lidded, flame proof casserole. Season the lamb shanks with salt and pepper then brown in the oil. Remove the shanks and drain on absorbent paper.
4. Fry the onion until lightly browned. Stir in the flour then cook for a minute or two before adding the ale and the chicken or lamb stock followed by the bouquet garni, raisins, date syrup or sugar and vinegar or verjuice.
5. Simmer for about 2 ½ to 3 hours or until meltingly tender.
6. Once the lamb is cooked, stir in the saffron infusion and chopped parsley. Adjust the seasoning by adding a touch more vinegar or verjuice if more acidity is needed.
7. Serve with mashed potato or rice.

Fool's Gold

Marinated Pork Chops with Saffron Mustard Sauce & Roasted Hazelnuts

A punchy sauce from Ancient Rome. I like to serve these pork chops with soft polenta. This is adapted from the recipe 'Mustard Wine Sauce for Braised Meats' in John Edwards' *The Roman Cookery of Apicius* (1993).

Ingredients (serves 2)
¼ tsp peppercorns
¼ tsp celery seed
¼ tsp caraway seed
¼ tsp salt flakes
1 tsp chopped savory or thyme
120 ml / 4 fl oz / ½ cup sweet white wine e.g. sauternes
1 tsp cider vinegar
2 pork chops (bone in), about 1-2 cm / ½-1 in thick (600-650 g / 1 ½ lb)
90 ml / 3 fl oz / ⅓ cup chicken stock
1 pinch / 20-30 saffron strands, crushed
1-2 tbsp olive oil
1 shallot, finely chopped
1 tsp plain flour
1 tbsp mustard, dijon for preference
salt & lemon juice to season
leaves from 2 sprigs thyme or savory
50 g / 2 oz / ½ cup chopped roasted hazelnuts or almonds

Method
1. In a large frying pan, toast the peppercorns, celery seed and caraway seed until fragrant. Convert to a fine powder in a spice grinder or with a pestle and mortar. Mix with the salt, chopped savory or thyme, sweet white wine and the cider vinegar. Pour this over the chops and leave in the fridge for at least four hours (or overnight if you prefer), turning once or twice to ensure both sides are infused with the flavours.
2. Warm the stock then pour over the saffron threads. Leave to infuse

Fool's Gold

(do this at the same time you prepare the marinade).
3. Preheat the oven to 200°C / 400°F / Gas 6.
4. Heat a tablespoon of olive oil in the same pan over a high heat. Remove the chops from their marinade then pat dry. Strain the marinade and reserve until required. Cook the chops for 2 to 3 minutes on each side or until they are golden brown. Transfer to a baking tray lined with foil and roast for 10 to 12 mins until thoroughly cooked.
5. While the chops are in the oven, fry the chopped shallots in the same pan over a medium heat until softened (add more oil if necessary). Add the plain flour then cook for a minute or two.
6. Pour in the reserved marinade followed by the saffron infused stock. Let it gently bubble away for a few minutes until it thickens.
7. Whisk in the mustard then season with salt and lemon juice to taste. Serve drizzled over the chops with the thyme or savory leaves and chopped nuts scattered over the top.

Pork & Fig Tart

The lid of this tart is cut and shaped to represent flames. It is a little fiddly but well worth the effort for the end result. Don't worry if some of the 'flames' decide to do their own thing while baking (real flames are rarely uniform in their appearance) as this adds to the attraction of the finished dish. Ideally make the filling a day ahead so that it has time to cool before you make the tart, the recipe for which is adapted from one for 'Flaumpeyns' in *Forme of Cury* (1390), and the design of which is inspired by one by Peter Brears in *Cooking and Dining in Medieval England* (2012).

Ingredients (serves 4-6)
150 ml / 5 fl oz / ⅔ cup golden ale plus 2 tbsp for the saffron
150 ml / 5 fl oz / ⅔ cup water

Recipes: Introduction

800 g to 1 kg / around 2 lb / piece pork belly (try to get a fleshier rather than a fatty bit)
6 dried figs (about 100 g / 4 oz)
1 sprig thyme
1 bay leaf
1 sprig parsley
1 star anise
2 cloves garlic, peeled and squashed
1 pinch / 20-30 saffron strands
1 quantity saffron hot water crust pastry (see page 278-9)
a little butter for greasing
1 ½ tsp powder douce (see page 276)
½ tsp ground black pepper
¼ -½ tsp salt
3 tbsp finely grated Parmesan
2 eggs, beaten
1 tbsp verjuice or white wine vinegar
1 egg, beaten to glaze the tart

Method

1. First prepare the filling. Bring the ale and the water to the boil in a lidded casserole deep enough to accommodate the pork belly
2. Place the pork belly, dried figs, thyme, bay leaf, parsley, star anise and garlic in the casserole and cook at 140°C / 275°F / Gas 1 for 2 hours or until the meat is really tender.
3. While the meat is cooking infuse the saffron in two tablespoons of ale.
4. When the meat is cooked allow it to cool slightly before removing the rind and as much excess fat as possible. Shred the meat while warm and roughly chop the figs discarding the stalks. Place shredded pork, figs and squashed garlic cloves in a bowl and allow to cool. Strain and reserve the cooking liquor. Discard the herbs and spice, and refrigerate the meat and stock when cool.
5. The following day preheat the oven to 200°C / 400°F / Gas 6. Place a baking tray wide enough to accommodate the cake tin in the oven at the same time.
6. To form the tart, take one third of the pastry and roll it out to a

Fool's Gold

thickness of 3 mm on a lightly floured board. Use the loose bottomed base of a 20 cm / 8 in x 4 cm / 1 ½ in cake tin to cut out a round lid. Cover and set aside until required.

7. Grease the inside of the cake tin and line the base with some baking parchment. Roll the remaining pastry and use it to line the cake tin leaving some pastry over hanging the top of the tin.
8. Add the powder douce, black pepper, salt and parmesan to the pork, giving the mixture a good stir. Beat the eggs with 3-5 tablespoons of the reserved cooking liquor, verjuice or vinegar and saffron infusion. Pour this onto the pork, stirring some more to ensure the ingredients are thoroughly combined.
9. Spoon the pork mixture into the prepared pastry case. Press it down firmly and smooth the top. You should have a small lip of exposed pastry at the top of the tart. Brush this with a little beaten egg reserved for glazing the tart to help the lid to stick.
10. Place the lid on the board. Using a sharp knife cut a line through the centre from the top of the disc down towards the outer edge keeping a 2 cm / 1 in margin around the outside of the circle. Do the same again but at 90 degrees to the original cut effectively making four quad-rants. Now cut each quarter into two remembering all the while to leave the 2 cm / 1 in perimeter around the edge of the disc.
11. Carefully lift the disc onto the tart. Press the outer edge of the disc against the exposed pastry of the base to create a seal. Trim away any excess pastry. This will create a gap in the middle but this is fine.
12. Brush the top of the tart with beaten egg. Peel each 'flame' back on itself to reveal the middle then the tips forward again to create a flame effect. Brush with a little more beaten egg.
13. Stand on the preheated baking tray and bake for 50 to 60 mins. You may need to reduce the temperature to 180°C / 350°F / Gas 4 after 40 minutes or so if the tips are getting too brown or you can lightly cover the top of the tart with foil.
14. Once the tart is baked you will need to let it cool a little before removing it from the tin. It can be eaten hot or cold.

Recipes: Introduction

Skink with Kale & Barley

This is one of those glorious one pot dishes that can be made ahead of time, then reheated and finished just prior to serving. It needs little else to go with it. It is inspired by the recipe 'To make French Broth called Kinck' in Hannah Woolley's *The Queen-Like Closet* (1670). The idea for the kale come from William Rabisha who added cabbage to his skink recipe some 20 years earlier.

Ingredients (serves 4-6)
2 pinches / 40-60 saffron strands, crushed
1 tbsp lemon juice and 1 tbsp orange juice or 2 tbsp Seville orange juice
100 g / 2 oz / ¼ cup pearl barley
4-6 tbsp vegetable oil
750 g / 1 lb 10 oz / 5 cups stewing beef
2 large leeks, trimmed and washed
2 cloves garlic, crushed with 2 pinches sea salt flakes
1 tsp ground ginger
2 tbsp flour mixed with ¼ tsp salt
1l / 1 ¾ pints / 4 ¼ cups beef stock
1 star anise
2 cloves
2 x 10 cm strips of orange zest
200 g / 4 oz / 1 ½ cups kale or cavolo nero, thick stalks removed and shredded
salt and pepper to season

Method
1. Infuse the saffron in the lemon or orange juice (or Seville orange juice if they are in season)
2. Place the pearl barley in a saucepan and cover with water. Bring to the boil and simmer for 45 minutes. It will be undercooked at this stage but that's fine as you will be adding it to the stew.
3. Heat a tablespoon of the oil in a large casserole. Brown about a third of the meat then remove with a slotted spoon and drain on absorbent

Fool's Gold

    kitchen paper. Repeat with the remaining meat using a tablespoon of oil each time.
4. While the meat is browning, split the leeks in half length ways then cut into half moons about 3-5 mm in width. Heat two tablespoons of the oil in the same pan you cooked the meat in but reduce the heat. Cook the leeks until soft then add the garlic, ground ginger, a dash of pepper and flour mixture. Stir for a minute or two to ensure the leeks are evenly coated in these ingredients.
5. Add the meat stock, star anise, cloves and strips of orange zest. Bring to the boil then reduce to a simmer. Cook for 30 to 45 minutes.
6. Add barley to the pan. Continue to simmer for a further 45 to 60 minutes or until the meat is really tender and the barley is thoroughly cooked. All of the above can be done ahead of time and reheated later if you wish.
7. About 5 to 10 minutes before serving, stir in the saffron citrus juice and shredded kale or cavolo nero. Once the kale has wilted add more seasoning (if required) then serve in warm bowls.

CAKES AND BREADS

Recipes: Cakes and Breads

Golden Cup Cakes with Saffron Icing

The recipe from Mary L. Allen's *Five O'Clock Tea* originally relied on turmeric and egg yolks to give this cake its golden hue, but I've replaced it with saffron.

Ingredients (makes 12)

For the cup cakes:
juice of one lemon
2 pinches / 40-60 saffron strands, crushed
225 g / 8 oz / 2 cups self-raising flour
1 tsp ground mace
pinch of salt
100 g / 4 oz / 1 stick unsalted butter, softened
225 g / 8 oz / 1 ¼ cups golden caster sugar
5 egg yolks
5 tbsp milk
zest of 1 orange

For the saffron icing:
2 pinches / 40-60 saffron strands, crushed
juice of half an orange
175 g / 6 oz / 2 sticks unsalted butter, softened
340 g / 12 oz / 3 cups icing sugar
gold glitter, balls, sprinkles or marigold petals to decorate

Method
1. Gently heat the lemon juice in a microwaveable bowl (say for around 10 seconds). Add the saffron and leave to infuse while you make the cake.
2. Preheat the oven to 180°C / 350°F / Gas 4. Line a twelve-hole muffin tray with with cup cake cases.
3. Sieve the flour, ground mace and salt together
4. Beat the 100 g / 4 oz / 1 stick butter and the golden caster sugar

together until light and fluffy (an electric hand whisk is handy for this). Add the egg yolks one at a time mixing well after each addition until thoroughly combined.
5. Add the flour to the batter alternating with the milk, beating well after each addition.
6. Finally add the saffron infused lemon juice and orange zest then mix thoroughly to combine. Divide between the cup cake cases
7. Bake for 12 to 15 minutes Allow to cool slightly in the tin before transferring to a wire rack to cool completely.
8. To make the icing infuse the saffron strands in the orange juice. Place the icing sugar in a food processor with the butter. Blitz to combine then add the saffron scented orange juice. Spread or pipe the icing onto the cakes then decorate with sprinkles or petals.

Apricot Cake

I was not convinced that the saffron would have that much of an impact in this recipe, adapted from Florence Jack's *Cookery for Every Household* (1914), as it is only in the icing. However, it pleasantly surprising what a difference it makes. Plus, this is an incredibly pretty cake when finished.

Ingredients (makes 8-10 slices)
1 x 420 g can tinned apricots, drained (reserve the syrup)
340 g / 12 oz / 1 ¾ cups granulated sugar
2 tsp vanilla extract
125 g / 4 ½ oz / 1 cup unsalted butter, softened
125 g / 4 ½ oz / ¾ cup caster sugar plus extra for dusting
3 eggs
225 g / 8 oz / 1 ¾ cups self raising flour, sieved
180 ml / 6 fl oz / ¾ cup apricot syrup
1 pinch / 20-30 saffron strands, crushed
2 tbsp lemon juice

Recipes: Cakes and Breads

25 g / 1 oz / ¼ cup pistachios, coarsely chopped
2 x Victoria sandwich tins (18-20 cm) greased & lined

Method
1. Drain the apricots reserving the syrup. You should be left with around 240 g / 8 ½ oz of fruit and 180 ml / 6 fl oz / ¾ cup of syrup. Preheat the oven to 180°C / 350°F / Gas 4.
2. First make the apricot 'marmalade'. Place the drained apricots in a food processor then blitz to a purée. Pour this into a pan then add 240 g / 8 ½ oz of the granulated sugar and half a teaspoon of vanilla extract. Bring to the boil then cook over a medium high heat until it reaches setting point (105°C / 221°F) stirring frequently. This should take around 5-8 minutes. If you don't have a thermometer you can test whether it has reached the jam stage by pouring a little onto a plate then pushing it with your finger. If it wrinkles, it should set. Pour the marmalade into a jar or a heat proof bowl and reserve until required.
3. To make the cake whip the butter to a cream then beat in the caster sugar. Add the eggs one at a time mixing well after each addition.
4. Add the flour in spoonfuls alternating with a bit of the leftover syrup from the tin of apricots. Finally add 1 ½ teaspoons of vanilla extract. Divide the mixture between the tins then bake for 10 to 15 mins or until well risen and brown (these are quite shallow cakes so don't panic if they look a little flat!). While the cakes are baking lightly dust some baking paper placed on top of a cooling rack with caster sugar. When the cakes are baked turn them out onto the sugared paper and allow them to cool completely.
5. Mix the crushed saffron with the lemon juice and leave to infuse.
6. Once the cakes are cool carefully cut each in half as if you were making a sandwich. Spread the bottom half of each cake with one third of the apricot marmalade then replace the top. Spread the remaining third of jam on top of one of the whole cakes then place the other sandwiched cake on top effectively creating four layers interspersed with apricot marmalade.
7. Gently heat the remaining 100 g / 4 oz / ½ cup granulated sugar and saffron infused lemon juice in a saucepan. Once the sugar has dissolved bring the syrup up to boiling point and cook until

thick. Allow the syrup to cool to lukewarm then pour it slowly over the cake, covering the top and allowing it to drip down the sides. Decorate with pieces of pistachio.

Gyngerbrede (A Fairing of Sorts)

Fairing was the name given to a piece of gingerbread bought at a fair. Gingerbread is one of the earliest confections around. During the medieval era it was made from a mixture of honey, breadcrumbs and spices. The curious thing about one of the earliest gingerbread recipes is that it contains cinnamon, pepper and saffron but no ginger. I have adapted a Cornish fairing recipe found in Edith Martin's *Cornish Recipes Ancient and Modern* using these flavourings.

Ingredients (makes 16)
150 g / 5 oz / 1 ¼ cups plain flour
1 ½ tsp ground cinnamon
½ tsp ground white pepper
50 g / 2 oz / ¼ stick butter, cubed
15 g / ½ oz lard, cubed (or more butter for a vegetarian version)
75 g / 3 oz / ⅝ cup golden caster sugar
75 g / 3 oz / ¼ cup runny honey
1 pinch / 20-30 saffron strands, crushed and soaked in 1 tsp boiling water
1 tsp bicarbonate of soda

Method
1. Preheat the oven to 180°C / 350°F / Gas 4. Line a large baking sheet with silicone or baking paper
2. Sieve the flour and ground spices into a bowl.
3. Rub in the butter and lard then stir in the sugar.
4. Gently heat the honey in a microwave for a few seconds to make it a little runnier. Stir in the saffron infusion followed by the bicarbonate of soda. It will fizz a bit. Mix this honey into the flour etc and bring together to form a dough. You can leave the dough for a while if you like.

Recipes: Cakes and Breads

5. Divide the dough into sixteen pieces. Roll each piece into a ball then flatten slightly with the palm of your hand. Place on the baking sheet well spaced apart (the biscuits will spread as they bake).
6. Bake for 8 to 10 minutes or until deeply golden. Allow to cool and firm up on the tray for a little while before transferring to a wire rack.

Risshewes

This is a recipe inspired by one found in *Two Fifteenth Century Cookery Books* (Harl MS 4016). Risshewes are sort of like a deep-fried medieval mince pie although you can eat them at any time of the year. They are amazing fried but I have provided instructions for a baked version below for those who don't like the idea of fried pastry.

Ingredients (makes 12)
1 pinch / 20-30 saffron strands, crushed
2 tbsp hot water
150 g / 5 oz / 1 cup dried figs, chopped
50 g / 2 oz / ⅓ cup dates, chopped
50 g / 2 oz / ½ cup currants
3 tbsp walnut oil or other light, mild flavoured oil
3 tbsp pine nuts
50 g / 2 oz / ¼ cup golden caster sugar
½ tsp ground cinnamon
½ tsp ground ginger
¼ tsp ground black pepper
¼ tsp ground mace
⅛ tsp ground cloves
⅛ tsp fine sea salt
1 quantity sweet saffron short crust pastry (see page 276)
1 egg, beaten
1 litre / 1 ¾ pints / 4 ¼ cups vegetable oil for frying
icing sugar for dusting

Fool's Gold

Method
1. Infuse the saffron in the hot water.
2. To make the filling, place the saffron infusion, dried figs, dates, currants and walnut oil into a small food processor. Blitz until you have a rough paste. If you don't have a food processor place the dried figs, dates and currants on a board then chop vigorously with a large knife until you have a rough paste (it will seem a little dry at this stage). Transfer to a bowl then add the walnut oil and saffron infusion.
3. Transfer the paste from the food processor to a small bowl. Add the pine nuts, sugar, ground spices and salt. Mix well until thoroughly combined. Divide the fruit paste into twelve piles (about 30 g / 1 oz each).
4. On a lightly floured board roll the saffron pastry out to a thickness of 2-3 mm. Stamp out twelve rounds using a 14-15 cm cutter. You will probably need to re-roll the pastry. Save any offcuts to test the temperature of the oil.
5. Lightly brush each round with egg. Place one pile of the fruit paste to one side of the circle, leaving 1cm around the top edge of the circle. Shape the past into a rough semi circle. Lift the bottom half of the dough up and over the paste, enclosing it like a small pasty. Press the edges firmly to ensure the pastry is sealed.
6. Heat the oil in a large wok over a medium-high heat. To see whether the oil is at an appropriate temperature fry a small piece of the leftover pastry. It should result in a spritely but not too ferocious sizzle (approximately 175°C / 350°F). Fry the pastries in batches, say three or four at a time, for around 4 minutes (if you have a deep fat fryer this time may be reduced). Turn them frequently. When they are done they will be a golden brown colour. Drain on kitchen towel before serving sprinkled with a little icing sugar.

Variation
If you don't like the idea of frying these pastries they can be baked in the oven at 175°C / 350°F / Gas 4 for 15 minutes. Brush the exterior with a little egg prior to cooking.

Recipes: Cakes and Breads

Saffron Drizzle Seed Cake

Seed cakes have a long-standing history in Britain. In their original incarnation the seeds (usually caraway) were added to enriched doughs before they morphed into a spongier form in the Victorian era. They appear to have fallen out of favour in the twentieth century. 'Why were those cakes always so dry,' lamented Elizabeth David in *Spices, Salt and Aromatics in the English Kitchen*. She was not alone in her aversion. In her recipe 'To make a fine Seed or Saffron cake' (which inspired the recipe below) eighteenth-century cook Hannah Glasse concluded that 'you may leave out the Seed if you chuse it, and I think it rather better without it; but you must do as you like'.

Personally, I do like to add seeds and not just caraway. As a nod to my Essex roots I have included both caraway and coriander seeds. As well as saffron the county was known for growing both of these crops which were used in medicine and condiments. The saffron appears in the form of a syrup. I defy anyone to accuse this cake of being dry.

Ingredients (makes a 900 g / 2 lb loaf cake)

For the cake:
150 g / 5 ½ oz / 1 ¼ cups plain (all purpose) flour
2 tsp baking powder
¼ tsp ground mace
¼ tsp ground cinnamon
pinch ground cloves (optional)
pinch of salt
25 g / 1 oz / ¼ cup ground almonds
175 g / 6 oz / ¾ cup soft unsalted butter
175 g / 6 oz / ¾ cup golden caster sugar
3 eggs
finely grated zest of 2 unwaxed lemons
1 tsp, lightly crushed coriander seeds
2 tsp caraway seeds

For the drizzle:
125 g / 4 ½ oz / 1 cup icing sugar, sieved

Recipes: Cakes and Breads

juice of 2 lemons (5-6 tbsp)
2 pinches / 40-60 saffron strands, crushed

Method
1. Preheat the oven to 180°C / 350°F / Gas 4. Grease and line a 900 g / 2 lb loaf tin.
2. Sieve the flour, baking powder and ground spices together into a bowl. Stir in the salt and ground almonds.
3. Cream the butter and sugar together until pale and creamy. Beat in one of the eggs followed by a third of the flour mixture. Repeat until all of the eggs and flour have been incorporated.
4. Fold in the finely grated zest along with the caraway and coriander seeds.
5. Bake for about 40 minutes. It should be golden and well risen when cooked and a skewer should come out clean when inserted into the cake.
6. While the cake is cooking gently heat the lemon juice, icing sugar and saffron to dissolve the sugar (do not boil). Leave to infuse until the cake is done.
7. As soon as the cake is cooked pierce the surface all over with skewer. Slowly pour the saffron-lemon syrup over the cake allowing the cake to drink up the syrup a little at a time. Once all the syrup has been absorbed leave the cake to cool completely in the tin before removing.

Saffron Macaroons

Another style of cake with a long history in Britain. These little almond biscuits-cum-cakes were often scented with rose or orange blossom water but saffron is great too. This is an adaptation of Marguerite Patten's recipe from *A Century of British Cooking*.

Ingredients (makes 12-14 medium or 35-40 mini macaroons)
1 pinch / 20-30 saffron strands, crushed
2 tsp hot water
2 egg whites

Fool's Gold

175 g / 6 oz / 2 cups ground almonds plus extra if required
175 g / 6 oz / 2 cups golden caster sugar
50 g /2 oz / ¼ cup dark chocolate pieces

Method
1. Infuse the saffron in the hot water.
2. Preheat the oven to 180°C / 350°F / Gas 4.
3. Place the egg whites in a clean bowl and beat to a froth with a fork (you are not making meringues so you are not looking for peaks of any description).
4. Stir in the ground almonds and caster sugar. Stir well then add the saffron infusion and mix to a stiffish paste. Small balls of the mixture should hold their form. If they don't then add a little more ground almond.
5. If you are making medium macaroons divide the mixture into around twelve balls about the size of an unshelled walnut (roughly 30 g / 1 oz each). For mini macaroons you'll need around a teaspoon of the mixture (roughly 10 g / ½ oz each). Lightly wet your hands to avoid the paste sticking then roll each portion into a ball (you may have to wet your hands repeatedly especially if you are making the smaller version). Place on a lined baking sheet, reasonably well spaced apart.
6. Bake medium macaroons for 12 to 15 minutes and mini macaroons for 8 to 10 minutes. They will brown slightly while they are cooking but make sure they don't get too dark. Allow to cool on the tray before transferring to cooling rack placed over a large sheet of greaseproof paper.
7. When the macaroons are cool melt the dark chocolate in a heatproof bowl suspended over a pan of barely simmering water. Dip a fork into the melted chocolate then flick over the cooled macaroons. Allow the chocolate to harden before serving.

Recipes: Cakes and Breads

Sarah Harrison's Saffron 'Cakes'

Nowadays we're used to saffron cakes containing fruit but a surprising number of old recipes contained seeds like this one from the eighteenth century.

Ingredients (makes 8-12 buns)
2 pinches / 40-60 saffron strands, crushed
100 ml / 3 ½ fl oz / half a cup of hot water
100 g / 4 oz / 1 stick unsalted butter, melted
150 ml / ¼ pint / ⅔ cup double cream
500 g / 1 lb 2 oz / 4 cups plain flour
2 x 7 g sachets fast action dried yeast
75 g / 3 oz / ⅜ cup caster sugar
1 tsp salt
2-3 tsp coriander seeds, coarsely crushed
2 eggs

Method
1. Infuse the saffron in the water. Allow to cool to room temperature.
2. Place the butter and cream in a saucepan. Heat until the butter has melted. Allow to cool to room temperature
3. Place the flour, yeast, sugar, salt and coriander seeds into the bowl of a food mixer with a dough hook attached. Mix until combined. If you don't have a food mixer stir the dry ingredients in a large bowl.
4. Beat the eggs into the butter/cream mixture. Add the saffron infused water. Pour the liquid onto the flour with the motor running slowly. Knead for 8-10 mins or until smooth and elastic. If you don't have a food mixer, add the liquid ingredients to the dry and bring the dough together with your hands. Transfer to a lightly floured board and knead for around 10 minutes until smooth and elastic before placing in a bowl.
5. Cover the bowl and leave to prove for 1½ to 2 hours or until doubled in size.
6. Shape into twelve buns (or eight pieces if you prefer larger buns!)

then place on a baking sheet leaving plenty of space between each bun. Cover with a clean tea towel and prove for 30 to 40 minutes.
7. Preheat the oven to 200°C / 400°F / Gas 6. Bake for around 15 mins (or slightly longer if making larger buns)

Variation: Saffron Cinnamon Buns

Ingredients (makes 6-7 buns)
1 x quantity Sarah Harrison's Saffron Cakes dough (above)
100 g / 4 oz / ½ cup soft dark brown sugar
1 ½ tbsp ground cinnamon
50 g / 2 oz / ½ stick really soft unsalted butter
1 ½ tbsp caster sugar
1 ½ tbsp lemon juice

Method:
1. Follow the instructions above to make the dough. While the dough is proving mix the brown sugar and ground cinnamon together.
2. On a floured board roll the dough into a large rectangle measuring 30 x 40 cm / 12 x 16 in. Spread it with the butter then sprinkle over the cinnamon sugar.
3. Roll the dough from the long side into a long sausage. Cut the very end of the roll off at an angle. Move along the roll 5-6 cm and make another cut slanting the opposite way. Imagine you are cutting a triangle that has lost its top (a trapezium). Continue making incisions along the roll every 5-6 cm / 2-2 ½ in ensuring that each diagonal cut is slanting in the opposite direction to the previous cut. You should end up with 6-7 buns. Arrange them flat on a lined baking sheet well spaced apart.
4. Cover with a clean tea towel and prove for 30-40 mins or until well risen.
5. Preheat the oven to 200°C / 400°F / Gas 6. Bake for around 20 mins.
6. Dissolve the caster sugar in the lemon juice by microwaving on high for 10 seconds. Brush the cinnamon buns with the solution when they first come out of the oven.

Recipes: Cakes and Breads

Spice Cake or Simnel Cake, for Mother's Day or Easter

Although it is not called a Simnel in *The English Huswife* (1615), Gervase Markham includes saffron in his Spice Cake, which contains many of the ingredients used in later recipes for Simnel Cake. It is Markham's recipe that I have used as the basis for my homage to the original Simnel. This produces a brioche like 'cake' more akin to a tea bread. I've included a marzipan layer, in keeping with modern tradition. You will also need a greased and lined 20 cm / 8 in springform tin, or a well buttered Kugelhopf mould.

Ingredients
400 g / 14 oz / 2 ½ cups mixed dried fruit (or opt for all currants or raisins)
5 tbsp sherry (medium to sweet if you have it but dry will do)
2-3 pinches / 40-60 saffron strands, crushed
1-3 tsp rosewater (depending on strength) and 1 tbsp water (or 2 tbsp water if you don't like rosewater)
100 g / 4 oz / 1 stick unsalted butter
100 g / 4 oz / ½ cups golden caster sugar
500 g / 1 lb 2 oz / 4 cups plain flour
1 tsp ground mace
1 tsp ground cinnamon
⅛ tsp ground cloves
1 tsp whole aniseeds, lightly crushed
½ tsp salt
1 whole egg
1 egg yolk (save the white for glazing before baking)
150 ml / 5 fl oz / half a cup double cream
150 ml / 5 fl oz / half a cup full fat milk
2 x 7g sachets fast action yeast
500 g / 1 lb 2 oz / 2 cups pre-made marzipan
apricot jam to glaze the top of the cake
1 tbsp icing sugar, sieved mixed with 1 tsp egg white (left over from the egg yolk above)

Fool's Gold

Method
1. Soak the dried fruits in the sherry several hours before (or even overnight, if you remember).
2. At the same time (or at least 30 minutes before you plan to make the dough) lightly crush the saffron strands in a small bowl then add the rosewater and water, or plain water.
3. Place the butter and sugar in a small saucepan. Heat gently stirring occasionally until the butter has melted and the sugar has dissolved. Allow to cool to body temperature (test it by dipping your finger in it).
4. Personally, I find it easiest to use a food mixer with a dough hook attachment as the dough is rather sticky (although you could knead it by hand). Sift the flour and ground spices into the bowl of a free-standing mixer. Stir in the aniseeds, salt and the fast action yeast. If you don't have mixer, combine all the dry ingredients in a large bowl.
5. Place a medium measuring jug on a set of digital scales (if you have them). Break the whole egg and yolk into the jug, measuring their weight in grams. Add the saffron infusion and the cream followed by enough milk to make up a total of 350 g / 12 ½ oz. Pour in the cooled melted butter and sugar stirring well to combine. Make a well in the centre of the spiced flour then add the the golden liquid. Mix to a rough dough – it will be very sticky. Continue to knead for 5 to 10 minutes with the food mixer on a low speed or by hand on a lightly oiled board. Cover the bowl and leave it to prove in a warm place for two hours
6. While the dough is proving sort out the marzipan. Cut one-fifth of the marzipan from the block. Divide into eleven pieces and roll each piece into a small ball to represent an 'apostle'. Cut the remaining marzipan in half. Roll into a rough circle about 20 cm / 8 in in diameter. Use the base of the springform tin to cut out a neater circle. Repeat with the remaining marzipan. Cover and set aside until required.
7. Tip the dough onto a lightly floured board. Knead in the macerated fruit. Divide the dough equally in two. Press one half of the dough into the bottom of a greased and lined 20 cm / 8 in springform cake tin.

Recipes: Cakes and Breads

8. Place one of the marzipan circles on top of the dough in the tin. Place the remaining dough on top of the marzipan and press it onto the edges of the tin. Ideally no marzipan should touch the sides of the tin. Leave the cake to prove again in a warm place for a further 30-40 minutes or until it has risen significantly.
9. While the cake is proving preheat the oven to 180°C / 350°F / Gas 4. Bake for about 45-60 minutes, covering lightly with a piece of baking paper or foil if the top is becoming too dark. Remove from the oven and allow to cool.
10. Once the cake is cooled brush the top with a little warmed apricot jam. Stick the remaining marzipan circle on top of the cake. Mix the icing sugar with the egg white. Use small bulbs of the icing to affix the balls to the top of the cake. Allow the icing to set for an hour or so before serving.

Like all yeast leavened cakes this will only stay fresh for a day or two. You can use any leftover cake to make the Simnel Pudding on page 238.

St Keverne Feast Buns

This recipe was given to Hettie Merrick by Mavis Sobey of St Keverne in Cornwall. Unlike other saffron cakes these ones are not yeast leavened. In her book, *Pasties and Cream: Memories and Recipes from a Cornish Childhood*, Merrick describes this recipe as a 'sort of saffroned heavy cake'. Think of these as being the Jaffa cakes of the saffron bun world – they fall somewhere between a biscuit and a cake. Like scones these buns are best eaten soon after they baked. However, they can be redeemed the following day if you split them and spread with some jam and clotted cream.

Ingredients (makes 12-14)
2 pinches / 40-60 saffron strands, crushed

Fool's Gold

150-180 ml / 5-6 fl oz / ½-¾ cup milk
225 g / 8 oz / 2 cups plain flour
225 g / 8 oz / 2 cups self raising flour
pinch of salt
250 g / 9 oz / 1 cup unsalted butter, cubed
200 g / 7 oz / 1 cups caster sugar
175 g / 6 oz / 1 cup mixed dried fruit
1 egg
1 tbsp golden syrup

Method
1. Dissolve the saffron in two tablespoons of the milk and leave to infuse.
2. Preheat the oven to 200°C / 400°F / Gas 6.
3. Sift the flours and salt into a large mixing bowl. Add the butter then rub it into the flour.
4. Stir in the caster sugar and mixed dried fruit. Add the saffron infused milk plus a little extra to make a dough that's a little softer than a pastry mixture.
5. On a lightly floured board roll out the dough to a thickness of 3cm. Stamp out 8cm rounds and place on a greased or lined baking sheet. Re-roll the trimmings to make more cakes.
6. Beat the egg with the golden syrup. Mark each of the buns with a cross on top (do not cut all the way through the dough).
7. Bake for 10-15 minutes until well risen and golden.

Traditional Saffron Buns (Or Cake)

This recipe comes from Elizabeth David's *English Bread and Yeast Cookery* (1977) which she describes as 'a variation on a Cornish saffron cake'. Having tried a lot of saffron cake recipes this came out on top as my favourite. Curiously, despite David's counselling regarding the dangers of putting too much saffron in recipes she includes a rather

Recipes: Cakes and Breads

generous amount here. This does produce an intense yellow colour but also a strong saffron flavour. You could reduce it by half if you are concerned that it is a bit much, although the finished buns will be much paler. It also makes great Hot Cross Buns for Good Friday (see the note at the end of the recipe).

Ingredients (makes 12 buns or a 900 g loaf cake)
150 g / ¼ pt / half a cup milk
½ tsp saffron strands, crushed (about 4 good pinches / 80-120 strands)
450 g / 1 lb / 4 cups strong white bread flour
7 g sachet fast action yeast
60 g / 2 oz / ¼ cups sugar
1 tsp mixed spice
1 tsp salt
2 eggs
120 g / ¼ lb / ½ cup clotted cream
125 g / 4 ½ oz / ¾ cup mixed vine fruits or currants (which is traditional)
1 tbsp finely chopped stem ginger in syrup (1-2 pieces)

Method

1. Bring the milk up to boil point then stir in the crushed saffron. Allow to infuse and cool to room temperature.
2. Place the flour, yeast, sugar, mixed spice and salt into the bowl of a food mixer with a dough hook attached. Beat the eggs into the cooled saffron milk then add this mixture and the clotted cream to the food mixer bowl. With the motor running slowly, mix until you have a stiffish dough (about 5-8 minutes). Add the mixed vine fruits and finely chopped stem ginger and continue to mix until thoroughly incorporated. If you don't have a food mixer place the dry ingredients (except the dried fruit and stem ginger) in a large bowl. Add the wet ingredients then knead on a lightly floured board for about 8 minutes before adding the dried fruit and continuing to knead for a further 3-4 minutes or until the fruit is thoroughly incorporated.
3. Leave the dough in a warm place for a couple of hours to prove. Alternatively, you could prove the dough overnight in the fridge (which is the method Elizabeth David uses).

Fool's Gold

4. Knock back the dough then either shape into twelve buns or place in a greased and floured 900 g loaf tin. Prove again for 40 minutes or so or until the dough has risen again.
5. Preheat the oven to 200°C / 400°F / Gas 6. Bake the buns for 15 minutes. A large cake will take around 30 to 40 minutes. Allow to cool on the tray or in the tin for a little while before transferring to a wire rack.

Variation: Saffron Hot Cross Buns

Make a loose paste from six tablespoons of plain flour, a tablespoon of caster sugar and four tablespoons of milk. Use an icing bag to pipe crosses of the paste on the buns before baking.

Anglo-Indian

Introduction

The Victorians were fond of a curry (even the Queen herself was reputedly a fan). The era saw the publication of a number of Anglo-Indian recipe books. I'm not sure any of them could claim to offer truly authentic recipes, in spite of their unfamiliar spellings, and some are most certainly better than others. The dishes were adapted to match British tastes and the ingredients available at home (hence the reliance on generic curry powder in some domestic cookery books). Books such as *Anglo-Indian Cookery at Home: A Short Treatise for Returned Exiles* (1895) by Henrietta Hervey were largely aimed at people who had lived in India. Hervey herself had spent twenty-three years living all over the country and felt that women like her were hankering 'now and again, after the fleshpots of the land of their exile'. The recipes in this section represent a very particular interpretation of the cookery of India and other south asian countries from a bygone era. For the most part the spellings used here are the same as those given by the cooks who published their adaptations.

Chicken Quorema

Forget the sickly-sweet chicken kormas you may have had in the past. This is a rich curry with the hint of a kick but is in no way cloying. Adapted from the recipe for Fowl Quorema in *The Indian Cookbook*, 1880.

Ingredients (serves 4 generously)
1-2 pinches / 20-60 saffron strands, crushed
juice of 1 small lemon
75 g / 3 oz / ⅓ cup ghee or butter
3 onions, sliced in half moons
¾ tsp crushed dried chillies
1 tsp coriander seeds
8 peppercorns

Fool's Gold

5 green cardamoms
3 cloves
1 large (10 cm / 4 in) or 2 small (5 cm / 2 in) cinnamon sticks
175 g / 6 oz / ¾ cup natural yoghurt
2 tsp cornflour
1 ½ small onions, finely grated or ground in a food processor or similar
2 large cloves garlic, crushed
½ tsp ground ginger
6-8 chicken thighs (800 g / 1 lb 12 oz), skinned and boned and each cut into 4-8 pieces
1-1 ½ tsp salt
2 bay leaves
1 blade lemongrass, lightly squashed
120 ml / 4 fl oz / ½ cup water plus a little extra if required
75 g / 3 oz / ¾ cup ground almonds
75 ml / 2 ½ fl oz / ⅓ cup double cream
1 tsp sugar (optional)

Method
1. Infuse the saffron in the lemon juice.
2. Heat 50 g / 2 oz / ¼ cup of the ghee or butter in a large saucepan or casserole. Fry the onion slices until crisp and brown. This will take a while so feel free to prepare the remaining ingredients while they are cooking. Remove with a slotted spoon and reserve until required.
3. Roast the chilli flakes and whole spices until fragrant then convert to a powder in a spice grinder or with a pestle and mortar.
4. Mix the yoghurt with cornflour.
5. Mix the ground or finely grated onion with the crushed garlic. Fry this purée in the same pan you cooked the onion in until fragrant (add more a little ghee if the purée looks like it is going to stick) then add the ground spices and ground ginger then continue to cook for a minute or two until fragrant.
6. Add the chicken to the pan, coating it in spices followed by the yoghurt and cornflour mixture, salt, bay leaves, lemongrass and water. Bring to the boil and simmer for 30 minutes or until the chicken is tender (add a little more water if it looks like the liquid

Recipes: Anglo-Indian

is evaporating). Don't worry if the sauce looks rather curdled at this stage. It will sort itself out when you add the remaining ingredients. Remove the lemongrass and bay leaves.
7. Stir in the saffron infused lemon juice, cream, almonds, sugar (if using) and half the browned onions then reheat gently. Serve garnished with the remaining browned onions.

Variation: Cauliflower Quorema

Sometimes I make a vegetarian version of this curry using roasted cauliflower. Preheat the oven to 200°C / 400°F / Gas 6. Remove the leaves from a large cauliflower or two small to medium cauliflowers (you can roast the leaves alongside the florets and use them as a garnish later). Break medium sized florets away from the tougher core which you can discard (you will need 700 to 800 g / 1 lb 9 oz to 1 lb 12 oz to serve four people as a main course). Toss in two tablespoons of vegetable oil, one coarsely chopped clove of garlic, and one teaspoon of coarsely ground coriander seeds. Season well with salt then roast for 20 to 25 minutes until just tender. Make the sauce as directed above (minus the chicken). Add the cooked cauliflower after you have stirred in the saffron, lemon juice, cream almonds and half of the browned onions then reheat gently. Serve garnished with the remaining browned onions (and roasted leaves if you are using them).

Lamb or Mutton 'Koftas' (Kubab Khutaree) with Fresh Mint Chutney

Adapted from Robert Flower Riddell's recipe for Kubab Khutaree in *Indian Domestic Economy and Receipt Book*, and Henrietta Hervey's recipe for Mint Chutney in *Anglo-Indian Cookery At Home*.

Ingredients (serves 4-6)
For the meatballs:

Recipes: Anglo-Indian

1-2 pinches / 20-60 saffron strands, crushed
100 g / 4 oz / ¼ cup double cream
4 cloves
10 cardamom pods
2 tsp coriander seeds
1 tsp ground pepper
500 g /1 lb 2 oz / 2 ¼ cups lamb or mutton mince
50g / 2 oz / ½ cup ginger, fresh, peeled and grated
1 small onion, peeled and grated
50 g / 2 oz / a little under ½ cup blanched almonds, roughly chopped
50 g /2 oz / ½ cup fresh white breadcrumbs
50 g /2 oz / ⅛ cup Greek yoghurt
1 egg beaten
1-2 tsp salt salt
50-100 g / 2-4 oz / ¼-½ cup ghee
juice of 2 limes

For fresh mint chutney:
2 packs mint sprigs, washed (28 g / 1 oz each)
4 spring onions, chopped
4 cloves garlic, chopped
4 whole hot green or red chillies, chopped (seeds and all)
2 tbsp tamarind paste

Method
For the meatballs:
1. Gently heat the saffron in the cream. Leave to cool and infuse for at least an hour.
2. Toast the whole spices then grind to a powder with the pepper.
3. Mix the mince with the onion and ginger. Add the ground spices and saffron infused cream along with the blanched almonds, yoghurt, egg and salt (start with one teaspoon) and the juice of a lime.
4. Take a little of the mixture and fry in some ghee. Taste the sample – if you think it needs more seasoning add more salt ensuring it is thoroughly mixed in. Roll the mixture into walnut-sized balls – you should get about twenty-four.

Fool's Gold

5. Heat the ghee in a frying pan over a medium heat. Fry the meatballs in batches until browned all over, keeping the cooked balls warm while you cook the next batch.
6. Serve sprinkled with the remaining lime juice then serve hot with the fresh mint chutney.

For the mint chutney:
1. Strip the leaves from the mint and place in a food processor with the remaining ingredients. Process to a coarse paste. You can add a tablespoon or so of water to help ease it along if you think it needs it. Serve cold with the meatballs. (It may not look like a vast amount but a little of this goes a long way!)

Tip
You can make these ahead of time and reheat them on a baking sheet at 180°C / 350°F / Gas 4 for 10-15 minutes. Make sure they are piping hot before serving.

Golden Bhoonee Kitcheeree

Kedgeree, that concoction of spiced rice, smoked haddock and eggs served as a brunch dish, takes its inspiration from 'kitcheeree' or 'khichari'. In her book *Curry: A Biography*, Lizzie Collingham notes that this dish of two grains (often rice and lentils although many regions in India had their own version according to which grain or pulse they commonly grew) was a 'staple food of rural peasants' during the sixteenth and seventeenth century. By the late nineteenth century the anonymous author of this recipe tells the reader that kitcheeree often replace boiled rice at breakfast and was served with 'fried fish, omelets, croquets [and] jhal freezee', so it is easy to see how it has morphed into the dish we know today.

Personally, I rather enjoy this recipe, inspired by one for 'Jurrud or

Recipes: Anglo-Indian

Yellow-tinted Kitcheeree' in *The Indian Cookbook* (1880), as a vegetarian main course, although it can be served as a side dish. Don't forget to soak your chosen pulse overnight.

Ingredients
2 pinches / 40-60 saffron strands, crushed
2 tbsp hot water
100 g / 4 oz / ½ cup yellow split peas or other pulse, soaked overnight
50 g / 2 oz / ¼ cup ghee or butter, plus a little extra just in case you need it
2 onions, sliced
175 g / 6 oz / 1 cup basmati rice
3 slices fresh ginger
3 peppercorns
1 tsp salt
3 cloves
4 cardamoms
1 cinnamon stick (5-8 cm long)
3 large bay leaves

Method
1. Infuse the saffron in the water.
2. Place the split peas in a saucepan and bring to the boil. Boil rapidly for 10 minutes then reduce the heat and cook for 30-40 minutes or until the peas are just tender. It's better for them to retain a little bite at this stage rather than being mushy.
3. Melt the ghee in a saucepan and fry the onions until crisp and brown. Remove with a slotted spoon and reserve.
4. Reduce the heat and fry the rice until it has absorbed the ghee (add a little more if the rice seems to be sticking). Add the cooked split peas, ginger, salt and spices. Pour in boiling water until the rice is just covered (about 350 ml / 12 fl oz / 1 ½ cups should do it). Cook over a low heat covered with tight fitting lid for around 15 minutes until the water has been absorbed.
5. Quickly stir in the saffron infusion then replace the lid and leave for 5 minutes. Serve sprinkled with the browned onions.

Fool's Gold

Fragrant Egg Curry (Bizah Sadah)

Adapted from Robert Flower Riddell's recipe in *Indian Domestic Economy* (1852).

Ingredients
1 pinch / 20-30 saffron strands, crushed
2 tbsp hot water
6-8 eggs (depending on size used)
50 g / 2 oz / ¼ cup ghee or butter
4 medium onions, sliced in half moons
½ tsp ground cinnamon
½ tsp ground cardamom
¼ tsp ground turmeric
¼ tsp ground cloves
¼ tsp ground black pepper
250 ml / 8 ½ fl oz /1 cup water boiling
juice from ½-1 lime (depending on size)

Method
1. Infuse the saffron in the hot water.
2. Boil the eggs for around 10 minutes or until hard. Drain off the hot water and run the eggs under the cold tap until cool enough to handle (this should also stop a dark ring forming around the yolk). Roll the egg on a board to crack the shell then peel it off. Halve each egg and reserve until required.
3. Melt the ghee in deep frying pan. Fry the onions in the ghee until golden.
4. Add the ground spices then fry for a minute or two until fragrant.
5. Add the water and bring back up to the boil. Add the saffron infusion then lower in the egg halves yolk side down initially. Gently simmer for about 10 minutes or until they are thoroughly heated through, turning the eggs once or twice.
6. Finish the dish with a good squeeze of lime juice before serving.

Recipes: Anglo-Indian

Mutton (or Lamb) and Mango Curry (Kulleah Umber)

Mutton is a much underused meat in my opinion. It seems to have acquired a reputation for being tough and fatty with a strong flavour. I find mutton none of these things and would urge you to use it in this recipe if you can source it. However, lamb can be used as an admirable substitute. This is a lovely mild curry, adapted from Robert Flower Riddell's recipe for Kullear Umber in *Indian Domestic Economy and Receipt Book* (1853), with a hint of sweetness, so it is perfect for anyone who doesn't like fiery curries.

Ingredients
1-2 pinches / 40-60 saffron strands, crushed
60 ml / 2 fl oz / ¼ cup double cream or coconut milk
2 tsp coriander seeds
½ tsp black peppercorns
4 cloves
10 cardamom pods
5-8 cm cinnamon stick
50 g / 2 oz / ¼ cup white granulated sugar
60 ml / 2 fl oz / ¼ cup water
1 large unripe mango (375-450 g / 13 oz-1lb)
1 lime, juiced
50 g / 2 oz / ¼ cup ghee
500 g / 1 lb 2 oz mutton or lamb chunks suitable for stewing
1 onion, sliced
5 cm / 2 in fresh ginger, grated
300 ml / ½ pint / 1¼ cups water
1 tbsp raisins
1-2 tsp salt
lime or lemon juice to season

Fool's Gold

Method
1. Infuse the saffron in the cream or coconut milk.
2. Lightly toast the whole spices in a frying pan then convert to a powder in a spice grinder.
3. Mix 50 g / 2 oz / ¼ cup granulated sugar with 60 ml / 2 fl oz / ¼ cup water. Heat gently until the sugar has completely dissolved. Peel and cut the mango into long slices. Add to the syrup with the lime juice and simmer until tender (about 10 to 15 minutes). Remove half of the mango slices from the syrup and purée them with one or two tablespoons of the syrup in a food processor.
4. Heat the ghee in a large saucepan over a high heat. Brown the lamb or mutton pieces in the ghee. Add the sliced onions, ground spices, grated ginger, raisins and salt followed by 300 ml / ½ pint / 1¼ cups water then simmer for 45 to 60 minutes or until the meat is tender.
5. Add the mango purée, reserved mango slices, saffron infusion and a little lime or lemon juice to season. Heat gently until hot. Adjust the seasoning adding more salt, syrup and lemon juice according to taste.

Pineapple Pilau

Adapted from a recipe by Mrs I. R. Dey in *Indian Cookery and Confectionery*, 1920.

Ingredients
1-2 pinches / 20-60 saffron strands
2 tbsp hot water
50 g / 2 oz / ¼ cup granulated sugar
100 ml / 3 ½ fl oz / ½ cup of water
juice ½ lemon plus extra if needed
200 g / 7 oz / 1 ¼ cups fresh pineapple pieces (prepared weight)
225 g / 8 oz / 1 cup basmati rice
large knob of ginger, peeled & chopped (10 g / ⅓ oz)
1 ½ tsp coriander seeds

Fool's Gold

1 tsp cumin seeds
2 cloves
5-8 cm cinnamon stick
2 cardamom pods
1 ½ tsp salt
50-100 g / 2-4 oz / ¼ to ½ cup ghee
300-400 ml / 10-13 ½ fl oz / 1¼-1½ cups boiling water
50 g / 2 oz / ⅓ cup toasted cashew nuts for garnish

Method
1. Infuse the saffron in the hot water
2. Place the the sugar in a pan with 100 ml / 3 ½ fl oz / half a cup of water and the lemon juice. Heat gently at first to dissolve the sugar then bring up to boiling point. Add the pineapple then simmer for 5-10 minutes or until the pineapple softens (it shouldn't be mushy). Drain but reserve the syrup and set the fruit aside until required.
3. Heat 50 g / 2 oz / ¼ cup ghee in a large lidded frying or sauce pan. Fry the ginger and spices until fragrant. Add the rice and cook until thoroughly coated in ghee. Add the salt and enough boiling water to just cover the rice. Cook for 15 minutes or so or until all the water has been absorbed.
4. Once the rice is just cooked stir in the drained pineapple, one to two tablespoons of the syrup, about two thirds of the cashews and the saffron infusion. Replace the lid and leave the rice to rest for a further 5 minutes or so.
5. Serve immediately garnished with the remaining toasted cashew nuts.

Tamarind Fish and Spiced Potato Wedges

Think of this recipe, taken from Henrietta Hervey's *Anglo-Indian Cookery at Home*, as a spicy, less calorific version of that British classic: fish and chips. This is one of the rare occasions where you do not have

Fool's Gold

to infuse the saffron first, although you do need to marinate the fish overnight so start this the day before you plan to eat it.

Ingredients
For the fish:
1-2 tsp chilli flakes (depending on how hot you like your food)
½ tsp sea salt flakes
2 cloves garlic, chopped
2 good pinches / 40-60 saffron threads
2 tbsp tamarind paste
2 tsp white wine vinegar
2 tsp granulated sugar
4 cod or haddock fillets, skin removed (150 g / 5 oz each)

For the spiced potato wedges:
4 jacket potatoes (175-200 g / 6-7 oz each)
½ tsp black peppercorns
1 tsp cumin seeds
1 tsp coriander seeds
½ tsp sea salt flakes
2 cloves garlic, chopped
4 tbsp vegetable oil

Method
For the fish:
1. Place the chilli flakes, sea salt, garlic, saffron, tamarind paste, vinegar and sugar in a spice grinder and blend to a smooth paste (or you could do this with a pestle and mortar with a bit of elbow grease).
2. Rub into the fish fillets then place in a non-metallic, oven-proof dish. Cover and leave to marinate in the fridge overnight.
3. When you are ready to cook the fish, pre-heat the oven to 200°C / 400°F / Gas 6. Bake the fish, uncovered with its marinade, for around 15 minutes or until just cooked.

For the potato wedges:
1. Place the whole jacket wedges in boiling water and cook for 10

minutes. Drain and allow to cool (you could do this the day before when you are preparing the fish).
2. Coarsely grind the black pepper, cumin and coriander seeds. A pestle and mortar is good here although you could give them a quick whizz in a spice grinder (they don't have to be super fine). Mix the crushed seeds with the salt, chopped garlic and two tablespoons of the vegetable oil.
3. Cut each potato into eight long wedges. Toss in the garlicky spiced oil.
4. Preheat the oven to 200°C / 400°F / Gas 6. Pour the remaining two tablespoons of the oil onto a non-stick baking sheet and place in the oven for 5-10 minutes.
5. Pour the spiced wedges onto the hot baking sheet. Bake for 25 minutes turning the wedges once or twice to ensure they are evenly browned and are cooked all the way through.

Prawn and Cucumber Curry

This curry is adapted from Henrietta Hervey's recipe for Malay Curry in *Anglo-Indian Cookery at Home*. Also referred to as a Ceylon (Sri Lanka) curry the original author pronounces this as 'a delicious preparation, and an agreeable change'.

Ingredients
400 ml / 13 ½ fl oz / 1 ⅔ cup coconut milk
2 pinches / 40-60 saffron strands, crushed
1 tsp coriander seeds
1 tsp sesame seeds
Large knob of fresh ginger, peeled and chopped (10 g / ⅓ oz)
2 hot green or red chilies, roughly chopped (including seeds)
½ onion, chopped
2 cloves garlic, chopped
½ tsp ground allspice
½-1 cucumber, deseeded (depending on size)

Fool's Gold

400 g / 14 oz / 3 cups large raw prawns, deveined
juice of ½-1 lime, depending on the size
salt to season
1 tbsp chopped coriander leaves to garnish

Method
1. Gently heat the coconut milk then pour over the saffron. Leave to infuse.
2. Grind the coriander seeds, sesame seeds, ginger, chilies, onion, garlic, allspice and a good pinch of salt to a paste in a spice grinder (add a little of the coconut milk if needs be).
3. Pour the infused coconut milk and curry paste into a large saucepan. Bring to the boil then simmer for 10 minutes.
4. Add the cucumber and prawns to the curry. Return to a simmer and cook again until the prawns are cooked (around 5 to 10 minutes). Season with salt and lime juice. Serve scattered with coriander leaves.

Fish Dishes

Recipes: Fish Dishes

Fennel Pollen Halibut with Fennel & Leek Broth

In the past it was common to serve pottages on top of a piece of bread (or sop, hence soup). Here I have replaced the bread with a piece of pan fried halibut lightly dusted in fennel pollen. Brian and Margaret of the Cornish Saffron Company produce fennel pollen as well as saffron and suggested using it with pan fried fish. This is a delicately spiced broth and wonderfully light. Feel free to use another white fish of your choice or even salmon fillets in place of the halibut. If you can't find fennel pollen used ¼-½ teaspoon of finely crushed fennel seeds instead. Adapted from the recipe 'Fenkel in Soppes' in *Forme of Cury* (1390).

Ingredients (serves 2)
1 pinch / 20-30 saffron strands, crushed
1 tbsp hot water
1-2 tbsp olive oil
1 leek, trimmed and sliced into ½ cm / ¼ in rounds
1-2 fennel bulbs (150-200 g / 5-7 oz each), trimmed but with most of the root left on, fronds reserved for decoration
½ tsp powder douce (see page 276)
pinch ground white pepper
100 ml white wine
400 ml fish or vegetable stock
1 tbsp finely chopped parsley
2 x 150 g / 5 oz fish fillets e.g. halibut, sea bass, skin on
½ tsp fennel pollen mixed with ¼ tsp fine salt
1 tbsp vegetable oil
15 g / ½ oz butter
salt and lemon juice to season

Fool's Gold

Method
1. Infuse the saffron in the hot water.
2. Heat the olive oil over a medium heat. Fry the leek until it begins to soften.
3. While the leek is cooking cut the fennel bulbs in half then slice them into half moons. Add to the pan with the leeks. Fry for five minutes before adding the powder douce, a pinch of white pepper, the wine and the stock. Bring to the boil then simmer for 20-30 minutes until the vegetables are tender. Add the saffron infusion and chopped parsley then keep the broth warm while you cook the fish.
4. Sprinkle the fish fillets with the fennel pollen mixture. Put the vegetable oil and butter in a non-stick frying pan over a medium heat, swirling the butter around the pan until melted and foaming, then turn up the heat. Once the butter starts bubbling, add the fish fillets to the pan, skin-side-down, and fry for 3 mins until crisp. Flip the fillets over, lower the heat slightly and cook for 1 to 2 mins more (depending on the thickness). The flesh should be opaque and flake easily when it is fully cooked. Quickly drain on absorbent kitchen paper.
5. To serve, divide the broth between two bowls ensuring the vegetables are equally distributed. Place the fish on top and decorate with fennel fronds.

Fish & Spinach Pie with Saffron & Seaweed Mash

Ingredients (serves 4 generously)

For the filling:
600 ml / 1 pt / 2 ½ cups full fat milk
1 pinch / 20-30 saffron strands, crushed

Recipes: Fish Dishes

2 cloves
1 onion, peeled and halved
1 bay leaf
1 blade of mace
600 g / 1 lb 5 oz / 4 cups mixed raw fish chunks (e.g. cod, salmon, smoked haddock)
50 g / 2 oz / ½ stick unsalted butter
50 g / 2 oz / a little under ½ cup plain flour
salt, pepper and lemon juice to season
450 g / 1 lb frozen, chopped spinach, defrosted

For the topping:
150 ml / 5 fl oz / a little over ½ cup double cream
2 pinches / 40-60 saffron strands, crushed
4 large potatoes (about 225 g / 8 oz each), peeled and quartered
75 g / 3 oz / ¾ stick unsalted butter
2 egg yolks
2 tsp seaweed flakes
a good grating of nutmeg
salt, pepper and lemon juice to season
50 g / 2 oz / ½ cup grated cheddar cheese

Method

1. To make the filling, heat a tablespoon of the milk in a microwave on full power for about 10 seconds the pour over the saffron.
2. Pour the rest of the milk into a large shallow saucepan. Stick a clove in each of the onion halves. Place them in the pan with the bay leaf, mace and fish chunks. Bring up to boiling point over a medium heat. Once the milk reaches boiling point turn off the heat then leave for 10 minutes. Strain the milk into a jug through a fine sieve. Reserve the fish pieces but discard the onion, bay leaf and mace.
3. Wipe the saucepan you used to cook the fish in clean then heat the unsalted butter until melted. Add the flour then stir over a medium heat until the paste smells biscuity. Remove from the heat.

Fool's Gold

4. Gradually add the warm milk to the flour paste stirring well after each addition to ensure there are no lumps. Once all the milk has been incorporated, return the pan to a medium heat and cook, stirring constantly, until the sauce has thickened. Season with salt, pepper and a good squeeze of lemon juice.
5. Squeeze out as much moisture as possible from the frozen spinach. Arrange the cooked fish interspersed with dollops of the spinach in the base of a large roasting dish. Pour over the sauce then leave to cool.
6. To make the topping, heat the cream either in the microwave on full power for about 30 to 40 seconds or in a small saucepan. Pour over the saffron strands.
7. Place the quartered potatoes in a large saucepan and cover them with water. Add a pinch of salt. Bring to the boil then cook until tender. This will take around 25 to 30 minutes from when you begin cooking them. Once they are cooked drain the potatoes.
8. While the potatoes are draining heat the butter until melted, then add the saffron infused cream. Pass the potatoes through a potato ricer or mash the potatoes by hand. Add the saffron butter and cream mixture, egg yolks, seaweed flakes and a good grating of nutmeg. Adjust the seasoning adding a little more salt if you think it needs it (the seaweed flakes are reasonably salty in themselves).
9. Dollop the saffron and seaweed mash on top of the filling (or pipe pretty swirls if you like). Scatter with the grated cheddar. This can be done ahead of time. If you are making this in advance refrigerate as soon as the pie is cool enough to do so.
10. When you are ready to cook the pie, preheat the oven to 180°C / 350°F / Gas 4. Bake in the centre of the oven for 25 to 30 minutes (give it an extra 5 to 10 minutes if you are cooking it from chilled) or until the top is golden and the sauce is bubbling.

Recipes: Fish Dishes

Grilled Oysters with Spiced Beer

Inspired by the recipe 'Oysters In Gravy Bastard' in *Two Fifteenth Century Cookbooks* (Harl. MS 279).

Ingredients (serves 4 as a starter)
a small pinch /10-15 saffron strands, crushed
150 ml / ¼ pint / ⅔ cup golden ale
15 g / ½ oz / ⅛ stick unsalted butter
1 shallot, peeled and chopped
½ tsp peeled and grated fresh ginger
pinch of ground white pepper
1 tsp plain flour
1-2 tsp caster sugar, to taste
½ -1 ½ tsp verjuice or white wine vinegar, to taste
4 tbsp fresh white breadcrumbs
2 tbsp finely grated parmesan
1 tbsp finely chopped parsley
12 oysters, opened but still in their shells

Method
1. Infuse the saffron in a tablespoon of ale.
2. Melt the butter in a small pan then fry the shallot and fresh ginger until golden. Add a good pinch of white pepper then stir in the plain flour followed by the remaining ale and one teaspoon of the sugar (there is no need to add salt as the oysters are salty enough). Gently simmer for 3 to 5 minutes until the mixture has thickened a little and is slightly reduced. Strain into a jug, squeezing out as much of the gingery juices as possible then add the saffron infusion and ½ to 1 ½ teaspoons verjuice or white wine vinegar (according to taste). Taste then adjust the sweetness or acidity by adding more sugar or verjuice/vinegar. The sauce will taste quite bitter at this stage but the sweetness of the oysters will balance this out.
3. Mix the breadcrumbs with the parmesan and parsley.
4. Place 1 to 1 ½ teaspoons of the gingery sauce in each oyster shell. Top

with half a tablespoon of the breadcrumb mix. Place under a hot grill for 1 to 2 minutes or until the breadcrumbs are just browning. Serve immediately.

Variation: Scallops

If you don't like the idea of eating oysters you can make this with scallops. Allow 2 to 4 scallops per person, (depending on their size). Pan fry scallops in a little oil for 20 to 30 seconds each side. Place them in small gratin dishes and pour over about two tablespoons of the ale sauce. Top with 1 ½ tablespoons of the breadcrumb mix then grill for 2 to 3 minutes. Serve immediately.

Mussels with Leeks, Almond Milk and Saffron

I like to use a roasted almond milk for this recipe although you could use the recipe on page 275 instead. My adaptation of this recipe, inspired by that for 'Cawdle of Muskels' in *Forme of Cury* (1390), first appeared in *Harvest*, Issue 2, Spring 2021.

Ingredients (serves 2 but can easily be scaled up)
1 pinch / 20-30 saffron strands, crushed
120 ml / 4 fl oz / ½ cup dry white wine
100 g / 4 oz / a little over ⅔ cup blanched almonds
250 ml / 8 ½ fl oz / 1 cup just boiled water plus 50 ml / 2 fl oz / ¼ cup cold water, or around 200 ml / 7 fl oz / just under a cup shop bought almond milk
1 kg / 2 lb 4 oz fresh mussels
1 ½ tbsp olive oil
1 trimmed leek (150-200 g / 5-7 oz), washed, halved lengthways and cut into half moons
1 clove garlic, chopped and crushed with a little sea salt

Recipes: Fish Dishes

¼ tsp ground ginger
⅛ tsp ground cinnamon
⅛ tsp ground black pepper
small pinch ground cloves
lemon juice and salt to season
1-2 tbsp chopped fresh parsley

Method
1. Steep the saffron strands in wine. The wine will take on a beautiful golden hue during this time.
2. Preheat the oven to 180°C / 350°F / Gas 4. Roast the almonds for 5 to 10 minutes until lightly golden (rather than brown).
3. To make the almond milk soak the almonds in the just boiled water for at least one hour. Place the almonds and water in a blender or food processor then blend until smooth. Line a sieve with muslin (or a clean tea towel) then pour the contents of the blender into the sieve. Rinse out the blender or food processor with the remaining cold water then pour this into the sieve too. Allow the liquid to drain then gather up the muslin and squeeze out as much liquid as possible. You should be left with around 200 ml / 7 fl oz creamy almond milk.
4. Place the mussels in a sink of cold water. De-beard them and discard any broken molluscs or any that refuse to close.
5. Gently heat the olive oil in a lidded pan large enough to hold the mussels. Sweat the leeks in the oil for 10 minutes. They should be softened but take on no colour. Add crushed garlic and the saffron infused wine, 120 ml / 4 fl oz / ½ cup almond milk and the spices. Bring to the boil then cover and reduce to a simmer for 10 minutes. If the sauce seems too thick add more almond milk but the mussels will make their own contribution as they cook. You can make the sauce ahead of time if you wish.
6. Add the cleaned mussels (reheat the sauce to boiling point first if you have made it ahead) and cook with the lid on for 5 minutes, shaking the pan from time to time until they've all opened (discard any that haven't). Season with salt (if needed) and a good squeeze of lemon juice. If you are still concerned that there

Recipes: Fish Dishes

is insufficient sauce then by all means add more almond milk (or water if you have used up all of your homemade batch). Divide the mussels between two bowls then scatter with parsley. Serve with lots of crusty bread to mop up the spicy juices.

Haricot Bean & Smoked Mackerel Salad

Adapted from the recipe 'Beans' in *A Perfect School of Instructions for the Officers of the Mouth* (1682) by Giles Rose.

Ingredients (serves 2 as a lunch dish)
2 spring onions, washed and trimmed
2 smoked mackerel (150-200 g / 5-7 oz / 2 cups)
1 x 400 g / 14 oz tin haricot beans in water
2 tbsp finely chopped herbs (I like to use parsley, tarragon and marjoram but parsley on its own is fine)
4-6 tbsp saffron vinaigrette (see page 280)
1 tbsp lemon juice
a couple of pinches of coarsely ground pepper and a little salt to season

Method
1. Cut the spring onions into thin roundels including the green bit.
2. Remove the skin from the smoked mackerel fillets then break the fish into chunks
3. Drain and rinse the beans. Place in a large bowl with the onions and mackerel. Add the herbs, saffron vinaigrette, lemon juice, a couple of pinches of coarse ground pepper and a little salt to taste.
4. Serve at room temperature.

Fool's Gold

Pilchard Pasties

'It is said that the Devil has never crossed the Tamar into Cornwall, on account of the well-known habit of Cornish women of putting everything into a pasty, and that he was not sufficiently courageous to risk such a fate!' Edith Martin includes a number of fillings in her Cornish recipe book (*Cornish Recipes: Ancient and Modern*, 1930) including a broccoli pasty, jam pasty and a star gazing pasty. The latter was a pilchard baked in a dough blanket with its head poking out of one end and the tail the other.

My version is perhaps a little more exotic taking its inspiration from the Mexican empanada. Lourdes Nichols author of *The Complete Mexican Cookbook* (1998) explains that the concept of the empanada came from Cornish miners who had travelled to Mexico to work in the gold, silver and copper mines. Saffron is included in the pastry and the filling although you could use shop bought puff pastry instead.

Ingredients (serves 8)
1 pinch / 20-30 saffron strands
1 tbsp cider vinegar
1 sweet potato (250-300 g / 9-10 oz)
1 tbsp vegetable oil
1 onion, finely chopped
1 clove garlic, crushed
1 tsp smoked paprika
1 tsp dried oregano
1 x 400 g / 14 oz tin pilchards in tomato sauce
50 g / 2 oz / ⅓ cup pimento stuffed olives, sliced
3 tbsp raisins
salt and a little cayenne to season
650 g / 1 lb 7oz saffron rough puff pastry (see page 277) or 500 g / 1 lb 2 oz block pre-made puff pastry
a little beaten egg to glaze

Recipes: Poultry and Game

Method
1. Infuse the saffron in the cider vinegar.
2. Peel the sweet potato then cut into small dice (around 1 cm / ½ in). Cook for five minutes in boiling water then drain.
3. Heat the oil in a frying pan. Fry the onion until soft then add the cooked sweet potato, garlic, smoked paprika and oregano. Cook for a minute or two then transfer to a bowl and allow to cool.
4. Mash the pilchards and their sauce then add to spiced vegetables along with the sliced olives, raisins and saffron infusion. Mix thoroughly and season with the salt and generous dash of cayenne.
5. Roll the pastry out to a thickness of 3 mm. Use a saucer to cut out circles. You will need to gather the off cuts and roll the pastry again in order to get eight circles.
6. Place an eighth of the mixture on half of the circle ensuring you leave around 1-2 cm / ½-¾ in gap to the edge. Brush the edge of the pastry with water then fold the other half over the top to enclose the filling. Press down firmly or crimp the edge to ensure it is completely sealed. Repeat this process with the remaining pastry and filling.
7. Once all of the pasties have been made place on a lined baking sheet in the fridge for at least 30 minutes.
8. Preheat the oven to 200°C / 400°F / Gas 6.
9. Brush the pasties with beaten egg then bake for around 20 minutes until puffed up and golden. Serve warm or cold.

Trout Fillets with Almonds & Currants

The original medieval recipe, 'Rygh In Sawse' in *Forme of Cury* (1390) calls for 'rygh' which has been interpreted as ruffe, a member of the perch family. I have opted to use trout fillets here although

Recipes: Fish Dishes

salmon fillets would work too. You could use whole rainbow trout if you don't mind dealing with the bones (I'm afraid I do). The original recipe suggests serving this dish cold but I prefer it hot.

Ingredients (serves 4)
1 pinch / 20-30 saffron strands, crushed
3 tbsp currants
150 ml / ¼ pint / ⅔ cup white wine
1 tsp powder fort (see page 275-6) or several pinches each of ground pepper and ground ginger
½ tsp fine sea salt
4 x trout or salmon fillets (130-150 g / 4 ½-5 oz each)
2-3 tbsp vegetable oil
50 g / 2 oz / ⅓ cup whole blanched almonds
1 large clove garlic, crushed with a little salt
250 ml / 8 ½ fl oz / 1 cup almond milk (see page 275)
lemon juice and salt to season

Method
1. Infuse the saffron and the currants in the white wine overnight
2. Mix ½ teaspoon of powder fort and ½ teaspoon of sea salt. Sprinkle over the flesh side of the trout or salmon fillets. Keep refrigerated until required.
3. Heat a tablespoon of the oil over a medium high heat in a large, non stick frying pan. Fry the almonds until lightly golden. Remove with a slotted spoon and set aside. Reserve the pan with the oil to cook the fish later.
4. In a different small frying pan heat a tablespoon of the oil over a medium to low heat. Gently cook the garlic until fragrant and softened. Add the remaining ½ teaspoon of the powder fort followed by the saffron wine soaked currants (and the wine) and the almond milk. Simmer for 5 to 10 minutes or until slightly reduced. Season with lemon juice and more salt if required.
5. To cook the fish heat the pan with the oil you cooked the almonds in over a medium high heat (add a little extra if you think you need it). Once the pan is hot cook the trout fillets skin

Recipes: Fish Dishes

side down for 2 to 3 minutes or until the skin is crisp. Flip the fish over and cook for another minute or so or until the fillets are just cooked.
6. To serve, pour the sauce over the fillets and garnish with the fried almonds.

Marinated Sole Goujons

Adapted from a recipe in Charles Carter's *The Compleat City and Country Cook, Or, Accomplish'd Housewife*, 1732.

Ingredients (serves four as a starter or 2-3 as a light lunch)
200 ml /7 fl oz / a little under 1 cup medium white wine
4 tbsp white wine vinegar
½ onion, peeled and sliced into half moons
1 pinch/20-30 saffron strands, crushed
1 tbsp caster sugar
½ tsp coriander seeds, lightly crushed
½ tsp sea salt flakes
4 lemon sole fillets (about 450-500 g / 1lb-1lb 2oz weight with skin on)
25 g / 1 oz / ¼ cup plain flour
salt, pepper and a pinch of mace
2-3 tbsp vegetable oil
1 tbsp chopped lemon thyme (or ordinary thyme)
1 tbsp chopped parsley
½ lemon, thinly sliced

Method
1. Bring wine, vinegar, onion, saffron, sugar, coriander seeds and salt to the boil for five minutes. Allow to cool.

Fool's Gold

2. Skin the sole fillets (you can ask your fishmonger to do this). Cut each skinned fillet into 6 to 8 strips.
3. Place the flour in a bag or on a plate with some salt, pepper and a pinch of mace. Toss the fish strips in the seasoned flour shaking off any excess,
4. Heat 2 tablespoons of the oil over a medium to high heat. When hot, fry the goujons on both sides until lightly coloured. Drain on absorbent kitchen paper. You will need to do this in batches.
5. Put the fish in a serving dish with the lemon slices and chopped herbs scattered over the fish. Strain the cooled marinade over the fish, cover and refrigerate overnight. Ideally bring the dish back up to room temperature before serving.

POULTRY AND GAME

Recipes: Poultry and Game

Gilded Chicken with Hazelnut Bread Sauce

The golden roasted birds and beasts of the medieval feast must have been a spectacular sight. Most recipes call for the birds to be basted with a mixture of egg yolks, saffron and other spices. This certainly achieved the gilded effect but at the expense of the wonderful crisp skin you get on a roasted chicken (which in my opinion is one of the best bits). So I have opted to use a saffron butter and a saffron wash to achieve a similar effect.

The hazelnut bread sauce is of a much later origin but makes a great accompaniment to all roasted birds from turkeys to partridges. It is quite sharp on its own but it goes wonderfully well with roasted chicken. The sauce is adapted from the recipe for 'Land fowl', e.g. turkey or pheasant, in *The Ladies Companion; Or Infallible Guide to the Fair Sex* (1740).

Ingredients

For the gilded chicken:
1 pinch / 20-30 saffron strands, crushed
3 tbsp white wine plus 300 ml / ½ pint / 1 ¼ cups
1 tsp granulated sugar
2 kg / 4 lb 7oz roasting chicken
75 g / 3 oz saffron & seaweed butter, softened (see page 278-80 or tip below)
2 cloves garlic, peeled but left whole and lightly squashed
1 stick celery, cut into three
1 small carrot, peeled and halved lengthways
1 onion, peeled and halved
450 ml / ¾ pint / 2 cups boiling water
bouquet garni of fresh herbs (e.g. 2 sprigs parsley, 2 sprigs thyme and a
  bay leave tied together)
2-3 tbsp plain flour
salt, pepper and lemon juice to season

Fool's Gold

For the hazelnut bread sauce:
1 pinch / 20-30 saffron strands, crushed
1 tbsp lemon juice and 1 tbsp orange juice (or 2 tbsp Seville orange juice when in season)
50 g / 2 oz crustless slice of bread
50 g / 2 oz / ½ cup blanched or roasted hazelnuts
100-200 ml / 3½-7 fl oz / ½-¾ cup stock (from the chicken)
¼ tsp salt, plus more to taste
¼ tsp ground white pepper
pinch of ground cloves, plus more to taste

Method

1. Infuse the saffron for the sauce in the citrus juices.
2. Cut the bread into chunks then place it in a bowl. Put the blanched hazelnuts in a separate bowl. Cover both the bread and hazelnuts with boiling water and set aside while you prepare the chicken.
3. Preheat the oven to 200°C / 400°F / Gas 6.
4. Infuse the saffron for the chicken in three tablespoons of the white wine along with the sugar.
5. Place your fingers between the skin and the breast of the chicken and gently pry them apart being careful not to tear the skin. Spread around 50 g / 2 oz of the saffron seaweed butter between the skin and flesh of the chicken. Smear the remaining 25 g / 1 oz over the chicken's legs and thighs.
6. Scatter the vegetables in the base of a roasting pan the place the chicken on top (if you have the giblets add these too). Roast for 20 minutes.
7. Remove from the oven and reduce the oven temperature to 180°C / 350°F / Gas 4. Pour the wine and boiling water around the base of the chicken. Brush the chicken with the saffron infused wine. Return to the oven for a further 40 to 60 minutes, brushing the chicken with the saffron wine glaze every 20 minutes or so. The chicken is thoroughly cooked when the juices run clear after a sharp knife or fork is inserted into the thickest part of the thigh.

Recipes: Poultry and Game

8. Remove the chicken to a carving board. Cover with foil to keep warm and leave it to rest while you finish the sauce. Strain the cooking liquor from the chicken into a jug. You should have around 600 ml / 1 pint / 2½ cups, a little of which will be used to make the hazelnut bread sauce and the rest transformed into gravy. Allow it to settle for a bit then skim off as much fat as possible (which will mostly be butter) and reserve both the fat and stock for the gravy and bread sauce.
9. Squeeze out as much moisture from the bread as possible. Drain the nuts. Place the nuts, bread, salt, pepper, cloves and citrus saffron infusion in a blender or food processor along with 100 ml / 3 ½ fl oz / just under ½ cup of the strained chicken stock. Blend until smooth. Place in a small pan and heat gently until hot. It will thicken as you do this so add a little more stock until you get the desired consistency (you should only need a further 100 ml / 3 ½ fl oz / just under ½ cup at most. The hazelnut bread sauce should be pretty thick like mayonnaise rather than a pouring sauce). The sauce can be served warm or at room temperature.
10. Place 2-3 tablespoons of the skimmed fat into another saucepan. Stir in the flour and cook for a minute or two. Gradually add all of the remaining skimmed chicken stock then cook, stirring constantly until you have a gravy. Season with salt and a little pepper.
11. Carve the chicken and serve with the gravy and hazelnut bread sauce.

Tip
If you don't want to make your own butter infuse one pinch / 20-30 crushed saffron strands in one tablespoon lemon juice for at least an hour. Combine with 100 g / 4 oz / 1 stick butter and 1 teaspoon of seaweed flakes plus a little salt if you feel it needs it. Use as directed above.

Fool's Gold

Milk Braised Chicken Thighs with Garlic & Saffron

Adapted from the recipe for 'Hennys in Gauncelye' in *Two Fifteenth Century Cookery Books* (Harl MS 279).

Ingredients (serves 4)
75 ml / 2 ½ fl oz / ⅓ cup double cream
2 pinches / 40-60 saffron strands, crushed
2 tbsp vegetable oil
8 x chicken thighs, skin on & bone in (or boned if you prefer)
2-4 garlic cloves, peeled and chopped (depending on their size)
2 bay leaves, lightly bruised (fresh if possible)
250 ml / 8 ½ fl oz / 1 cup whole milk
2 egg yolks
1 tsp cornflour
salt, pepper & lemon juice to season
2 tbsp chopped parsley

Method
1. Heat the cream in the microwave for 20 to 30 seconds until very warm then add to the saffron. Allow to infuse.
2. Heat the oil in a large, flameproof, lidded casserole. Season the chicken well with salt and pepper. Brown the thighs then drain off the excess oil.
3. Return the chicken to the pan with the garlic, bay leaves and milk.
4. Cover then bring to the boil (keeping an eye on the casserole to ensure it doesn't boil over) then simmer for 25 to 30 minutes or until the chicken is tender and cooked through.
5. Remove the chicken from the sauce and keep warm. The milk will have curdled but this doesn't matter. Strain the sauce into a clean pan, discarding the garlic pieces and bay leaves.
6. Bring the sauce back up to boiling point. Meanwhile, beat the egg yolks and cornflour together then add to the saffron infused cream. Pour this mixture on to the hot sauce stirring continuously until it begins to thicken (it should be the consistency of single cream). Add

a good squeeze of lemon juice then adjust the seasoning to taste. Just before serving stir in the chopped parsley.

Pheasant and Chorizo Stew with Saffron Rice

Although saffron was not used extensively in savoury English cookery by the nineteenth century it does crop up in recipes every now and then particularly where rice or 'foreign' dishes are concerned. This recipe is based on 'Pheasants with rice à l'espagnole' in *The Modern Cook* (1846) by Charles Elmé Francatelli, who briefly worked for Queen Victoria as her chef.

Ingredients (serves 4)
For the pheasant:
1 medium to large onion, peeled and cut in half
1 whole clove
3-4 tbsp olive oil
1 carrot, peeled and diced
1 stick celery, diced
8-12 mini chorizo sausages
2 pheasants jointed i.e. 4 breasts, 4 legs, seasoned (reserve the carcass for the stock – see note below)
3 tbsp plain flour, well seasoned with salt and ground black pepper
120 ml / 4 fl oz / ½ cup medium-dry sherry
500 ml / 17 fl oz / 2 cups pheasant or chicken stock
1 tbsp sherry vinegar
2 sprigs thyme
1 x 10 cm strip orange peel
1-3 tsp cornflour mixed with 1-2 tbsp water
salt, ground black pepper and lemon juice to season
thyme leaves to garnish

Recipes: Poultry and Game

For the saffron rice:
2 pinches / 40-60 saffron strands, crushed
2 tbsp hot water
2 tbsp olive oil
½ onion, peeled and chopped (left over from preparing the pheasant)
1 clove garlic peeled and crushed with ¼ tsp sea salt flakes
1 tbsp tomato purée
A good pinch each of cayenne pepper and ground cloves
225 g / 8 oz / 1 cup white basmati rice
about 350 ml / 12 fl oz / 1 ½ cups hot pheasant or chicken stock

For the pheasant stock:
(You can use chicken stock (homemade or shop bought) for this recipe but if you have the pheasant carcasses and the time it is worth making a stock from those instead)
2 pheasant carcasses whole or roughly chopped
1 onion, peeled and coarsely chopped
1 carrot, peeled and roughly chopped
1 celery stick, peeled and roughly chopped
1 bouquet garni (2 sprigs thyme, 2 sprigs parsley and 1 bay leaf tied together)
about 1.8 litres / 3 pints cold water

Method
For the pheasant:
1. Preheat the oven to 160°C / 300°F / Gas 2.
2. Roughly chop half the onion then set aside for the rice and stick the clove in the other half.
3. Heat a tablespoon of the oil in a large, lidded flameproof casserole. Fry the diced carrot and celery until just starting to turn brown. Remove from the oil with a slotted spoon and drain on absorbent kitchen paper.
4. Heat another tablespoon of oil in the casserole then brown the mini chorizo sausages. Remove with a slotted spoon, drain as before and put to one side with the vegetables.
5. Depending on how much oil is left in the pan (the sausages may produce a bit) add another 1 to 2 tablespoons of olive oil to the pan.

Fool's Gold

Toss the pheasant pieces in well seasoned flour shaking off the excess. Then fry until browned all over drain on absorbent kitchen paper.
6. If there seems like excessive oil left in the pan drain this off. Return the vegetables and chorizo sausages (and any left over flour) to the pan along with the onion half stuck with a clove, the sherry, stock, vinegar, thyme and orange peel. Bring to the boil then return the browned pheasant portions to the casserole. Place in the oven for 1 to 1½ hours or until the pheasant is really tender. You can do this first and keep the casserole warm while you prepare the rice.
7. If you wish to thicken the sauce further remove the cooked pheasant to a plate, cover with foil then place it somewhere warm. Discard the onion half, thyme sprigs and orange peel. Bring the sauce to the boil then add some cornflour mixed with water, stirring until it reaches the desired consistency.

For the saffron rice:
1. Infused the saffron in the hot water.
2. Heat the oil in a lidded saucepan.
3. Fry the chopped onion and garlic until beginning to turn golden
4. Add the tomato purée, cayenne and cloves and cook for a further minute or two.
5. Add the rice and stir to ensure it is coated in the tomatoey oil.
6. Pour over the hot stock (it should just cover the rice). Once the stock is boiling replace the lid and reduce the heat. Cook for 15 minutes or so or until all the water has been absorbed.
7. Once the rice is just cooked stir the saffron infusion. Replace the lid and leave the rice to rest for a further 5 minutes before serving with the pheasant and chorizo sausages.

For the pheasant stock:
1. Place all of the ingredients in a large, deep saucepan. Bring to the boil then simmer for one hour. Strain the stock through a sieve and use as directed in the recipe above. Any left over stock may be frozen.

Recipes: Poultry and Game

Spiced Venison Stew with Herb Dumplings

This stew is adapted from the recipe 'Beef y-Stywyd' in *Two Fifteenth Century Cookbooks* (Harl. MS 279). The dumplings are inspired by the recipe for 'Jusshell' in *Forme of Cury* (1390).

Ingredients
For the stew:
1 cinnamon stick 5-8 cm long
2 cloves
1 blade mace
½ tsp grains of paradise (or black peppercorns)
½ tsp cubebs (or whole allspice)
2 tbsp balsamic vinegar
800 g / 1 ¾ lb stewing venison or beef, cubed
2 tbsp vegetable oil
2 onions, chopped
1 ½ tbsp plain flour
500 ml / 17 fl oz / 2 cups venison or beef stock
2 pinches / 40-60 saffron strands, crushed
2 tbsp boiling water
1 tbsp chopped fresh parsley
1 tbsp chopped fresh sage
salt to season
1 tsp sugar (optional)

For the herby 'bread' dumplings:
1 pinch / 20-30 saffron strands, crushed
2 tbsp boiling water
250 g / 9 oz / 2 cups stale white breadcrumbs (not dried)
3 eggs, beaten
1 tbsp chopped fresh parsley
1 tbsp chopped fresh sage
1 tbsp chopped chives
½ tsp salt
well flavoured meat or vegetable stock or salted water to cook

Fool's Gold

Method
For the stew:
1. Grind the whole spices (except the saffron) to a fine powder in a spice mill (or use a pestle and mortar). Mix with the vinegar then rub the spice paste into the meat and leave to marinate in the fridge overnight.
2. The following day heat the oil in a large flameproof casserole over a medium heat. Add the chopped onions and fry until brown.
3. Once the onions have browned stir in the flour. Cook for a minute or two before adding the stock and the spiced venison or beef. Bring up to the boil then reduce to a gentle simmer for 1½ to 2 hours or until the meat is meltingly tender. Adjust the seasoning adding the sugar if you feel it is required. You can make this in advance if you prefer and reheat it later.
4. Meanwhile, infuse the saffron in the boiling water.
5. Just before serving stir in the saffron infusion and chopped herbs. Serve with dumplings.

For the dumplings:
1. Infuse the saffron in two tablespoons of boiling water.
2. Mix all of the ingredients (except the stock/salted water) to form a stiff paste.
3. Wet your hands to prevent the dough from sticking and form 16 dumplings (they will expand considerably when cooked). Press the dumplings between your palms to make sure they're nice and compact. Bring a large, wide pot of well flavoured stock or lightly salted water up to boiling point – it should be barely simmering rather than rapidly bubbling to avoid the dumplings disintegrating. Carefully drop the dumplings into the liquid and cook for five minutes. Carefully lift them out with a slotted spoon and serve with the stew.

Recipes: Poultry and Game

Trespassers Pie

Given the grief that rabbits and hares cause saffron growers it feels apt to include a recipe for a trespassers pie. You can replace the rabbit with chicken if you prefer. I make this like a pithivier (there is something quite liberating about a free-form pie) but you could use a 30 cm / 12 in enamel pie dish instead. It's best to make the filling a day ahead so that it can cool before you make the pie.

Ingredients
1 pinch / 20-30 saffron strands, crushed
2 tbsp white wine
1 tbsp oil
50 g / 2 oz streaky bacon, chopped (I use smoked by preference but unsmoked is fine too)
1 medium onion, chopped
1 clove garlic, crushed
½ tsp ground ginger
½ tsp ground cinnamon
½ tsp ground mace
pinch of ground cloves
2 tbsp plain flour
1 tsp sugar
150 ml / 5 fl oz / ⅔ cup white wine
450 ml / 15 fl oz / 2 cups chicken stock
2 wild rabbits, jointed (this may seem a lot for 4 people but there isn't an awful lot of meat on a wild rabbit) or 6-8 (600 g / 1 lb 5oz) boned and skinned chicken thighs, cut into chunks
2 sprigs thyme or savory
salt and pepper to taste
650 g / 1 lb 7 oz saffron rough puff pastry (see page 277) or 1 ½ x 500 g blocks pre-made puff pastry
1 egg, beaten
1-2 tsp cornflour mixed with 1 tablespoon water

Fool's Gold

Method
1. Infuse the saffron in the wine.
2. Heat the oil then fry bacon and onion over a medium heat until the bacon has browned and the onion has softened.
3. Add the garlic and ground spices. Cook for a minute or two before adding the flour and sugar.
4. Combine the wine and the stock then gradually add to the pan, stirring all the time. Bring to the boil then add the rabbit joints or chicken pieces and thyme or savory. Season with a little salt and pepper. Cook the rabbit for 60 to 90 minutes and the chicken for 30 minutes or until tender.
5. Once the rabbit or chicken is cooked lift it out of the stock using a slotted spoon. If you are using rabbit remove the meat from the joints being careful to ensure there are no small bones present. Cut the rabbit meat into chunks.
6. Strain the cooking liquor into a jug. Adjust the seasoning then add the saffron infusion. Discard the thyme but add the vegetables and bacon to the meat. Moisten the meat with a few tablespoons of the cooking liquor – you'll probably need around three to five tablespoons. Don't add too much as it may escape during the cooking process. Reserve the rest to serve with the pie. Allow the filling to cool completely before assembling the pie.
7. Divide pastry in two with one piece a bit bigger than the other. Roll the smaller piece to a thickness of 3-5 mm then cut out a 23 cm / 9 in circle for the base. Do the same with the slightly larger piece and cut out a circle measuring 25 cm / 10 in for the top. I use the bases of my spring form cake tins for this but you could use dinner plates of similar sizes.
8. Place the smaller disc on a baking sheet lined with silicone or baking paper. Brush the edge of the smaller disk with water. Pile the pie filling in the middle of the circle forming a nice meaty mound. Carefully lay the larger circle over the top pressing down to seal the edges. I like to place the upper part of a 20 cm / 8 in loose bottomed sandwich cake tin over the dome and cut around it to neaten the base of the pie (this isn't absolutely necessary. If you leave it as it is you will have a larger pastry rim).

Recipes: Poultry and Game

Pinch the edges of the base to create a crimped effect. Use a small knife to make a small hole in the centre of the dome to allow steam to escape. If you like you can re-roll the pastry trimmings to cut out decorations which you can affix to the pie with a little water.

9. Put the pie into the fridge to rest for an hour
10. Preheat the oven to 200°C / 400°F / Gas 6. Brush the pie with beaten egg. Bake for 10 minutes then reduce the temperature to 180°C / 350°F / Gas 4 for a further 30 to 40 minutes.
11. Shortly before the pie is cooked reheat the reserved cooking liquor. If you prefer a thicker gravy stir in 1 to 2 teaspoons of cornflour mixed with a tablespoon of cold water then stir over a gentle heat until thickened further.

Seared Pigeon Breast with Pancetta & Grape Salad

Adapted from the recipe 'Hochepoche of Pigeons' in *A Perfect School of Instructions for the Officers of the Mouth* (c. 1682) by Giles Rose.

Ingredients (serves 2 as a light lunch)
1 pinch / 20-30 saffron strands, crushed
¼ tsp ground ginger
¼ tsp ground nutmeg
1 small clove garlic, peeled and crushed with ¼ tsp sea salt flakes
Pinch of ground black pepper
2 tbsp verjuice or white wine vinegar
4 pigeon breasts, skin on
1 tbsp vegetable oil
50 g / 2 oz sliced smoked pancetta or smoked streaky bacon (about 3-4 rashers), snipped into small pieces
100 g / 4 oz / ⅔ cup seedless red or black grapes, halved
80 g / 3 oz pack mixed salad leaves

Fool's Gold

2 tbsp saffron vinaigrette (see page 280)
salt and pepper to season

Method
1. Mix the saffron, ground spices, crushed garlic, and a pinch of pepper with the verjuice or white wine vinegar. Rub this into the pigeon breasts and leave to marinate in the fridge for a few hours or even overnight.
2. Heat the oil in a large, non stick frying pan over a medium to high heat. Pat the pigeon breasts dry on some kitchen paper. Once the pan is hot, add the pigeon breasts skin-side down and cook until golden brown – this will take 1 to 3 minutes for each side depending on the size of the breasts and how well done you like your meat. Remove the breasts from the pan and leave to rest somewhere warm, lightly covered with foil, for approximately 5 minutes.
3. Reduce the heat slightly then add the pancetta or bacon pieces to the pan. Cook until crisp and brown, stirring frequently. Drain on some absorbent kitchen paper.
4. In a large mixing bowl, toss the grapes and salad leaves with the saffron vinaigrette. Add the crispy pancetta then divide between two plates. Top with the pigeon breasts and serve immediately.

Dessert

Recipes: Dessert

Almond Furmity with Drunken Apricots

This is adapted from Hannah Woolley's recipe 'Furmity with almonds', in *The Queen-Like Closet; or, Rich cabinet stored with all manner of rare receipts for preserving, candying & cookery* (1670). Furmity or Frumenty was a thick, medieval pottage that was commonly served with roasted venison or porpoise on a fish day. It was frequently made with cracked wheat but barley makes an admirable alternative. By the seventeenth century it took on a more luxurious form enriched with cream and sugar making it more like rice pudding than a risotto.

This is a very rich pudding particularly if you make your own almond milk (although you can use shop bought almond milk). It is lovely warm but I like to serve it chilled.

Ingredients (serves 6-8)
250 g / 9 oz / 1 ¼ cups dried apricots
200 ml / 7 fl oz / just under 1 cup sweet white wine
1 clove
4 cardamom pods
2 cinnamon sticks, 5-8 cm in length
2 pinches / 40-60 saffron strands
150 ml / ¼ pint / ⅔ cup double cream or almond milk (see page 275) plus a little extra if needed
150 g / 5 oz / ¾ cup pearl barley
900 ml / 1 ½ pints / 3 ¾ cups almond milk (see page 275)
100 g / 4 oz / ½ cup caster sugar
1 blade of mace (or a generous pinch of ground mace if you can't source the whole spice)
a good grating of nutmeg
1-2 tsp rosewater (optional)
2 tbsp toasted flaked almonds

Fool's Gold

Method
1. Preheat the oven to 140°C / 275°F / Gas 1.
2. Put the apricots, wine, clove, cardamom and one of the cinnamon sticks into a shallow oven proof dish. Place the dish into the oven, covered with either a lid or some tin foil, and bake for one hour. The apricots will have plumped up and absorbed most of the liquid. Allow to cool to room temperature.
3. Infuse the saffron in 150 ml / ¼ pint / ⅔ cup double cream or almond milk. Personally, I find homemade almond milk is rich enough but cream definitely adds another level of luxury.
4. Place the barley in a saucepan. Cover with water and boil for 10 minutes then drain.
5. Place the part cooked barley, 900 ml / 1 ½ pints / 3 ¾ cups almond milk, caster sugar, remaining cinnamon stick, mace and a good grating of nutmeg in a large, deep saucepan. Bring to the boil then simmer gently for 45 to 60 minutes or until the barley is tender. Keep an eye on it so that it doesn't boil over and stir it frequently towards the end to prevent it from sticking to the saucepan.
6. Once the barley is cooked stir in the saffron infused cream or almond milk and 1 to 2 teaspoons of the rosewater (if using). Add a little extra cream or almond milk if it seems a bit thick (if you are planning to serve this chilled it will thicken considerably as it cools so be prepared to add more liquid to loosen it up a bit).
7. Serve the furmity in bowls or glasses with a few of the drunken apricots on top sprinkled with some toasted flaked almonds.

Almond Pudding

This is a proper rib sticker of a pud of a similar ilk to the Christmas variety (although more nutty than fruity). Hannah Glasse's original recipe, 'Almond Hogs Pudding', in *The Art of Cookery Made Plain & Easy* (1746), calls for the mixture to be boiled in pigs intestines leading

Recipes: Dessert

to the name 'hogs pudding' although it contains no meat per se only suet. Hannah Glasse suggests interspersing layers of the almond pudding mixture with candied citron (for which I have substituted mixed peel) although other recipes add dried currants to the mix. Both versions are delicious.

You can make this as one large pudding or eight individual puddings which take less time to cook. However, the longer you cook this mixture the deeper gold it becomes.

Ingredients (serves 8)
120 ml / 4 fl oz / ½ cup medium sherry
2 pinches / 40-60 saffron strands, crushed
25 g / 1 oz / ¼ stick soft unsalted butter for greasing
a little plain flour for dusting
175 g / 6 oz / 1 ¾ cups ground almonds
100 g / 4 oz / a little under 1 cup fresh white breadcrumbs
200 g / 7 oz vegetable or beef suet
140 g / 5 oz / ¾ cup golden caster sugar
2 tsp mixed spice
1 tsp baking powder
180 ml / 6 fl oz / ¾ cup double cream
2 eggs
1 tsp orange blossom water
100 g / 4 oz / 1 heaped cup chopped mixed peel, or 50g / 2 oz currants / ½ cup and 50 g / 2 oz / ⅓ cup raisins

> ** You will need a 1.2 litre or 2 pint pudding basin or 8 individual pudding basins plus some baking parchment.*

Method
1. Gently heat the sherry until warm but not boiling. Pour over the saffron then leave to infuse.
2. Use the butter to thoroughly grease the pudding basin or basins. Cut out a circle of baking parchment to fit in the base of each pudding basin (this will help ensure it doesn't stick) then lightly dust the inside of the basin with flour.

Fool's Gold

3. Mix the ground almonds, breadcrumbs, suet, caster sugar, mixed spice and baking powder in a bowl.
4. Beat together the double cream, eggs, orange blossom water and saffron infusion. Add to the dry ingredients and mix thoroughly.
5. If you are making a large pudding place one quarter of the mixture in the prepared basin then sprinkle with one third of the chopped mixed peel. Place another quarter of the pudding mixture in the basin followed by another third of the peel. Continue this until all of the pudding mix and peel has been used ensuring that you finish with a layer of the pudding mixture. Alternatively, mix the chopped peel or currants and raisins into the pudding mixture then place in the pudding basin or basins.
6. Cover the pudding or puddings with lightly buttered foil. Place in a steamer basket that sits over a saucepan about one third full of boiling water (or stand the pudding on top of an up turned saucer in the base of a saucepan if you don't have a steamer basket). Steam for four hours (for a large pudding) or 45 minutes to 1 hour for individual puddings. Make sure you check the water regularly so that the pan doesn't boil dry – always top up with boiling water. You can also bake the individual puddings in the oven in a deep roasting dish half filled with water then covered with one piece of buttered foil. The cooking time will be the same.
7. Turn the pudding or puddings onto a serving plate. Remove the paper disc if is attached to the pudding. Serve hot with custard, cream or with 100 g / 4 oz each of sherry, brown sugar and butter melted together.

Baba au Rhum

Baba recipes make frequent appearances in Victorian cookbooks. There are a number of theories behind the origins of this dessert which hails from eastern Europe (particularly Poland). The general upshot seems to be that the boozy syrup was introduced to rescue a less than fresh cake.

Fool's Gold

And boy, what a thirsty cake this can be. I have been quite conservative with the syrup but you can increase the quantity if you prefer a more drenched cake or cakes.

Ingredients (makes 1 large cake or 12 individual cakes)
For the cake:
1 pinch / 20-30 saffron strands, crushed
2 tbsp hot water
25 g / 1 oz / a little under ¼ cup sultanas or raisins
25 g / 1 oz / a little under ¼ cup currants
grated zest of half a lemon
3 tbsp madeira
1 ½ tbsp dark rum or brandy
250 g / 9 oz / 1 cup plain flour
7 g / ¼ oz sachet fast action yeast
½ tsp salt
25 g / 1 oz / ⅛ cup caster sugar
60 ml / 2 fl oz / ¼ cup lukewarm water
60 ml / 2 fl oz / ¼ cup double cream
2 eggs, beaten
150 g / 5 oz / 1 ½ sticks soft unsalted butter, diced plus extra for greasing

For the rum syrup:
300 g / 10 ½ oz / 1 ½ cups granulated sugar
150 ml / ¼ pint / ⅔ cup water
1 ½ tsp coriander seeds, lightly crushed
2 x 5 cm / 2 in strips of lemon peel
4-6 tbsp kirsch or rum (according to taste)

Method
For the cake:
1. Infuse the saffron in the hot water.
2. Put the dried fruit and lemon zest in a small saucepan with the madeira and rum. Heat gently just to boiling point then leave the fruit to infuse for one hour or so. Alternatively marinate the fruit in the alcohol (unheated) overnight.

Recipes: Dessert

3. Mix the flour, yeast, salt and sugar in the bowl of a food mixer with a dough hook attachment.
4. Mix the water, cream, beaten eggs and saffron infusion. With the motor running on slow pour onto the flour and knead until combined. Gradually add the soft butter until you have a soft sticky dough. If you don't have a food mixer, make a well in the centre of the dry ingredients then add all the liquid ingredients. Mix well to combined before gradually kneading in the softened butter. Place in a bowl and leave in a warm place to double in size (about ninety minutes to two hours).
5. Knead the dough by hand on a lightly floured board, this time incorporating the macerated fruit. Divide between 12 buttered and floured kugelhopf/bundt moulds (they should be filled a little less than half) or one 20 cm / 8 in kugelhopf/bundt or savarin ring mould. Leave the babas in a warm place to rise again (about 40 to 60 minutes or so).
6. Preheat the oven to 180°C / 350°F / Gas 4. Bake individual babas for 15 minutes until well risen and golden. A larger baba will take 25-30 minutes. Allow to cool slightly in the moulds before removing and drenching in the syrup.

For the rum syrup:
1. Bring the sugar, water, coriander seeds and lemon peel to the boil then simmer rapidly for 10 to 15 minutes until you have a thick syrup.
2. Remove from the heat and strain into a shallow dish. Stir in the kirsch or rum. If you have made individual babas dip them into the syrup while warm, repeating as necessary until they are saturated to your satisfaction. For a large baba, repeatedly pierce the underside with a skewer then drizzle over some of the syrup. Flip the baba over so it is the right way up and place on a serving plate. Pierce the top with the skewer in the same way then drizzle over more syrup until it has reached the desired level of saturation.

Fool's Gold

Curd Pancakes

Homemade curds are simple to make with a little planning ahead. I use Angela Clutton's method of adding white wine vinegar to whole milk from her insightful book *The Vinegar Cupboard* (2019). These lightly spiced fritters, adapted from Hannah Glasse and Maria Wilson's Curd Fritters in *The Complete Confectioner* (1800), are rather like thick pancakes. With that in mind I have replaced some of the eggs with a little milk and added some baking powder to make them a little lighter.

Ingredients (makes around 16 x 10 cm pancakes)
For the pancakes:
1 pinch / 20-30 saffron strands, crushed
120 ml / 5 fl oz / ½ cup milk
75 g / 3 oz / ⅔ cup flour
½ tsp powder douce or mixed spice
1 tsp baking powder
25 g / 1 oz / ⅛ cup caster sugar
2 eggs, beaten
200 g / 7 oz / just under 1 cup fresh curd cheese (see below)
A knob or two of butter
Honey or maple syrup

For the curds:
1 litre / 1 pt 13 ½ fl oz / 4 cups full fat milk
pinch of salt
25 ml / ¾ fl oz (about 5 tsp) white wine vinegar (I like to use tarragon vinegar when I have it in the cupboard)

Method
To make the pancakes:
1. Heat the milk in a saucepan until hot. Pour over the saffron then leave to cool to room temperature.
2. Sieve the flour, powder douce or mixed spice and baking powder into a bowl. Place in a blender or food processor with the eggs, sugar, fresh curds and milk. Blend until smooth. If you don't have a blender, combine the saffron infused milk with the beaten eggs and curd

Recipes: Dessert

cheese. Stir the sugar into the sieved spiced flour. Gradually add the wet ingredients to the dry beating well between each addition until you have a thick, smooth batter.

3. Heat a large flat griddle or a frying pan over a medium to high heat. Melt a little butter on the hot griddle or pan then pour puddles of the batter (about two tablespoons per pancake) onto the hot surface. Depending on the size of your griddle or frying pan you should be able to cook three to four pancakes in one go. Cook for a minute or two until you see bubbles begin to appear on the top of the pancake then use a thin fish slice or slotted turner to flip them over for a further minute or so. You will need to cook the pancakes in batches so keep them covered in a low oven while you cook the rest (unless of course you have some willing diners available to eat them as soon as they are cooked). My brood likes these drizzled with runny honey or maple syrup.

Tip
These pancakes freeze well. To reheat, loosely wrap the pancakes in foil then place in a low oven (140°C / 275°F / Gas 1) for 10-15 minutes.

To make the curds:
1. Heat the milk in a saucepan with a good pinch of salt. You need to bring it almost to the boil. If you have a thermometer it should be approximately 85°C / 185°F. If you don't, look for small bubbles on the surface and steam. Once it reaches this stage, take the pan off the heat then add the vinegar. As you stir you should see the curds beginning to form and separating from the whey (if this isn't the case add a smidge more vinegar). Cover and put to one side for three hours.
2. Line a colander or sieve with a piece of damp muslin and suspend it over a bowl. Ladle the curds and whey into the colander and leave it to drain for an hour. The longer you leave it the firmer the curds will be. Fresh curd cheese can be stored in the fridge for up to four days. I like to use the whey in place of water when I make bread.

Fool's Gold

Rhenish Cream

This is a bit of a deviation from Hannah Glasse's original version, found in *The Complete Confectioner, Or, Housekeeper's Guide* (1800), which uses calves feet and eggs as the setting agents but the flavourings are the same. I have used gelatine but you could replace this with a vegetarian setting agent like agar-agar. You will need enough to lightly set 600 ml / 1 pint of liquid. I've gone for rather a soft set like a panna cotta.

Ingredients (serves 6-8)
2 pinches / 40-60 saffron strands, crushed
150 ml / ¼ pint / ⅔ cup medium-sweet white wine e.g. Liebfraumilch
400 ml / 13 ½ fl oz / 1 ⅔ cups double cream
2 tsp finely grated lemon zest
2 large bay leaves, lightly crushed to release their aroma
½ tsp lightly crushed coriander seeds
1 x 5-8cm cinnamon stick
25-50 g / 1-2 oz / ⅛-¼ cup caster sugar (depending on how sweet the wine is)
3 leaves gelatine or a vegetarian equivalent
Berries to serve

Method
1. Infuse the saffron in the wine
2. Gently heat the cream, lemon zest, bay leaf and spices and sugar to boiling point. Infuse for one hour. Strain into a jug.
3. Soak the gelatine leaves in cold water for 5 minutes. Squeeze out the excess water. Heat the gelatine with the saffron infused wine stirring until the gelatine has dissolved. Combine this solution onto the strained cream then pour into moulds or small ramekins. Refrigerate for several hours or overnight (particularly if you plan to turn the creams out).
4. To remove from the moulds briefly dip in hot water. Serve with some berries on the side and perhaps a short bread biscuit or two.

Recipes: Dessert

Saffron & Orange Blossom Soufflé with Nougat Ice Cream

Louis Eustache Ude (1769-1846) was a French chef who was counted the Earl of Sefton and the Duke of York (King George III's second son, Prince Frederick Augustus) as his employers before finding fame as the chef at Crockford's Club in the early nineteenth century. He provides a number of methods for making soufflés in his book *The French Chef* including this one which uses mashed potato rather than flour as its base (others use rice flour or breadcrumbs). It's not nearly as odd as it sounds, I promise, plus it's gluten-free. The nougat ice cream is adapted from a recipe in *The Alice B Toklas Cookbook* (1954).

Ingredients (serves 6)

For the soufflé base:
1 large floury potato (200 g / 7 oz in weight)
2 pinches / 40-60 saffron strands, crushed
1 tbsp lemon juice
1-2 tsp orange blossom water (or plain water if you prefer a less floral scented dessert)
50 g / 2 oz / ½ stick softened unsalted butter
25 g / 1 oz / ⅛ cup golden caster sugar for dusting, plus 50 g / 2 oz / ¼ cup
250 ml / 9 fl oz / 1 cup whole milk
5 cm / 2 in strip of lemon zest
3 egg yolks

For the meringue:
6 egg whites
a few drops of lemon juice
50 g / 2 oz / ¼ cup golden caster sugar
icing/confectioner's sugar for dusting

For the nougat ice cream (makes about 600 ml / 1 pint):
50 g / 2 oz / ½ cup shelled, unsalted pistachios
50 g / 2 oz / ¼ cups blanched almonds

Fool's Gold

300 ml / ½ pint / 1 ½ cups single cream
3 egg yolks
150 g / 5 oz / just under ½ cup orange blossom honey
2 egg whites
1 tsp orange blossom water
150 ml / 5 fl oz / ¾ cup double cream

Method
For the soufflé:
1. Preheat the oven to 180°C / 350°F / Gas 4. Pierce the potato all over, then bake until soft for about 1 hour or until there is no resistance when you pierce the potato with a small knife. Allow to cool before scooping the potato out of its skin and then passing it through a potato ricer or mashing it until smooth. You will need 100 g / 4 oz / ⅓ cup cold mashed potato without any butter or milk added for this recipe. This can be done up to three days ahead.
2. Infuse the saffron in the lemon juice and orange blossom water (if using). The strength of the latter varies according to the brand so start with one teaspoon. You can add a little more if you want a stronger flavour.
3. Use half the butter to grease six individual soufflé dishes (about 10 cm diameter, 200 ml / 7 fl oz capacity). Use 25 g / 1 oz / ⅛ cup of the caster sugar to dust the inside of the soufflé dishes. This will help ensure an even rise. Chill in the fridge until required.
4. Place the remaining butter, milk and lemon zest in a small sauce pan. Heat until the butter has melted. Discard the zest and whisk in the riced or mashed potato.
5. Whisk the egg yolks and 50 g / 2 oz / ¼ cup caster sugar together until thick and creamy. Combine this with the potato mixture. Return to the heat then cook until thickened. Pass through a sieve into a clean bowl pushing all the potato through. Cover the surface with cling film and allow this mixture to cool to room temperature (this can be done in advance, even the day before, just remember to refrigerate the 'custard').
6. When you are ready to assemble the soufflés, preheat the oven to 180°C / 350°F/ Gas 4.

Recipes: Dessert

7. Make the meringue by whisking the egg whites with a few drops of lemon juice to stiff peaks. Add the golden caster sugar one teaspoon at a time until thoroughly incorporated. Fold the meringue into the cooled soufflé base. Divide the mixture between the prepared soufflé dishes. Run your thumb around the rim of each dish to help ensure an even rise.
8. Place the dishes in a large roasting dish and fill the tin halfway with boiling water. Place in the oven for about 13-15 minutes. The soufflés should be lightly golden on top and puffed up. Remove the soufflé dishes from the water bath and serve immediately dusted with a little icing sugar and with the nougat ice cream on the side.

For the nougat ice cream:
1. Preheat the oven to 150°C / 300°F / Gas 2. Roast the nuts for 5 to 10 minutes until lightly golden. Coarsely chop.
2. In a saucepan, heat the cream to boiling point. Meanwhile whisk the egg yolks and the honey together in a heatproof bowl. Pour the hot cream over the eggs and honey. Return the combined mixture to the saucepan then stir over a gentle heat and until thickened. Cool the custard quickly by placing the bowl in a sink containing cold water (just enough to come half way up the exterior of the bowl containing the custard). Once the custard had cooled, chill in the refrigerator.
3. Whip the egg whites to stiff peaks. In another mixing bowl, add the orange blossom water to the double cream. Using the same beaters whisk the double cream to soft peaks. Fold the cream into the cooled custard first followed by the egg whites and the chopped nuts. Ensure everything is thoroughly combined then pour the mixture into a container (you'll need one that has a capacity of at least 1 litre). Place in the freezer overnight.
4. Remove the ice cream about 10 to 15 minutes before you plan to serve it. As soufflés don't like to hang around it is best to scoop out six portions and place them on a plate in the fridge (or freezer if your kitchen is particularly warm) while the soufflés are baking.

Recipes: Dessert

Spiced Apple Fritters

Like crêpes these fritters, adapted from a recipe in Gervase Markham's *The English Huswife* (1615), are best eaten as soon as they are cooked. You can keep them warm in a low oven but they will lose some of their crispness. The original recipe uses an ale balm leavened batter but I'm afraid my household is far too impatient to wait for the yeast to do its work so I've used baking powder instead.

Ingredients (serves 4-6)
1 pinch / 20-30 saffron strands, crushed
2 tbsp sherry
125 g / 4 ½ oz / 1 cup plain flour
1 tsp baking powder
Pinch cloves
½ tsp cinnamon
¼ tsp nutmeg
¼ tsp mace
pinch of salt
1 tbsp caster sugar
75 ml / 2 ½ fl oz / ⅓ cup double cream
75 ml / 2 ½ fl oz / ⅓ cup ale
1 whole egg
1 egg yolk
6-8 eating apples
about 1 litre / 1 pt 13 ½ fl oz vegetable oil for deep frying

For the topping:
4 tbsp caster sugar
1 tsp cinnamon

Method
1. Infuse the saffron in the sherry.
2. Sieve the flour, baking powder, spices and salt into a bowl. Stir in a tablespoon of caster sugar and make a well in the centre.
3. Combine the cream and ale then beat in the egg and the yolk followed by the saffron infused sherry.

Fool's Gold

4. Pour the liquid ingredients into the well then gradually whisk in the spiced flour until you have a thickish batter then put to one side while you prepare the apples. You can make the batter in advance (I usually leave it for an hour or so before I use it).
5. You can peel the apples if you prefer but I don't always bother. Cut the apples into thick discs about ½-1cm/¼-½in thick. Depending on the size of your apples you should get around four slices. Remove the core with a 2 cm / 1 in cutter so that you have a ring. Leave in water until ready to cook. Mix the caster sugar and ground cinnamon together for the topping in a small bowl.
6. Heat the oil in a wok or deep saucepan (if you have a deep fat fryer feel free to use that) over a medium to high heat. To see if is hot enough fry a small cube of bread. If it sizzles seductively and gradually turns golden brown then you are good to go.
7. Pat several of the apple rings dry on a clean tea towel. Dip them into the batter letting the excess drain off (use a couple of forks to do this to keep your hands clean). Fry for 1-2 minutes then use a fork or silicone spatula to flip each one over and cook for a further 1-2 minutes.
8. Remove with a slotted spoon and drain on kitchen paper. Liberally sprinkle with cinnamon sugar before eating.

Simnel Pudding

As lovely as yeast leavened cakes are they do not have the keeping power of other cakes. This is a great way to use up any left over Simnel cake or any other type of saffron bun (and yes it is essentially a riff on bread and butter pudding). If you are using an unfruited saffron bun (like the Sarah Harrison variety on page 151) scatter over 50-75 g / 2-3 oz dried fruit like currants or raisins. I like to add a little saffron to the 'custard' but you can omit this if you prefer.

Ingredients
1 pinch / 20-30 saffron strands crushed (optional)

Recipes: Dessert

2 tbsp warm brandy (or you can use hot water if you prefer)
butter for greasing the baking dish
250-300 g / 9-10 oz Simnel cake or saffron buns cut into 2-3cm/1in chunks
150 ml / 4 fl oz / a little over ½ cup whole milk
150 ml / 4 fl oz / a little over ½ cup double cream
25-50g / 1-2 oz / ⅛-¼ cup golden caster sugar
3 eggs beaten

Method
1. Infuse the saffron in the brandy or hot water if using.
2. Preheat the oven to 180°C / 350°F / Gas 4. Butter a shallow baking dish with a capacity of around 1 litre.
3. Scatter the pieces of Simnel cake or saffron buns in the dish. Beat together the milk, double cream, caster sugar (if you are using Simnel cake 25 g / 1 oz should be ample but use more for a less sweet saffron bun), eggs and the saffron infusion. Pour over the cake pieces then bake in the oven for 25-30 minutes or until set. Serve with more cream or custard if you like (it seems my brood can never have enough custard).

Strawberry & Saffron Tarts

Saffron-coloured custard was a popular filling for medieval tarts, as can be seen from this recipe adapted from *Two Fifteenth Century Cookery Books* (Harl MS 279. Here it is paired with a spiced strawberry layer. These deep filled tartlets were known as 'daryoles' but you can make one large tart if you prefer.

Ingredients (makes 12 small tarts or one 23 cm / 9 in tart)
1 pinch / 20-30 saffron strands, crushed
130 ml / 3 ½ fl oz / just over half a cup sweet white wine
250 g / 9 oz / 1 ¾ cups strawberries hulled
30-35 g / just over 1 oz dates, finely chopped (2-6 dates depending on size

Fool's Gold

and variety used)
1 ½ tbsp golden caster sugar
½ tsp powder douce (see page 276) or ¼ tsp each cinnamon & ginger plus a pinch of cloves
1 tsp arrowroot or cornflour mixed with 2-4 tsp sweet white wine or water
1 x quantity sweet saffron short crust pastry (see page 276)
300 ml / ½ pt / 1 ¼ cups double cream
5 egg yolks
50g / 2 oz / ¼ cup golden caster sugar
12 extra saffron strands (optional)

Equipment: 12 hole muffin tin or a 23 cm / 9 in loose bottomed tart tin

Method

1. Infuse saffron in 100 ml / 3 fl oz / just under half a cup of the sweet white wine.
2. Cut the strawberries into small dice. Place in a small saucepan with the chopped dates, 2 tablespoons of the sweet wine, 1 ½ tablespoons golden caster sugar and the spices. Gently bring up to boiling point then cook until the strawberries are soft and pulpy with a few pieces retaining their shape. This should take around 3-4 minutes.
3. Mix the arrowroot or cornflour with 2-4 teaspoons of sweet white wine or water. Stir into the simmering strawberry sauce then stir until thickened. Turn off the heat and allow to cool completely. If possible make the strawberry mixture the day before you plan to make the tarts and store in the fridge.
4. Roll out the pastry to a thickness of 3 mm / ⅛ in. Stamp out 12 x 11 cm rounds. Place each round in a muffin hole. This should be more or less level with the top of each hole. Using your fingers, press down into the base of each hole pushing the pastry upwards. This will cause it to sit slightly proud of the hole (it will shrink back during while baking). Place in the refrigerator while you preheat the oven.
5. Preheat the oven to 200°C /400°F /Gas 4. Place a baking tray in the oven large enough for the muffin or large tart tin to sit on.
6. Prick the base of each tart case then line it with baking paper or a neutral coloured muffin case. Fill each one with baking beans then place the

Recipes: Dessert

muffin tin on top of the hot tray and bake for 15 minutes. Once cooked remove the baking beans and lining paper from each case.

7. While the tart cases are baking, make the custard. Heat the cream and saffron infused wine in a small saucepan to boiling point. Meanwhile beat the yolks and 50 g / 2 oz / ¼ cup golden caster sugar together with a balloon whisk in a large jug until combined. Pour the hot cream mixture over the egg yolks, whisking as you go.

8. Place about a teaspoon of the strawberry mixture in the base of each pastry case. Pour the warm saffron custard over the strawberry mix filling almost to the top. If you like to can dlelicately place a single saffron strand on top of each custard tart. Bake at 200°C / 400°F / Gas 4 or 15 minutes. The custard will have risen and should still have a slight wobble. If it still seems a little loose reduce the temperature to 180°C / 350°F / Gas 2 for a further 5 minutes. Allow to cool in the tin before taking out. Although these tarts do keep for a day or two they are best eaten on the day they are baked.

Variation

To make one large tart, line a 23 cm / 9 in loose bottomed tart tin with the sweet pastry leaving a little pastry over hanging the top of the tin. Prick the base, line with baking paper and baking beans then bake as directed above for 15 minutes. Remove the paper and beans then return to the oven for a further 5 minutes. Use a vegetable peeler to level off the top of the pastry case by scraping away at the overhanging pastry.

As this tart will take longer to cook you need reduce the oven temperature to 150°C / 300°F /Gas 2. To fill the tart, spread the strawberry filling over the base then top with the warm custard mixture. You may want to do this when the tart case is in the oven by pulling the shelf out slightly to make it easier to fill. Bake for around 40-45 minutes until the filling is just set but still has a bit of a wobble and the top has browned a little.

Fool's Gold

Autumnal Tart

This is adapted from the recipe 'Tartes In Applis' in *Forme of Cury* (1390).

Ingredients (serves 8)
1 pinch / 20-30 saffron strands, crushed
2 tbsp hot water
1 x quantity sweet saffron short crust pastry (see page 276)
2-3 eating apples (at least 225 g in total weight)
1-2 pears (at least 225 g in total weight)
1 ½ tsp powder douce (see page 276) or mixed spice
3 tbsp runny honey
75 g / 3 oz / ½ cup raisins or sultanas
75 g / 3 oz / ½ cup dried figs, roughly chopped
1 egg, beaten (to glaze the tart)

Method
1. Infuse the saffron in the hot water.
2. Preheat the oven to 180°C / 350°F / Gas 4.
3. Grease a 23 cm / 9 in loose bottomed flan tin. Roll out two thirds of the pastry then use it to line the tin. The remaining third can be used to create a lattice for the top of the pie.
4. Peel and core the apples and pears. Chop into small pieces then place into a large bowl. Mix with the saffron water, spice, honey, raisins and figs. Spoon into the pastry case.
5. Roll out the remaining pastry and create a lattice for the top of the tart by either cutting strips and arranging them on top of the tart or using a special lattice cutter. Trim away any excess pastry then brush with beaten egg.
6. Bake in the oven for 35 to 40 minutes until the pastry is golden brown. Serve warm or cold with cream or vanilla ice cream.

Vegetarian

Recipes: Vegetarian

Courgette & Ginger Soup

Courgettes are easy to grow but can be ridiculously prolific. This recipe adapted from one in Giles Rose's *A Perfect School of Instructions for the Officers of the Mouth* (1682), is a great way to use up a glut of courgettes, and can be frozen. If you cook courgettes long and slow they virtually melt into the butter and need very little stock to produce a soup (I picked this tip up from fellow food writer Kathy Slack's fabulous book *From the Veg Patch*). Like Giles Rose I have added a little cheese but you can omit this and switch the butter for olive oil for a vegan version.

Ingredients (serves 3-4)
2 pinches / 40-60 saffron strands, crushed
300 ml / ½ pint / 1 ¼ cups vegetable stock plus a little extra if required
50 g / 2 oz / ½ stick butter (or 3 tbsp olive oil)
800 g / 1 lb 11 oz / 4 cups courgettes, coarsely grated
1 onion, sliced
1 tbsp chopped fresh ginger
1 tsp ground ginger
4 tbsp finely grated parmesan
1 tbsp sugar (optional)
1 tbsp lemon juice
1 tbsp chopped fresh chervil (or slightly less chopped tarragon)
salt & white pepper to season

Method
1. Infuse the saffron in the stock.
2. Gently melt the butter in a large lidded, deep frying pan or casserole over a gentle heat. Sweat the courgettes, onions, fresh and ground ginger for 30 to 40 minutes or until the vegetables are really soft.
3. Add the parmesan, sugar (if using) and lemon juice.
4. Blend the cooked courgettes with saffron infused stock and chopped chervil or tarragon. You can add more stock if the soup is too thick

for your tastes. Season well with salt and white pepper. Reheat gently, without boiling, before serving.

Chickpea & Saffron Dip

Serve this dip, based on a recipe in *Forme of Cury* (1390) with crudités, pitta bread or crisps.

Ingredients
1 pinch / 20-30 saffron strands, crushed
75 ml / 2 ½ fl oz / ⅓ cup white wine
75 ml / 2 ½ fl oz / ⅓ cup light olive oil
1 fat clove garlic, chopped
1 x 340 g tin chickpeas, drained
½ tsp powder fort or ¼ tsp each ground black pepper and ground ginger (plus extra if desired)
½ tsp fine sea salt plus more to taste
a good squeeze of lemon juice
1 tbsp finely chopped parsley

Method
1. Infuse the saffron in the wine (it's fine to do this when the wine is at room temperature).
2. Heat the olive oil in a saucepan over a gentle heat. Cook the garlic for 1 minute then add the chickpeas, powder fort or spices, saffron infused wine and salt. Bring to the boil and simmer for 10 minutes. Place in a food processor with the lemon juice (or a bowl and use a stick blender) then blitz until smooth. Add a little water if it seems too dry. Stir in the chopped parsley before serving. This can be made ahead of time then refrigerated, but it should be served at room temperature.

Fool's Gold

Brie or Camembert Tart

Brie is generally an exceedingly polite cheese. Its mild mannered nature means it rarely makes its presence known in the fridge (unless you get a particularly aged, bolshy one). That's not to say it's not flavoursome and it lends itself well to this rich cheese tart. But if you do want something a bit bossier by all means use a ripe Camembert instead. This recipe adapted from one for 'Tart of Bry' in *Forme of Cury* (1390), is very rich so a little goes a long way. Try serving it with the pickled pears on pages 121-4.

Ingredients (serves 6-8 as a starter or light lunch)
2 pinches / 40-60 saffron strands, crushed
1 clove garlic, peeled, left whole but lightly squashed
1 sprig rosemary, bruised
200 ml / 7 fl oz / just under 1 cup double cream
400 g / 14 oz ripe brie or camembert, straight from the fridge
500 g / 1 lb 2 oz block puff pastry or use the saffron rough puff pastry on page 277, you'll need about two thirds of this
4 egg yolks
¼-½ tsp ground ginger
1 tsp icing sugar
salt

Method
1. Place saffron, garlic and rosemary in a small pan with the cream. Heat to boiling point then leave to infuse for about one hour.
2. Preheat the oven to 180°C / 350°F / Gas 4.
3. Remove the rind from the brie. Cut into chunks and place in bowl suspended over a pan of barely simmering water. Heat until melted stirring occasionally to help it along.
4. While the cheese is melting, roll out the puff pastry to a thickness of 3mm then line 23cm/9in loose bottomed tart tin with puff pastry.
5. Place the egg yolks in a bowl. Strain the cream onto the egg yolks, discarding the garlic and rosemary. Add the ginger, sugar and a little salt. Mix well then stir this into the melted cheese.
6. Pour the cheese mixture into the puff pastry

Recipes: Vegetarian

7. Bake for 30 to 40 minutes or until the pastry has puffed up and the filling has set. Allow to cool for 10 minutes or so before serving.

Pasternak Fritters with Verde Sawse

'Pasternak' is an old word for parsnips. I like to use gram (chickpea) flour here but regular plain flour is fine. You could use celeriac in place of the parsnips if you like. Verde Sawse is a medieval green sauce that is great with these fritters but also works well with lamb, fish or chicken This recipe is based on 'Frytour of Pasternakes of Apples' and 'Verde Sawse' in *Forme of Cury* (1390).

Ingredients
For the fritters:
1 pinch / 20-30 saffron strands, crushed
150 ml / 5 fl oz / ⅔ cup ale
120 g / 4 ½ oz / 1 cup plain flour or gram flour
½ tsp ground ginger
½ tsp fine sea salt
2 eggs, beaten
500 g / 1 lb 2 oz parsnips, peeled, quartered
1-2 eating apples (200 g / 7 oz), cored but leave the peel on
2 tbsp snipped chives
oil for frying

For the verde sawse:
25 g / 1 oz / ¼ cup fresh white breadcrumbs
75 ml / 2 ½ fl oz / ⅓ cup cold water
1 pinch / 20-30 saffron strands, crushed
1-2 tbsp white vermouth or medium dry white wine, plus a little extra if needed
2 generous handfuls fresh green herbs to include mint, parsley, sage and thyme, washed and thoroughly dried
1 clove garlic, crushed
¼ tsp ground ginger

Recipes: Vegetarian

¼ tsp ground black pepper
⅛ tsp ground cinnamon
2 tbsp mild olive oil
1-2 tbsp verjuice or white wine vinegar
½-1 tsp salt (according to taste)
a little lemon juice to season

Method
To make the fritters
1. Infuse the saffron in the ale. As the ale will be cool make sure you do this well ahead of time to allow the flavour and colour to diffuse.
2. Sieve the flour, ginger and salt into a bowl. Make a well in the centre then break the eggs into it. Beat the eggs into the flour adding the saffron infused ale as you go. You will end up with quite a loose batter.
3. Coarsely grate the parsnips and apples then fold into the batter along with the chives.
4. Pour enough oil to just cover the base of a large non-stick frying pan. Heat over a medium to high heat. Place two tablespoons (one on top of the other) of the pasternak mixture then flatten slightly (they should be around 8-10 cm wide). You should get another two or three in the same pan. Cook for 2-3 minutes before flipping over and cooking for a further 2-3 minutes. They should be nice and golden if a little raggedy at the edges. Keep warm in a low oven while you cook the rest of the fritters.

To make the verde sawse
1. Put the breadcrumbs in a small bowl. Pour over the water then soak for an hour.
2. Steep the saffron in the white vermouth or wine also for an hour.
3. Remove any woody stems from the herbs. Place in a food processor with the remaining ingredients and process until you have a smooth purée. Add more vermouth/water to achieve the desired consistency.

Tip
You can make the fritters in advance and reheat them at 180°C / 375°F / Gas 4 for 10 to 15 minutes.

Fool's Gold

Onion & Almond Soup with Cheesy Croutons

There are several versions of 'Soupes Dorry' from the medieval period. Some contain saffron and others contain onions but I have chosen to use both here in a recipe based on one in *Two Fifteenth Century Cookbooks*. Both use an almond milk stock as the basis of the broth. 'Sops' were pieces of bread placed in the bottom of a dish over which a pottage would be poured. Ideally begin this a day ahead.

Ingredients
2 pinches / 40-60 saffron strands, crushed
180 ml / 6 ½ fl oz / ¾ cup dry white wine
2 tbsp olive oil
900 g / 2 lb white onions
1 tsp powder douce (see page 276) or mixed spice
2 bay leaves
1 litre / 1 ¾ pints / 4 cups hot, light vegetable stock
200 g / 7 oz / 1 ½ cups blanched almonds
four slices of baguette or sourdough (about 2 cm thickness), that will fit on top of your serving bowls
100 g / 4 oz / 1 cup grated cheese e.g. cheddar or gruyère
1-2 tbsp snipped chives

Method
1. Soak the saffron in two tablespoons of the white wine.
2. Take two of the onions. Peel and halve then cut into half moon slices. Heat a tablespoon of the olive oil in a frying pan over a medium to high heat. Cook the two sliced onions until brown. Drain on absorbent paper and put to one side until required. These will be used to garnish the soup when you serve it.
3. Peel and half the remaining onions then cut into half moon slices. Heat the remaining oil in a saucepan, this time over a gentle heat. Sweat the onions until softened stirring frequently to ensure they do

Recipes: Vegetarian

not take on too much colour. This will take 20 to 30 minutes. It's better to to go low and slow here to ensure the onions don't brown.

4. Once the onions have softened add the powder douce or other spices then cook for a minute or so before adding the bay leaves, the rest of the white wine and vegetable stock. Bring to the boil then simmer for 15 minutes.
5. Place the blanched almonds in a heat proof bowl or jug. Strain the hot onion broth over the almonds squeezing the onions to get out as much liquid as possible. Leave the nuts to soak for at least an hour (or even overnight if you prefer). Discard the bay leaves but reserve the boiled onions.
6. Place the almonds and their soaking liquid in a blender (you may need to do this in batches depending on the size of your blender). Process until smooth then pass the mixture through a sieve lined with muslin or a jelly bag to extract the 'milk' squeezing every so often.
7. Rinse out the blender then add a ladle of the strained almond milk, and around one third of the boiled onions. Blend until smooth then transfer to a saucepan along with the remaining, un-puréed onions, almond milk and saffron and wine infusion. Reheat gently until hot but do not boil.
8. While the soup is reheating toast the bread on each side. Sprinkle one of the toasted sides with grated cheese then grill until melted and bubbling. Ladle the soup into warm bowls and top with the cheesy croutons. Scatter each bowl with some of the browned onions and snipped chives. Serve immediately.

Pea Tarts with a Parmesan Crust

Pea tarts (or pies) appear to have been a popular addition to the dinner table from the late sixteenth century through to the eighteenth century. The saffron gives the pea filling an extra vibrancy. Sugar features in most of the recipes I have seen although it is hard to know just how much was used or how sweet the resulting tart would have been. Elizabeth Grey, Countess of Kent, who included a version of this recipe in her book *A Choice Manuall, or Rare and Select Secrets in Physick and Chyrurgery*

Fool's Gold

(1653), recommends icing the tarts but for me this is a step too far even with the addition of verjuice in her recipe to temper the sweetness.

These are wonderful as a pre-dinner nibble and can be prepared well in advance so that there is minimal fussing before you serve them.

Ingredients (makes 20 canapé size tarts)
1 pinch / 20-30 saffron strands, crushed
1 tbsp lemon juice
200 g / 7 oz / 1 ⅔ cups plain flour
1 good pinch salt
100 g / 4 oz / ½ cup chilled unsalted butter, diced
30 g / 1 oz / ¼ cup parmesan, finely grated
2 egg yolks
2-4 tbsp iced water
200 g / 7 oz / 1 ½ cups frozen peas
3 tbsp extra virgin olive oil
¼ tsp salt
¼ tsp ground white pepper
1 spring (salad) onion, chopped
1 tbsp chopped fresh savoury leaves (or thyme)
a few pinches of caster sugar
parmesan shavings to decorate (optional)

Method
1. Infuse the saffron in the lemon juice.
2. Preheat the oven to 180°C / 350°F / Gas 4. Cut out 24 small squares of baking paper just large enough to line each indentation of a 24-hole mini muffin tin.
3. Sieve the flour and salt into a bowl. Add the butter then rub it in with the tips of your fingers until it resembles breadcrumbs. Stir in the parmesan then add the yolks and enough iced water to bring the dough together. You can use a food processor to make the pastry if you prefer. Chill for at least an hour.
4. Roll the pastry out to a thickness of 3 mm / ⅛ in. Use a 6 cm / 2 in cookie cutter to cut out rounds of pastry then use them to fill the holes in the mini muffin tin (re-roll the offcuts if necessary). Press

Recipes: Vegetarian

down to ensure the pastry is moulded to the indentations then prick the base of each case with a fork. Line the raw pastry cases with the paper squares then fill with a few baking beans. Bake for 7 minutes. Remove the paper and beans then return to the oven for a further 7-10 minutes. The cases should be cooked through and golden. Allow to cool before removing from the tin and filling.

5. Place the peas in a bowl. Cover with boiling water then leave for 3 minutes. Drain thoroughly.
6. Return the peas to the bowl or place them in a food processor. Add the saffron infusion, olive oil, salt, white pepper, spring onion and chopped savory or thyme leaves. Use a stick blender (or processor) to produce a rough purée – it doesn't need to be super smooth. This can be done in advance the refrigerated until required.
7. Just before you are ready to serve the tarts place a good teaspoon of the pea mixture into each parmesan pastry case. The purée mixture should provide enough to fill 18-20 tarts (you will have a few extra tart cases just in case of any breakages prior to filling). Once you have the tarts on the serving plate lightly sprinkle the tops with a little caster sugar (I know this sounds odd, but trust me, it does work and won't make the tarts sweet unless you are over enthusiastic with your sprinkling!). Top each tart with a small piece of shaved parmesan before serving.

Variation

If you don't have the time to make your own pastry, the pea purée makes a lovely topping for bruschetta. Brush 4 medium slices of sourdough with olive oil then season with salt and pepper. Bake at 180°C / 350°F / Gas 4 for 10 to 15 minutes or until lightly browned and crisping up (the time will be dependent on the freshness of the bread). Top each slice with the pea mixture, then sprinkle with sugar and parmesan shavings as described above.

Fool's Gold

Vegetarian Toad in the Hole with Golden Onion Gravy

Ingredients (serves 4)
300 ml / ½ pt / 1 ¼ cups milk
2 individual pinches / 40-60 saffron strands, crushed
2 tbsp hot water plus extra for the porcini
10 g / ½ oz dried porcini
500g / 1 lb 2 oz large flat chestnut mushrooms
3 red onions
1 sprig rosemary or thyme plus 3 tsp chopped fresh rosemary or thyme, according to preference
4 tbsp vegetable oil
2 cloves garlic, chopped
25 g / 1 oz butter
175 g / 6 oz / 1 ½ cups plain flour plus 2 tbsp
2 eggs
grated zest of half a lemon
¼ tsp fine sea salt
black pepper to season
2 tbsp flour
120 ml / 4 fl oz / ½ cup white wine
480 ml / 16 fl oz / 2 cups hot vegetable stock
salt, pepper and lemon juice to season

Method
1. Pour the milk into a saucepan then heat to boiling point. Stir in 1 pinch / 20-30 crushed saffron strands and leave to cool.
2. Infuse the remaining crushed saffron strands in the hot water. In a separate bowl pour hot water over the dried porcini then leave to soak for at least 30 minutes.
3. Pre-heat the oven to 200°C / 400°F / Gas 6. Cut the mushrooms into 1 cm thick slices. Peel one of the red onions then cut into half moon slices and set aside with the mushrooms. Peel the two remaining red onions then cut into half moon slices and set aside for the gravy.
4. Toss the mushrooms and onions with two tablespoons of the

vegetable oil, the chopped garlic and 1 ½ teaspoons of chopped rosemary or thyme. Place the vegetables in the same roasting tin that you intend to cook the 'toad' in then roast for 20 to 30 minutes or until the mushrooms are tender. They will exude a bit of moisture so cook them until this has almost disappeared (a little left in the bottom of the dish won't matter).

5. Melt the butter in a deep frying pan over a medium heat. Fry the onions reserved for the gravy with a sprig of thyme or rosemary until brown. This will take around 20 to 25 minutes.
6. While the mushrooms are roasting, sieve 175 g / 6 oz / 1 ½ cups plain flour into a large jug or bowl. Make a well in the centre then break in the eggs. Gradually whisk in the cooled saffron infused milk, beating well to ensure there are no lumps.
7. Drain the soaked porcini mushrooms then finely chop. Stir the porcini into the batter along with the remaining chopped rosemary or thyme, lemon zest, salt and pepper. Set aside until required.
8. Drizzle the roasted mushroom mixture with the remaining vegetable oil, then place it back in the oven for five minutes to ensure the oil is hot. Quickly pour over the prepared batter then return to the oven. Bake for 25 minutes until well risen and set.
9. While the mushroom 'toad' is cooking and once the onions for the gravy have browned, remove the rosemary or thyme sprig then reduce the heat and stir in the remaining two tablespoons of flour. Mix well. Combine the wine and stock then gradually pour onto the onion and flour mixture stirring well after each addition until all the liquid has been incorporated. Continue to stir over a gentle heat until the gravy thickens. Keep this gently bubbling away until you are ready to serve the 'toad'. Just before serving stir the saffron and water infusion into the onion gravy. Season with salt, pepper and lemon juice before serving.

DRINKS

Recipes: Drinks

Usquebaugh

The name is usquebaugh is believed to be derived from the Gaelic *uisce bae* meaning water of life or *aqua vitae*. It was often flavoured with liquorice, fennel or aniseed (or a combination of all three). By the eighteenth century it was frequently coloured with saffron too. Many recipes use brandy as the base, but vodka is also used. What follows is an amalgam of several recipes. From its appearance in domestic manuals of the time usquebaugh seems to have been popular both for recreational and medicinal purposes. George II's wife, Queen Caroline, was given usquebaugh on her death bed in 1737.

This is a spirit so I would recommend diluting it (although I'm not sure they did in the eighteenth century). My husband likes it with tonic water. I sometimes mix two tablespoons of usquebaugh with two teaspoons of icing sugar and a tablespoon of finely chopped mint, then drizzle it over sliced or balled melon – a great foil for parma ham.

Ingredients (makes around 700 ml / 24 fl oz)
1 stick (4-6g) liquorice, broken into pieces
2 tsp fennel seeds
2 tsp aniseed
1 tsp coriander seeds
75 g / 3 oz / ½ cup raisins
30 g / 1 oz / about ¼ cup (approximately 2) dried figs, roughly chopped
700 ml / 25 fl oz vodka or brandy
½ tsp saffron strands, crushed

Method
1. Place the liquorice, fennel, aniseed, raisins and figs in a jar. Pour over vodka or brandy (keep the bottle so that you can use it for the finished usquebaugh). Leave to infuse for eight days in a dark place. If you remember give it a gentle shake every other day or so.
2. Place the saffron into the original bottle. Strain the infused alcohol

onto the saffron. I usually leave the usquebaugh for at least 24 hours before trying it. It may look a little murky and brown in the bottle but once it's diluted it turns a beautiful gold.

Daffodil Cocktail

Eliza Smith's recipe 'To make the true Daffy's Elixir' contains many of the same ingredients as usquebaugh plus some a few extra ingredients some of which have laxative properties (like senna, which for obvious reasons are not included here). As the recipe below clearly isn't as complex as the original Daffy's Elixir it felt wrong to give it that name. I received some interesting suggestions for its name on various social media channels but have decided to go with 'daffodil' as that is what the colour reminds me of. I often serve this cocktail in vintage Babycham glasses which are quite small. If you are using a more capacious martini glass follow the larger measurements. The quantity of sugar syrup required will depend on how sweet you like your drinks. Some people prefer to do without it.

Ingredients (serves 1)
½-1 tbsp usquebaugh, chilled
1-2 tbsp rhubarb purée, chilled (see below)
½-1 tsp simple sugar syrup, chilled, optional (see below)
sparkling wine e.g. Cava, Prosecco or Champagne (if you're feeling flush!)
edible flower e.g. violet, primrose or borage for decoration (absolutely not essential but they do look pretty)

Method
1. Pour the usquebaugh, rhubarb purée and a little simple sugar syrup (if using) into the base of your glass. Give it a little stir.
2. Add a good splash of the sparkling wine. Give it another gentle stir to amalgamate the ingredients. It will fizz quite a bit so go easy as you continue to fill the glass.
3. Float an edible flower on top of your cocktail and enjoy!

Fool's Gold

Hypocras Cocktail

Don't be afraid to use verjuice if you have it. I promise it won't leave an unpleasant taste!

Ingredients (serves 1)
1 tbsp hypocras syrup (see below)
1-1½ tsp verjuice or lemon juice
100-125 ml / 3½-4 fl oz sparkling white wine

Method
1. Pour the syrup into a champagne flute.
2. Add a teaspoon of verjuice or lemon juice. Give it a good stir then top with sparkling white wine. Add more verjuice or lemon juice if you think it needs it.

Hypocras Syrup

Sweetened spiced wines have been served as digestives for centuries. Herbs and spices were steeped in wine then filtered through conical flannel filter bags which supposedly resembled the sleeves of Hippocrates, the ancient Greek physician. They were initially sweetened with honey although sugar was used in later centuries. The recipe below is inspired by John Edwards adaptation of Apicius' *Conditum Paradoxum* ('Extraordinary Spiced Wine'). It makes an admirable sparkling wine cocktail (which I'm sure is far less sweet than the Roman's would have liked it). The syrup's spicy undertones endear it to mulled white wine in the winter. Just add four of five tablespoons of the syrup (or more or less according to taste) and a few slices of lemon to a bottle of dry white wine then gently heat until hot (but don't let it boil).

Ingredients (makes around 250 ml / 8 ½ fl oz / 1 cup)
8-10 cm cinnamon stick
1 ½ tsp black peppercorns or 3 whole long peppers

Recipes: Drinks

½ tsp saffron strands
250 g / 9 oz / ¾ cup runny honey
150 ml / ¼ pint / ⅔ cup dry or medium white wine
2 large bay leaves, crushed
4 slices of fresh ginger

Method
1. Lightly crush the cinnamon, peppercorns and saffron in a pestle and mortar. You are looking for broken pieces rather than a fine powder.
2. Place the crushed spices, honey, wine, bay leaves and ginger in a small sauce pan. Bring to the boil then simmer for five minutes.
3. Strain through a very fine sieve (preferably lined with muslin if you have it) into a jug. Decant the syrup into a bottle and reserve until required. I keep mine in the fridge although it should keep for a good while in a dark, cool cupboard.

Saffron Tea

Among its many reputed medicinal qualities, saffron was believed to quell stomach complaints which explains why it appeared in the recipes for surfeit waters found in the eighteenth century. The recipe below for the less glamorous sounding Antispasmodic Tea (a cure for indigestion) comes from Charles Elmé Francatelli. The lemon juice is my addition although this (and the brandy) could be omitted if you prefer.

Ingredients (serves 1)
5-15 saffron strands (depending on the size of the cup and according to taste)
2-3 tsp brandy or spirit of choice
2-3 tsp lemon juice (optional)
150-200 ml / 5-7 fl oz / ⅔-¾ cup boiling water (or more if you prefer)

Method
1. Personally I don't think you need to crush the saffron beforehand (I rather like to see them floating in the cup) but you can do so if you wish.
2. Mix the saffron with the brandy and lemon juice (if using) in your cup.

Fool's Gold

Leave for a good 10 minutes (or longer) to kick start the infusion process.
3. Top the cup up with boiling water. You will need to leave it for a further 5-10 minutes to cool down before drinking by which time it will have developed a wonderful golden glow.

Rhubarb Syrup

This will provide enough for several cocktails.

Ingredients
200 g / 7 oz sticks of rhubarb, chopped into 2cm/1in chunks
25 g / 1 oz / ⅛ cup caster sugar
2 tbsp water

Method
1. Place the rhubarb, sugar and water in a saucepan. Cook over a medium to low heat until the rhubarb is soft and falling apart. Allow to cool completely.
2. Use a stick blender to reduce the rhubarb to a smooth purée or rub through a sieve using the back of a spoon. Chill before use.

Simple Sugar Syrup

Again this will make far more than you need but it will keep for a good while in the fridge.

Ingredients
100 g / 4 oz / ½ cup caster sugar
100 ml / 3 ½ fl oz / ½ cup water

Method
1. Place the sugar and the water in a small saucepan. Bring to the boil then simmer for about 3-5 minutes or until slightly reduced. Cool then chill before use.

Miscellaneous

Recipes: Miscellaneous

Almond Milk

Homemade almond milk is far creamier than the shop bought stuff so it really is worth the effort to make your own. You can scale this recipe up or down according to the quantity required.

Ingredients (makes about 450-500 ml)
100 g / 4 oz / ¾ cup whole blanched almonds
600 ml / 1 pint / 2 ½ cups boiling water

Method
1. Place the almonds in a bowl or jug then pour over the boiling water. Leave to soak for at least one hour or overnight if you prefer.
2. Pour the nuts and water into a blender. Blend for a minute or so or until a creamy milk is produced. Strain the milk through a jelly bag or a sieve lined with muslin. Gently squeeze the fabric to extract as much of the milk as possible. The more moisture you extract from the nuts the creamier the milk will be.
3. Store the almond milk in the fridge for up to three days giving the bottle a gentle shake before using.

Medieval Spice Blends

Many medieval recipes call for particular spice blends although these were also sprinkled over dishes as a final flourish just before they were served.

Powder Fort

As the name suggests this 'strong' powder packs a punch. Think of it as a medieval precursor to cayenne pepper.

Ingredients
3 tsp ground ginger
1 tsp ground black pepper
1 tsp ground white pepper
1 tsp ground nutmeg
¼ tsp ground cloves

Method
Mix all the above together and use as directed in the recipe. Store in a jar.

Powder Douce

This is a much milder blend. Try a pinch or two sprinkled over some fresh strawberries or add it to stewed apple.

Ingredients
3 tsp ground ginger
1½ tsp ground cinnamon
1½ tsp icing sugar, sieved
¼ tsp ground cloves
½ tsp ground nutmeg

Method
Mix all the above together and use as directed in the recipe. Store in a jar.

Pastry Recipes

Most pastry recipes should be made with cold ingredients (hot water crust varieties being an exception to this rule). For this reason you should always ensure that you prepare your saffron infusion well ahead of time. Once cooled it should ideally be chilled in the fridge before you make the pastry.

The quantities of saffron in each of the recipes below vary quite considerably. The more you use the greater intensity of colour your pastry will have but be mindful that it will also affect the flavour. Given how important colour was in food during the medieval era I suspect our forebears erred on the generous side. Nevertheless, even one pinch of saffron will be enough to create a more golden crust.

Saffron Short Crust (sweet)

Ingredients (makes 500g)
250 g / 9 oz / 2 cups plain flour
3 tbsp icing sugar
125 g / 4 ½ oz / ½ cup cold unsalted butter cubed
1 egg

Recipes: Miscellaneous

1-2 pinches / 20-60 saffron strands soaked in 4 tbsp hot water then allowed to cool completely

Method

Sieve the flour and icing sugar into a bowl. Rub in the butter until the mixture resembles breadcrumbs. Add the egg and 2 to 3 tablespoons of the saffron infusion to bind the pastry (add a little more of the saffron infusion if necessary). Alternatively, blitz the flour, icing sugar and butter in a food processor then add the egg and 2 to 3 tablespoons of the saffron infusion (again adding more of the saffron infusion if necessary). Form the dough into a ball, cover and refrigerate for at least one hour.

Saffron Short Crust (savoury)

Ingredients
250 g / 9 oz / 2 cups plain flour
1 pinch fine sea salt
125 g / 4 ½ oz / ½ cup cold unsalted butter or half butter/half lard, cubed
1 pinch / 20-30 saffron strands soaked in 2 tbsp hot water then allowed to cool completely
2-4 tbsp cold water

Method

Sieve the flour and fine sea salt into a bowl. Rub in the fat until the mixture resembles breadcrumbs (or use a food processor). Add the saffron infusion followed by enough cold water to bring the dough together. Form the dough into a ball, cover and refrigerate for at least one hour before use.

Saffron Rough Puff Pastry

Ingredients (makes around 650 g)
2 pinches / 40-60 saffron strands, crushed
150 ml / 5 fl oz / just over ½ cup hot water
1½ tsp lemon juice
300 g / 10 oz / 3 ¼ cups plain flour
a couple of pinches of salt
125 g / 4 ½ oz / a little over 1 stick cold unsalted butter

Fool's Gold

100 g / 4 oz / 1 stick cold lard or more butter or vegetable fat for a vegetarian version

Method
1. Infuse the saffron in the hot water and lemon juice for at least one hour. Allow to cool completely then refrigerate until required.
2. Sift the flour into a bowl then add the salt.
3. Cut the butter and lard into 1 cm / ½ in cubes then stir into the flour.
4. Add the cold saffron water then mix to a rough dough ensuring that the fat is not rubbed in.
5. Roll the dough out on a well floured board into a long rectangle roughly 15 x 40 cm long. Fold the top third down then bring the bottom third up to cover the top section. Turn the pastry 90 degrees so that the bottom fold is on the left then re-roll the dough as before. Repeat this process four times then cover the dough and leave it to rest in the refrigerator. Some cooks like to leave the dough to rest for 10 to 15 minutes in the refrigerator in between each fold but I have never found this necessary. After the dough is rested it will be ready to use.

Saffron Hot Water Crust

Ingredients (makes 650 g)
100 g / 4 oz / 1 stick of lard or butter
180 ml / 6 fl oz / ¾ cup of water or ale
3 good pinches / 60-90 saffron strands, crushed
340 g / 12 oz / around 3 cups of plain flour
¾ tsp salt
1 egg yolk
1 ½ tbsp caster sugar

Method
1. Place the lard or butter, water or ale and saffron together in a saucepan and bring to the boil
2. Sieve the flour into a large bowl with the salt. Mix in the egg yolk and caster sugar
3. Make a well in the middle of the flour and pour in the fat and water mixture. Using a wooden spoon, mix thoroughly to form a dough

4. Cover the dough with cling film and leave to rest at room temperature for 20 minutes before using. It easiest to work with this type of pastry while it is still warm.

Saffron & Seaweed Butter

Saffron was used in the dairying process to colour butter and cheese. It was also used by the likes of Thomas Dawson to colour diary free almond butter which was useful during Lent.

So long as you have an electric mixer or whisk, butter is easy to make at home. The seaweed adds a saltiness to the butter but could be substituted with a tablespoon of mixed herbs or some finely crushed garlic (just remember to add salt if you don't use seaweed).

Ingredients (makes about 175 g / 6 oz)
1 pinch / 20-30 saffron strands, crushed
1 pinch sea salt flakes
1 tbsp lemon juice
300 ml / ½ pint / 1 ¼ cups double cream
1 ½ tsp seaweed flakes
1 pinch / 20-30 saffron strands (optional)

Method
1. Place a large jug of water in the fridge.
2. Crush a pinch of saffron strands with a pinch of sea salt flakes then infuse in the lemon juice.
3. Beat the cream with an electric whisk or in a free standing mixer until the milk solids separate from the butter milk.
4. Strain the butter through a fine sieve ideally lined with some muslin. Squeeze out as much of the buttermilk as possible from the solids using the back of a ladle or even your hands. The solids should form a nice ball and the buttermilk can be used for cooking or baking (it's great in scones). Place the butter in a clean bowl then pour over some of the ice cold water from the fridge. Squeeze again to remove more of the buttermilk. Discard the water and repeat this process another two to three times or until the water is clear when you squeeze the butter.
5. Return the butter to a bowl or place in a small food processor. Add

the seaweed and the saffron and lemon juice infusion. Process until combined. I like to add a further pinch of saffron strands (not soaked or crushed) then pulse a few times to incorporate in the butter. This will provide flecks of orange in the butter.

Saffron Vinaigrette

In his book *Acetaria: A Discourse of Sallets* (1699) John Evelyn notes that German housewives sprinkle their salads with honey and saffron although he admits that the English 'little encourage its admittance into our sallets.' I think it makes a rather charming addition to a humble vinaigrette.

Ingredients
1 pinch / 20-30 saffron strands, crushed
2 tbsp white wine or cider vinegar
1 clove garlic, peeled and chopped
½ tsp sea salt flakes
1 tsp caster sugar
1 tsp Dijon mustard
a good pinch of ground black pepper
3 tbsp light but fruity olive oil, rapeseed oil or grape seed oil
3 tbsp walnut oil (or more of the oil above)

Method
1. Infuse the saffron in the vinegar.
2. Crush the garlic with the sea salt flakes using the flat side of a large knife. Put the garlic paste in a jar with a screw top lid.
3. Add the sugar, mustard, pepper, oils and saffron infusion. Tightly secure the lid on the jar then give it a vigorous shake. If you prefer, you can strain this vinaigrette before using (to remove the garlic). The vinaigrette will keep for up to a week in the fridge but remove it a little while before you want to use it to bring it up to room temperature.

Acknowledgements

Being a writer and food historian is generally a solitary existence. This is not a plea for sympathy. I thrive on being squirrelled away in a library or archive (it is my default setting). I am immensely appreciative of the assistance I have received from the staff at the British Library, Cambridgeshire Archives, the Gibson Library, Kresen Kernow and Saffron Walden Museum archives, not to mention numerous other county archives available online. Thanks to these wonderful people this project was not as lonely as it could have been at times. I am also grateful for the inspiration I have received from fellow food historians such as Andrea Broomfield, Angela Clutton, Dr Annie Gray and Andrew Hann of English Heritage.

This book would not have been possible without the encouragement and support of my publisher Catheryn Kilgariff and the diligence of my editor, Brendan King. Each time I write a cookbook it is a huge learning curve. I am indebted to a number of my peers in the Guild of Food Writers for their valuable insights and for casting their eyes over these recipes. In particular I am grateful to Celia Brooks, Fanny Charles, Julie Friend, Jan Fullwood, Orlando Murrin, Ruth Nieman, Emily Quah, Joy Skipper and Ruth Watson for their help.

One of the most fascinating aspects of this project has been talking to the modern day crokers. They have been incredibly generous with their time and in sharing their knowledge about growing this rare commodity. Their passion for English saffron was highly infectious and our discussions have made me love this spice all the more. My hope is that this book will prompt you to try some saffron grown on English soil so do seek it out. It is a treasured ingredient and deserves to be remembered.

Peter & Douglas Gould, Cheshire Saffron (greatbritishsaffron.co.uk)
Brian & Margaret Eyres, Cornish Saffron (cornishsaffroncompany.co.uk)
David Smale & Penny Atwood, English Saffron (englishsaffron.co.uk)
Andrew Bodey, Kentish Saffron (kentishsaffron.co.uk)
Sally Francis, Norfolk Saffron (norfolksaffron.co.uk)

Fool's Gold

Sandlings Saffron (sandlingssaffron.com)
Sophie Tod, Sussex Saffron (sussexsaffron.co.uk)

There are likely more saffron growers around the country which I am yet to encounter so please forgive any omissions.

As ever my family have travelled with me on this saffron paved road, critiquing my culinary efforts along the way. Thankfully we have all survived the experience without succumbing to fits of hysteria or turning yellow.

Picture Credits

All photographs by Sam Bilton unless otherwise stated below:

page 15: '*Colchicum autumnale L., Colchicaceae.* Autumn crocus, meadow saffron, naked ladies.' Photographed in the Medicinal Garden of the Royal College of Physicians, London. © Wellcome Collection / Dr Henry Oakeley. Attribution 4.0 International (CC BY 4.0).

page 19: 'Saffron crocus (*Crocus sativus L.*): flowering stem with separate floral segments and bulb and a description of the plant and its uses. Coloured line engraving by C.H. Hemerich, *c.* 1759, after T. Sheldrake.' © Wellcome Collection.

page 57: '*Tacuinum Sanitatis.* Peasant picking saffron.' © Alamy.

page 64: '*Carthamus tinctorius L. Asteraceae.* Safe Flower, False Saffron by Dr Henry Oakley.' © Wellcome Collection / Dr Henry Oakeley. Attribution 4.0 International (CC BY 4.0).

Notes

Introduction
1. Graves (1984), pp. 21-4.
2. Harrison (1994), pp. 348-56; Skinner (1911), pp. 95-6.
3. Liger (1706), pp. 262-3.
4. Ovid (1812), 152.
5. Bernhardt (2008), pp. 56-8.
6. Harrison (1994), pp. 348-56.
7. Dalby, A. and Dalby, R. (2017), p. 28.
8. Leyel (1938), p. 330.
9. Francis (2020), pp. 2-9.
10. Francis (2020), pp. 2-9. In some climates the flowers appear before the leaves,
11. Francis (2020), p. 5.
12. Culpeper (2007), p. 246.
13. *Rick Stein's Cornwall*, S01E13, BBC 2, 20 January 2021.

Chapter One
1. In my youth this game was known as Chinese Whispers, but I have chosen to use the more acceptable modern name here. The principle of the game, however, is the same.
2. Harley MS 913, British Library. 'The Land of Cockayne' was a poem about an imaginary world believed to have been written in the early fourteenth century by a Franciscan monk. This fantasy contains, among other things, a house made of pie and cake, and a spice tree:

   > In its garden is a tree,
   > A very pleasant sight to see:
   > Ginger and galingale the roots,
   > And zedoary all the shoots,
   > The flowers are mace, quite excellent,
   > Cinnamon gives the bark its scent,
   > Cloves are the fruit, whose taste is rare.
   > There's no lack of cubebs there.

3. Morant (1748), p. 543; 'Medieval Walden', Visit Saffron Walden <https://www.visitsaffronwalden.gov.uk/wp-content/uploads/2021/03/TIC_MW_8ppDL_V6_WEB.pdf>
4. Cromarty (1967), p. 109.
5. Stacy (1973) pp. 1-2; Evans & Starte (2009).
6. 'William Harrison', The Hundred Parishes Society <http://www.hundredparishes.org.uk/people/detail/william-harrison>
7. Harrison (1994), p. 355.
8. Ibid., p. 348.
9. Crone (2020).
10. Hakluyt (1589), pp. 299-300.
11. Mandeville (1900), quotes from p. 5 and p. 86. Tortouse was the name for the port city of Tartus in modern day Syria.

12 Webb (2002), p.20, 78; Sumption (2003), p. 239-243; Essex Record Office, Will of John Bataill, Reference D/DBa T2/11.
13 Webb (2002), pp.78-113; Sumption (2003), pp. 244-45.
14 Webb (2002), pp.114-122; 'Saffron from San Gimignano: the precious flowers that built the towers', UNESCO, <https://visitworldheritage.com/en/eu/saffron-from-san-gimignano-the-precious-flowers-that-built-the-towers/521a62e8-89c1-4c01-b881-9d098588c4de> ; Riley (2007), pp.463-6.
15 Toussaint-Samat (2008), pp.518-23; Sevilla (2019), pp.48-49; 'The English Version of the Book V (*Codex Calixtinus*)', *Codex Calixtinus* <https://codexcalixtinus.es/the-english-version-of-the-book-v-codex-calixtinus/>; Webb (2002), p.23 adds: 'The Compostela pilgrimage may well have benefited from the increasing European publicity given to the wars of reconquest which were intermittently waged by the Christian kings of Spain against the occupying Muslims. Those who joined in the Spanish struggle were awarded the spiritual privileges of "crusaders"'.
16 Webb (2002) pp.143-4; Sumption (2003), pp. 260-6. Furnival (1867), p.60.
17 Wey (1857), p. 5.
18 Stacy (1973), p. 1.
19 Sowan (2018), pp. 50-1. Mills (1991), pp. xi, xii, 98. To further muddy the waters there is a village in Cambridgeshire (arguably a more logical place for the Romans to have grown saffron) called Croydon. This village is listed as Crauuedene in the Domesday Book which means 'valley frequented by crows'.
20 Theophrastus (1926), p. 337.
21 Pliny (1951), p. 185-189; Bird (2012), pp. 87-90. A samian vessel found at the upper end of the Walbrook valley contained a stamp which reads 'Lucius Iulus Senex's saffron salve (crocodes) for granulation of the eye lids' – evidently a very unpleasant eye disease in the Roman era which could lead to blindness. However, tests on colluyrium stamps from a late 2nd-early 3rd century grave near Lyon found no evidence of saffron in the ones stamped crocodes so perhaps 'saffron' only applies to the colour rather than the spice.
22 Edwards (1993), p. 11.
23 Cunliffe (1981), p. 97.
24 Cunliffe (1981), pp. 98-9.
25 Jashemski (1970-71), pp. 97-115. The line in Virgil's poem 'The crocus by Cilician field' has been interpreted as referring to the saffron crocus.
26 Cunliffe (1981), pp. 104-7.
27 Cunliffe (1981), p.106; Bird (2012), pp. 87-90; Pliny (1951), p.183.
28 Schoff (1912), pp.31, 110-111; Miller (1969), pp. 201-207.
29 Harden (1962), pp.147, 162.
30 Harden (1962), pp. 170-1.
31 Edmonds (1868), p. 4
32 Thirsk (1997) p.7.
33 Thirsk (1997) pp. 16-8.
34 Wilson (1991), p. 19.
35 Bradley (1726), pp. 49-50. Saffron was definitely being grown in England long before Sir Walter Raleigh's time.

Chapter Two
1 Bradley, R. 22 September 1727, Sloane MS 4049, pp. 31-32.

Notes

2 A stamp duty on all newspapers and pamphlets had been introduced in 1712. It had been argued that the duty would dissuade the publication of licentious documents. Queen Anne was concerned about the number of libellous and scandalous publications being published and demanded parliament find a remedy. However, the stamp duty was actually used to fund a national lottery although the income derived from the tax was very small. See Downie (1979), Chapter 7.
3 'Sir Hans Sloane', The British Museum <https://www.britishmuseum.org/about-us/british-museum-story/sir-hans-sloane>
4 Martyn (1730), p. 1; Egerton (2005).
5 Bradley, R. 27 September 1727, Sloane MS 4049, pp. 38-9.
6 Bradley, R. 23 June 1722, Sloane MS 4046, pp. 251-2.
7 Bradley, R. 6 November 1726, Sloane MS 4048, pp. 212-3. It is difficult to decipher the letter following the number eight in the letter, but it looks like an 's' for shilling.
8 Egerton (1970), p. 61.
9 Bradley (1720), p. 125.
10 This contemporary version of John Gardener's *The Feate of Gardeninge* was translated by Ellice de Valles. <'https://ellicesblog.wordpress.com/2017/10/30/a-feate-on-gardening/>
11 Howard (1678), pp. 945-9; Douglass (1727), p. 566-74.
12 Cromaty (1966), p. 4; Rosen, Keeling, and Meekings (1978), pp. 80-105.
13 Camden (1722), p. 425; Neale (1996), 234; Brown (1969), p.39-40; Evelyn (1901), entry for 31 August 1654, p. 302.
14 ERO D/ACR5/107/2; ERO D/ACR4/183/4; ERO D/DGh T29; ERO D/Dtu 164; Neale (1996), p. 235
15 Thirsk (1997), p. 66; Braybrooke (1836), pp. 146-7; ERO Q/SR 103/18,19 Indictments, 11 November 1587 (also Q/SR 103/15).
16 Brightwen Rowntree (1951), pp. 19-23; Braybrooke (1836), p. 89. Lord Brayrooke explains that Charles II had planned to buy Audley End from Lord Suffolk and is mentioned by Samuel Pepys in his diary, 'The King and Duke are to go to Audley End tomorrow, in order to buy it of my Lord Suffolk'. Braybooke places this date as 1665/6 following an outbreak of the plague. The royal family had taken refuge in Oxford but found London still in chaos on their return prompting them to visit Audley End.
17 Harrison (1994), pp. 348-56; Neale (1996), pp. 237-8.
18 Brightwen Rowntree (1951), p. 24; Brown (1969), p. 39; Percival (1989), pp. 79-80.
19 Rosen, Keeling, and Meekings, 'Parishes: Hinxton' (1978), pp. 220-30; Camden (1695), p. 402; Barker, Morris and Maynard (1913).
20 Schama (2001), p. 53; Jones and Stallybrass (2000), pp. 63-8.
21 Howell (1650), p. 4; Moryson (1617), p. 180; Camden (1695), pp. 1045-6; Jones and Stallybrass (2000), pp. 63-8.
22 Frances Howard (1590-1632) was the grand-daughter of Thomas Audley, 1st Baron Audley of Walden. She had been married to Robert Devereux in her teens and sought an annulment on the grounds that their union had never been consummated due to his impotence. She is buried at the Church of St Mary the Virgin in Saffron Walden.
23 Schama (2001), p. 52-4. Much has been written on this scandal from contemporary accounts like *The Poysoning of Sir Thomas Overbury* to a fictionalised version of the story by Lucy Jago called *A Net for Small Fishes* (2021).
24 Jones and Stallybrass (2000), p. 63-8; Bellany (1995, pp.179-210) explains that the prosecution claimed the astrologer, physician and necromancer, Simon Forman (1552-1611), had instructed Anne and Frances in the dark art of love-magic with a view to

making the Earl of Essex impotent.
25 Howell (1650), p. 4. In his letter to his father he notes that the Earl and Countess of Somerset were fortunate to escape the noose receiving life sentences for their roles in the murder. Frances particularly feared the Lord Chief Justice 'would have made white Broth of them'. Fortunately, 'Prerogative kept them from the Pot.' King James was very fond of Carr and the couple were released a few years after their incarceration. It certainly helps to have friends in high places.
26 D'Ewes (1845), p. 79.
27 Speed (1611), p. 37.
28 Brome (1700), pp. 57-58.
29 Rosen, Keeling, and Meekings (1978), pp. 256-63; Barker, Morris & Maynard (1913), no page.
30 Rosen, Keeling, and Meekings, (1978), pp. 230-246.
31 Rosen, Keeling, and Meekings (1978), pp. 230-46; CCA KP96/1/1; Palmer (1912), p. 161.
32 Bradley (1727), pp. 158-9; Rosen, Keeling, and Meekings (1978), pp. 80-105.
33 Lysons (1808), p. 36.
34 Heard (1984), p. 98. Heard claims that Cornwall consumed twenty per cent of all the saffron produced in England. Unfortunately, she does not provide a source or a timeframe for this statement so it has not been verified.
35 Worgan (1811), p. 3.
36 Carew (1811), p. 12-5
37 Hanson and Hanson (1997), p. 10, 16; Worgan (1811) pp. 8-9. The third type is loam of various 'texture, colours and degrees of fertility', including clay.
38 Heard (1984), p. 98
39 Hawkey (1871), p. 38.
40 A jointure arrangement occurs when an estate has been settled on a wife for the period during which she survives her husband, in lien of a dower.
41 Thrush and Ferris (2010), 'Treffry, John (1595–1658), of Place, Fowey, Cornw.'; Thrush and Ferris (2010), 'Trefusis, John (*c.* 1586–1647), of Trefusis, Mylor, Cornw.'; Keast (1950), pp. 58-63.
42 KKA TF/567; KKA TF/568. It is not clear whether this saffron meadow is same one William Major leased but my assumption, given the term, is that it is. The period of 99 years was common for land. After this time the land would revert back to the lessor. Sometimes a term of lives was also included (e.g. three) although this is not stated on these particular leases.
43 Thompson (1991), p. 4-12; KKA EN/472.
44 KKA CF/1/210
45 Harrison (1994), p. 348; GHH D760/9; GHH D1957/T1; BCA D-CN/9/10/1/3; WSA Add Mss 37193
46 BA L5/1091. The English Heritage property Wrest Park now sits on the site of these manorial lands; SA HB8/5/327; SA HB8/5/101; Page (1906) pp. 317-328; Blomefield (1808), pp. 267-82; Francis (2020) pp. 22-3. Francis's book contains a wealth of information on the botany of the *Crocus sativus* as well as the spice's history in Norfolk; *Pigot's Directory of Norfolk*, 1839, p. 453; Camden (1695), p. 391-2.
47 Hilda Leyel (1938, p. 329) writes: 'Saffron Hill in Holborn also takes its name from the Saffron plant; but probably because it was for so long the Italian quarter, and Italians colour their risotto with this yellow powder.'

Notes

Chapter Three

1   Wale (1883), pp. 5-6.
2   CCA 71/T101; Wale (1883), pp. 76-8.
3   Douglass (1728), p, 567; Wale (1883), pp. 132-4.
4   Wale (1883), p. 133.
5   Barker, Morris and Maynard (1913).
6   Bradley (1726), pp. 48-9; Howard (1678), pp. 945-6; Douglass (1728), p. 567; Wale (1883), p. 135.
7   Howard (1677), p. 948; Wale (1883), p. 135; Neale (1996), p. 237; Harrison, 1994, p. 348. It appears that progressively fewer saffron corms were planted per acre between the sixteenth and eighteenth centuries. In Harrison's day twenty quarters of corms were planted per acre 'placed in ranks two inches one from another'. By Howard's time the corms were spaced a little further apart. Around a century later, Clarke announced that only six quarters of heads were required per acre (he expected to pay anywhere between eight and fourteen shillings per quarter for the bulbs). This seems rather low given Howard's and Harrison's estimates. Like Harrison, Clarke says the corms should be planted two inches (about 5 cm) apart, although there is a greater distance between the rows. I do wonder whether the six quarters listed in the 1883 book have been incorrectly transcribed.
8   Ellis (1747), p. 116. Although this work is attributed to Ellis it is a revision of an earlier work by Samuel Trowell (*A New Treatise of Husbandry, Gardening, and other Curious Matters relating to Country Affairs*, 1739). This particular information comes from 'A Supplement on the Chapter on Saffron', so it is assumed to have been written by Ellis rather than Trowell,
9   Douglass (1728), p. 569; Francis and Ramandi (2001), p. 57; Wale (1883), p. 133; Braybrook (1836), p. 145.
10 Wale, 1883, p. 133.
11 Howard (1677), pp. 945-9; Ellis (1747) p. 116; Harrison (1994), pp. 350-1; Douglass (1728), p. 568; Wale (1883), p. 132; ERO Q/SR 76/22.
12 Howard (1677), pp. 945-6; Douglass (1728), p. 567; Bradley (1726), p. 108; Wale (1883), pp. 133-4.
13 Bradley (1726), p. 111; Wale (1883), p. 134.
14 Bradley (1726), p. 109-10.
15 Bradley (1726), p. 109-10.
16 Douglass (1728), pp. 570-2; Bradley (1727), pp. 159-161.
17 Bradley (1726), pp. 109-10.
18 Bradley (1727), p159; Wale (1883), p. 134.
19 Douglass (1728), p. 572, Bradley (1727), p. 161.
20 McKenny Hughes (1917), p. 103; Harrison (1994), p. 352. Harrison also uses the term 'ross' to describe the outer layer of skin on a corm.
21 Douglass (1728), p. 573; Harrison, 1994, p. 352.
22 Douglass (1728) p. 573; Wale (1883), p. 134. The rent for an acre of saffron ground was a little lower in Clarke's time at 13s 6d per year.
23 Pliny (1951),p. 185.
24 Beckmann (1846), pp. 179-180.
25 Turner (1687), p. 194. Marigold is frequently found in medicinal recipes sometimes alongside true saffron. Francis (2020, p. 12) notes that marigold petals have been used to

Notes

gently colour dairy products in the past but lacks saffron's aroma or vibrancy.
26 Harrison, (1994), p. 352-353; Beckman, (1846), p. 180; Bradley (1727), p. 103; Wale (1883), p. 134; Carew (1607), p. 38
27 Pliny (1951), p. 185; Harrison (1994), p. 353-354; Beckman (1846), p. 180.
28 Milmo (2022); David (1977), p. 147.
29 Francis and Ramandi (2021), pp. 18-9.
30 David (1977), p. 147.
31 Webb (2015).
32 Francis & Ramandi (2021), pp. 17-20.

Chapter Four

1 Pliny (1951), p. 261. There was a theory that uterus could 'wander' around the body and attach itself to different organs thereby causing a number of female complaints including hysteria. In 1603, English Physician and Chemist Edward Jorden published an entire pamphlet on the subject called *The Suffocation of the Mother* (the 'mother' was another name for the womb). Jorden argued that the fits suffered by women accused of witchcraft were a result of a medical condition rather than an affiliation with the devil.
2 Dioscorides (2000), p. 30.
3 Jouanna (2012), p. 338.
4 Elmer (2004), pp. 2-7.
5 Elmer (2004), pp. 8-9; Culpeper (2007), pp. 399, 374. Johannitius (809-873), a Nestorian Christian from southern Iraq, described the external factors (i.e. those things that are not natural to the human body) that affect the body as the six non naturals.
6 Grant (2000), p. 15.
7 Bradwell (1636), p. 17-28.
8 Martin (1994), p. 37.
9 Kleineke (2015), pp. 511-24. To put the Duchess's debt into context, during the same period a craftsman or labourer could expect to earn between 3d and 8d a day.
10 Francis & Ramandi (2021), p. 1-4, 67-68 Herdodt was of the opinion that too much saffron could also cause pallor, food aversions and dim vision.
11 Nagy (1988), pp. 44-7.
12 Tallamy (1735) f.17.
13 Blencowe (1925), pp. 41-60.
14 Leong (2008), p. 161.
15 Anselment (2001), pp. 187-8. Lady Norton was Elizabeth Freke's younger sister, Frances and hungary water is a distillate of rosemary flowers and wine.
16 Leong (2008), pp. 157-8.
17 Leong (2008), pp. 160-2.
18 Wilson (2006), p. 180.
19 Pollock (1993), pp. 132-3.
20 Wilson (2006), pp. 189-191.
21 Leong (2008), p. 154.
22 Duffy (1675), title page.
23 Wilson (2006), p. 208-210; Gosse (1886), pp. 167-8; p. 175.
24 Le Fèvre (1664), p. 6; pp. 37-8. There are various spellings of the alchemist's name including Nicasius le Febure, Nicolas le Febure or Nicasius le Fevre.
25 Digby (1668), p. 115, pp. 57-9, p. 244. 'An Excellent Remedy to procure Conception'

Notes

on pp. 239-40 involved combining a variety of seeds, syrups, preserved roots, dates, pistachios and spices (including saffron) to make an electuary. It concluded with the following advice: 'Take of this Electuary the quantity of a good Nutmeg in a little Glass-full of White-wine, in the morning fasting, and at four of the clock in the afternoon, and as much at night going to bed; but be sure not to do any violent exercise.'

26 Digby (1668), pp. 223-5.
27 Kleineke (2015), pp. 519-520; Pepys (1986), p. 506.
28 Grey (1653), pp. 132-4.
29 Pliny (1963), p. 299; Wilson (2006), p. 181; Francatelli (1846), p. 50.
30 Pollock (1993), p. 136.
31 Anselment (2001), p. 330.
32 Anselment (2001), p. 329-330.
33 Anon, 'London, April 15', *Newcastle Courant,* Wednesday, 16 April 1712, p. 3. Elizabeth Freke mentions Gott's death in her diary but appears to believe that he hung himself. According to Anselment the *Norwich Gazette* reported that Gott had taken laudanum and then 'tyed the Tail of his Shirt about his Neck' (see Anselment, 2001, footnote 224 on page 284).
34 Pollock (1993), p. 110.
35 Wilson (2006), pp. 234-241; Raffald (1794), p. 318; p. 336.

Chapter Five

1 Housman (1930), p. 212. Captain the Honorable Colwyn Erasmus Arnold Philipps, Royal Horse Guards, Flanders, November 13, 1914.
2 Duffett (2011), pp. 453-73. Bully beef is a variety of salt cured or 'corned' minced beef mixed with gelatin. Hard tack biscuits were hard, dry biscuits made from wheat flour, water and salt.
3 Housman (1930), p. 79. From a diary letter describing the Battle of Arras. Rev. Creighton was eventually killed by an aeroplane bomb in France on 15 April 1918 at the age of 35.
4 Housman (1930), p. 212. Captain the Honorable Colwyn Erasmus Arnold Philipps, Royal Horse Guards, Flanders, November 13, 1914 Captain Philipps was killed in action in Flanders, on 13 May, 1915 at the age of 27. Although the available food was dull it was initially plentiful. However, there were shortages towards the end of the war.
5 KKA DCNEW/243/47. A note on the Kresen Kernow archives date base suggests that the letter was written by Lance-Corporal Fred H Passmore reported dead in the *Newquay Express,* 17 May 1918. He is recorded as husband of Mrs Passmore who managed the Domestic Bazaar, and son of late Baptist minister, Reverend FT Passmore. He was killed in France on 1 May 1918 and had been in France for two years. Prior to this he worked for Mr Robert E. Pearce, chemist.
6 'Parcels For the Boys', *Newquay Express,* 14 December 1917, p. 8.
7 KKA DCNEWQ/243/79 Kresen Kernow archives. Ennor was reported in the *Newquay Express,* 13 October 1916, as being as being 'well known in soccer circles as the Cornwall County half-back'. He was the son of John Ennor surveyor to the Newquay Urban Council. His brother Reginald died on the front line in 1916, aged just 24.
8 Duffett (2011), pp. 453-73.
9 KKA DCNEW/243/43
10 Courtney (1890), p. 6; Clinnick (1926), p. 31.
11 Courtney (1890) p. 1; Woods (2013), pp. 76-7.

Notes

12 Martin (1930), pp.18-9.
13 Quiller Couch (1963), p. 124.
14 Edwards (1965), pp. 35-80. Despite his assertion that 'I *bear* the rich and love the poor; therefore I spend *almost all* my time with them,' (September 20, 1764) Wesley was actually dismissive of the agricultural classes. He believed agricultural labourers to be 'grossly stupid', and considered them to be on the same level 'as a turk or a heathen' in terms of their religious understanding.
15 'John Wesley and Methodism', Cornwall Guide <https://www.cornwalls.co.uk/history/people/john_wesley.htm> (accessed 30 December 2021).
16 Edwards (1965), p. 67
17 Thompson (2005), pp. 74-5. John Wesley himself was against tea drinking and wrote a pamphlet in 1748 warning of the ill effects of this beverage.
18 Merrick (2010), p. 47; Courtney (1890), p.26.
19 Markham (1998), p. 115.
20 Dawson (1587) No page given.
21 Herrick, Robert. 'To Dianeme. A Ceremony In Gloucester', luminarium.org <http://www.luminarium.org/sevenlit/herrick/simnel.htm> (accessed 30/12/21)
22 Chambers (1864), p. 336.
23 Boorde (1542), p. 261.
24 Boorde (1542) p.80; Wilson (1985), pp. 46-52.
25 Brillat-Savarin (1994), p. 13.
26 Woolgar (2018), pp. 1-20.
27 Woolgar (2018), pp. 1-20.
28 Wilson (1991), pp. 17-25. *Kitāb al-Tabīkh* was translated by A. J. Arberry in 1939 and for a long time was the 'only medieval Arabic cookery book known to the English speaking world'. It was reissued in 2001 by Prospect Books as 'A Baghdad Cookery Book' in *Medieval Arab Cookery*.
29 Woolgar (2018), p. 3.
30 Craig, W.J., (ed.) *The Winter's Tale*, Act Act IV. Scene II. *The Complete Works of William Shakespeare*, London: Oxford University Press: 1914.
31 Cosman (1995), p.71. Aromatic herbs like parsley were also used to create green breads and sanders (produced from the red sandalwood tree) was added to create pink or red tinged breads. Woolgar (2018), pp. 15-6.
32 Woolgar (2018), pp. 15-6; Woolgar (1992), p. 14. For details of the Countess of Norfolk's household accounts, see Ridgard (1985), pp. 86-128. Bond (2017), p. 72.
33 Woolgar (1992), pp. 7-8. While the wardrobe accounts dealt with the luxuries the diet accounts kept a record of the daily incomings and outgoings of the household. This included the pantry, buttery, kitchen and marshalsea. The expenses were entered for each day – *per dietas* – hence diet or week by week.
34 Ridgard (1984), pp. 103-4.
35 Ridout (2011), pp. 1-6. Officers for King Henry III's household had visited the fair in 1250 to buy cloth. Kings Hall bought provisions from the fair including saffron, almonds and mustard seeds.
36 KKA AR/37/41/1.
37 Cokayne, G. E. *The Complete Peerage of England, Scotland, Ireland, Great Britain and the United Kingdom, Extant, Extinct, or Dormant*, London: St Catherine's Press. (1910) pp. 374-5. This assault was far from an isolated incident. Cokayne adds 'In August 1397 he was accused by the Abbot of Hartland of breaking into the latter's houses, assaulting

Notes

him and chasing him into his chamber, and ill-treating his servants.' KKA AR/37/44.
38 Woolgar (2018), pp. 1-20.
39 Austin (1888), p. 23. Dairy and almond milk were excellent at taking on colour.
40 Woolgar (2018), p. 15.
41 Pegge (2008), p. 81. Serpell was a name for wild thyme. The addition of saffron makes this sauce the most vivid green.
42 Austin (1888), p. 35. Curiously, despite the title of the recipe there is no ginger in it. Woolgar (2018, p. 8) notes that Saracen dishes were often coloured red with Sandalwood.
43 Austin (1888), p. 93. A little further on in the manuscript a similar recipe called 'Risshewes de Frut' instructs the cook to make a paste (pastry) including saffron.
44 Wilson (1991), p. 19-20; Woolgar (2018), p. 13. *Le Ménagier de Paris* was an instruction manual written by a wealthy, older gentleman for his very young wife who was inexperienced in household matters.
45 Austin (1888). See p. 47 'Tartes de Chare' and p. 40 'Cokyntryce' respectively.
46 Austin (1888), p. 81.
47 Cosman (1995), p. 63.
48 Pegge (2008), p. 94. Note that the initial instruction is to make a green batter with parsley although saffron, which would produce a golden colour, is suggested as a substitute.
49 Cosman (1995), pp. 63-4; Power (1928), p. 310.
50 Anon (1740), p. 355.
51 Byron (1915), p. 117.
52 Woolley (1670), p. 74.
53 Marshall (1894), advertising appendix p. 23. The Food Standards Agency website explains that food colours were being used to disguise poor quality food and to mislead the consumer into believing they were buying something else. As a result, food poisoning was common and in 1851, approximately 200 people were poisoned in Britain, 17 of them fatally, as a result of eating coloured lozenges. This would eventually lead to the introduction of the Adulteration of Food and Drink Act of 1860. <https://www.safefood.net/food-colours/history>

Chapter Six

1 Harrison (1994), pp. 355-6.
2 Clarke (1887), p. 14. Clarke says the word 'croaker' used to describe a grumpy person could well be derived from 'croker'.
3 Norden (1840), p. 8.
4 Thirsk (1997), p. 252.
5 Clarke (1887), pp. 9-16.; Fitch (1895); 'Died', *Cambridge Chronicle and Journal*, 8 June 1827.
6 Clarke (1887), pp. 9-16. There was farmer called John Knott living Moor Lane in Duxford in the 1841 census who was born around 1795, who would be the right age to be the croker's grandson. Interestingly, his eldest son, also called John, was born in 1828, a year after the last saffron grower died. This John Knott died in 1875.
7 Harvey (1678), p.120. Harvey also notes that India-Saffron (which he calls Crocus Orient) was just 3s 6d per pound. Whether this was true saffron though is anyone's guess.
8 Braybrooke (1836), p. 146; Thirsk (1997), pp. 147-8.
9 Alexander (1770), p. iii, pp. 88-92. Alexander embarked on his saffron experiment as he

Notes

had heard of a 'lunatic who swallowed a very large quantity of it without being hurt'. This led him to the conclusion that saffron was pretty ineffective as a medicine. After his own trials though he did concede that his excrement was strongly tinged with saffron but that was about the only discernible effect he could detect.

10 Clarke (1887), p. 13
11 Beeton (1861), p. 1055.
12 Leyel (1938), p. 228. Both Cato and Pliny valued coleworts (cabbages and the like belonging to the brassica family) for their medicinal qualities. In *Acetaria: A Discourse of Sallets* (1699) John Evelyn also praised the cabbage for its effectiveness against intoxication. A 'lohoch' was a type of medicine that, as Leyel explains on p. 15, is 'thicker in consistency than a syrup but not as thick as an electuary'.
13 Francis & Ramandi (2021), p. 25-26; Thirsk (1997), p. 236; Panda (2018), pp. 18-22.
14 Du Maurier (2016), Chapter 8, 'Tinners'; Heard (1984), p. 100.
15 Shepro (2021), p. 308.
16 Thirsk (1997), p. 140.
17 Francis, (2020), Preface.
18 Thirsk (1997), p. 225.
19 The numbers of brown hares in the UK declined drastically during the twentieth century although there are some indications that their numbers may slowly be increasing. (See https://www.gwct.org.uk/research/species/mammals/brown-hare/trends-in-brown-hare-numbers/)
20 Dandan et al (2020).
21 Souret and Weathers (2000), pp. 25-35.
22 Harrison (1994), p. 348
23 Shepro (2021), p. 308.
24 Blith (1649), p. 248.

Bibliography

General

Alexander, William. *Experimental Essays on the Following Subjects*, London: Dilly, 1770.

Allen, Katherine. 'Hobby and Craft: Distilling Household Medicine in Eighteenth-Century England', *Early Modern Women,* 2016 11(1): 90-114.

Anselment, Raymond A. *The Remembrances of Elizabeth Freke, 1671-1714,* Cambridge: Cambridge University Press, 2001.

Barker, Mabel; Morris, George and Maynard, Guy. *Regional Survey of Saffron Walden*, Saffron Walden Museum Archives, 1913.

Beckmann, Johann. *History of Inventions Discoveries and Origins,* tr. William Johnson, London: Bohn, 1846.

Bellany, Alistair. 'Mistress Turner's Deadly Sins: Sartorial Transgression, Court Scandal, and Politics in Early Stuart England', in *The Huntington Library Quarterly*, 58 (2), 1995.

Bernhardt, P. *Gods and Goddesses in the Garden,* New Brunswick: Rutgers University Press, 2008.

Bird, David. 'Croydon, Crocus and Collyrium', *London Archaeologist,* Spring 2012, 13 (4): 87-90.

Blomefield, Francis. *An Essay Towards A Topographical History of the County of Norfolk, Volume 9,* London: W. Miller, 1808

Bond, James. 'Production and Consumption of Food and Drink in the Medieval Monastery', in *Monastic Archaeology*, edited by Graham Keevill, Mick Aston, Teresa Hall, Oxford: Oxbow Books, 2017.

Boorde, Andrew. *The fyrst boke of the introduction of knowledge made by Andrew Borde, of physycke doctor. A compendyous regyment; or, A dyetary of helth made in Mountpyllier (1542),* edited by F. J. Furnivall, London: Early English Text Society, 1870.

Bradley, Richard. *The Country Gentleman and Farmer's Monthly Director,* London: James Woodman and David Lyon, 1726.

Bradley, Richard. *The Country Housewife and Lady's Director,* Dublin: J. Watts, 1727.

Bradley, Richard. *New Improvements of Planting and Gardening, both Philosophical and Practical*, London: W. Mears, 1720.

Bradwell, Stephen. *Physick for the Sicknesse, Commonly called the Plague,* London: Benjamin Fisher, 1636.

Braybrooke, Richard Griffin. *The History of Audley End. To Which are Appended Notices of the Town and Parish of Saffron Walden in the County of Essex*, London: S. Bentley, 1836.

Brightwen Rowntree, Charles. *Saffron Walden: Then and Now*, Saffron Walden: C. Brightwen Rowntree, 1951.

Brome, James. *Travels over England, Scotland and Wales giving a true and exact description of the chiefest cities, towns, and corporations*, London: Abel Roper, 1700.

Brown, A. F. J. *Essex at work 1700-1815,* Chelmsford: Essex County Council, 1969.

Camden, William. *Camden's Britannia, newly translated into English, with large additions and improvements*, second edn, London: Edmund Gibson, 1722.

Carew, Richard. *Carew's Survey of Cornwall,* London: T. Bensley, 1811.

Carew, R. A. *World of Wonders: or an Introduction to a Treatise touching the Conformitie of Ancient and Moderne Wonders,* London: John Norton, 1607.

Chambers, Robert. *The Book of Days: A Miscellany of Popular Antiquities*, Vol 1, London: W. & R. Chambers, 1864.

BIBLIOGRAPHY

Clarke, Joseph. 'Notes on the Saffron Plant (*Crocus sativus, L.*) and in Connection with the Name of the Town Saffron Walden', *Essex Naturalist,* 1, 1887: 9-16.

Clinnick, Antony Allen. *The Cornish Year. Something to remember on each day of the year of noteworthy events in Cornish history, festivals, and folklore*, Truro: A. W. Jordan, 1926.

Cosman, Madeleine Pelner. *Fabulous Feasts*, New York: George Braziller, 1995.

Courtney, Margaret Ann. *Cornish Feasts and Folk-Lore*, Penzance: Beare and Son, 1890.

Cromaty, Dorothy. *The Fields of Saffron Walden in 1400*, Chelmsford: Essex County Council, 1966.

Cromarty, Dorothy. 'Chepyng Walden 1381-1420, A Study from the Court Rolls,' *Essex Journal*, 2 (2), 1967: 104-113.

Crone, G. R. 'Richard Hakluyt', *Encyclopedia Britannica*, 19 Nov. 2020 <https://www.britannica.com/biography/Richard-Hakluyt> [Accessed 16 September 2021].

Culpeper, Nicholas. *Culpeper's Complete Herbal,* London: Wordsworth Editions, 2007.

Cunliffe, Barry. 'Roman Gardens in Britain: A Review of the Evidence', in *Ancient Roman Gardens, Dumbarton Oaks Colloquium on the History of Landscape Architecture VII*, ed. by Elisabeth B. Macdougall and Wilhelmina F. Jashemski, Washington: Dumbarton Oaks, 1981.

Dalby, Andrew and Dalby, Rachel. *Gift of the Gods: A History of Food in Greece*, London: Reaktion Books, 2017.

Dandan Chen, Bingcong Xing, Haojun Yi, Yanjing Li, Bingsong Zheng, Ying Wang, Qingsong Shao, 'Effects of different drying methods on appearance, microstructure, bioactive compounds and aroma compounds of saffron (*Crocus sativus L.*)', *LWT: Food Science and Technology*, 120, February 2020.

Dewar, Mary. *Sir Thomas Smith: A Tudor Intellectual in Office,* London: Athlone Press, 1964.

Douglass, James. 'An Account of the Culture and Management of Saffron in England', *Philosophical Transactions*, Vol. 35 (1727–28): 566-574.

Downie, J. A. *Robert Harley and the Press*, Cambridge: Cambridge University Press, 1979.

Du Maurier, Daphne. *Vanishing Cornwall*, London: Virago, 2016.

Duffett, Rachel. 'Beyond the Ration: Sharing and Scrounging on the Western Front', *Twentieth Century British History,* 22 (4), December 2011: 453-473.

Durbach, Nadja. 'The parcel is political: the British government and the regulation of food parcels for prisoners of war, 1914–1918', *First World War Studies*, 2018, 9 (1): 93-110.

Edmonds, Richard. *Phoenician Tin Trade of Cornwall*, Plymouth: Isaiah W. N. Keys & Sons, 1868.

Edwards, Maldwyn. 'John Wesley', in *A History of the Methodist Church in Great Britain,* edited by Rupert Eric Davies, London: Epworth, 1965.

Egerton, Frank, 'Richard Bradley's Relationship with Sir Hans Sloane', *Notes & Records of the Royal Society of London*, 25, June 1970: 59-77

Egerton, Frank. 'Richard Bradley', *Oxford Dictionary of National Biography,* 2004.

Ellis, William. *The Farmer's Instructor; or, the husbandman and gardener's useful and necessary companion*, London: J. Hodges, 1747.

Elmer, Peter; and Grell, Ole Peter (eds.). *Health, Disease and Society in Europe 1500-1800: A Source Book,* Manchester: Manchester University Press, 2004.

Evans, M. and Starte, M. *The Saffron Crocus: A Brief History*, Saffron Walden: Saffron Town Council and Saffron Walden Museum, 2009.

Evelyn, John. *The Diary of John Evelyn, Volume I*, edited by William Bray, London: M. Walter Dunne, 1901.

D'Ewes, Simonds. T*he Autobiography and Correspondence of Sir Simonds d'Ewes,* edited by

Bibliography

James Orchard Halliwell-Phillipps, London: R. Bentley, 1845.

Digby, Sir Kenelm. *Choice and Experimented Receipts in Physick and Chirurgery,* translated by George Hartman, London, 1668.

Dioscorides. *De materia medica,* tr. Tess Anne Osbaldeston, Johannesburg: Ibidis Press, 2000.

Duffy, Anthony. *Elixir Salutis: The Choice Drink of Health,* London: W. G., 1675.

Le Fèvre, N. *A Discourse Upon Sr Walter Rawleigh's Great Cordial,* translated by Peter Melon, London: Printed by J.F. for Octavian Pulleyn, 1664.

Fitch, E. A. 'Mr Joseph Clarke, Obituary', *Essex Review,* 4, 1895: 205-210.

Francis, Sally. *Saffron: the Story of England's Red Gold,* Burnham Norton: Sally Francis, 2020.

Francis, Sally; and Ramandi, Marie Teresa (eds.), *Crocologia: A Detailed Study of Saffron, The King of Plants,* Leiden: Brill, 2021.

Furnival, Frederick (ed.). *The Stacions of Rome and the Pilgrims Sea-Voyage,* London: Early English Text Society, 1867.

Gentil, F. *Le Jardinier solitaire, the Solitary or Carthusian Gard'ner,* London: B. Tooke, 1706.

Gerard, John. *Gerard's Herbal: John Gerard's History of Plants,* edited by Marcus Woodward, Twickenham: Senate, 1998.

Gosse, Edmund. *Raleigh,* London: Longmans, Green & Co., 1886.

Grant, Mark. *Galen On Food & Diet,* London: Routledge, 2000.

Graves, Robert. *Greek Myths,* London: Penguin, 1984.

Grey, Elizabeth, Countess of Kent. *A Choice Manual of Rare and Select Secrets in Physick snd Chyrurgery Collected and Practised by the Right Honorable, the Countesse of Kent,* London: Printed by G.D, 1653.

Harvey, Gideon. *The Family Physician, and The House Apothecary,* London: Printed for M. R., 1678.

Hakluyt, Richard. *The Principal Navigations, Voyages, Traffiques and Discoveries of the English Nation, Volume V: Central & Southern Europe,* Edinburgh: E. & G. Goldsmid, 1887.

Hanson, John; and Hanson, Pat. 'To Clothe the Fields with Plenty: Farming in Cornwall at the end of the 18th century, viewed through the life and times of George Wilce of St Kew', Truro: Landfall Publications, 1997.

Harden, Donald. *Phoenicians,* New York: Praeger, 1962.

Harrison, William. *The Description of England: The Classic Contemporary Account of Tudor Social Life (1577),* London: Constable, 1994.

Hawkey, Charlotte. *Neota,* Taunton: C. Hawkey (privately printed), 1871.

Herm, Gerhard. *The Phoenicians: The Purple Empire of the Ancient World,* New York: Morrow, 1975.

Housman, Laurence (ed.). *War Letters of Fallen Englishmen,* New York: E.P. Dutton, 1930.

Howard, Charles. 'An Account of the Culture, or Planting and Ordering of Saffron', *Philosophical Transactions,* 138, 25 March 1678: 945-949.

Howell, James. *Epistolæ Ho-Elianæ Familiar Letters Domestic and Forren Divided into Sundry Sections, Partly Historicall, Politicall, Philosophicall, Vpon Emergent Occasions,* London: Humphrey Mosely, 1650.

Jashemski, Wilhelmina F. 'Tomb Gardens at Pompeii', *Classical Journal,* 66 (2), 1970-1971: 97-115.

Jones, Ann Rosalind, and Stallybrass, Peter. *Renaissance Clothing and the Materials of Memory,* Cambridge: Cambridge University Press, 2000.

Jouanna, J. *Greek Medicine from Hippocrates to Galen,* London: Brill, 2012.

Keast, John. *The Story of Fowey,* Exeter: James Townsend & Sons, 1950.

BIBLIOGRAPHY

Leong, Elaine. 'Making Medicines in the Early Modern Household', *Bulletin of the History of Medicine*, 2008, 82 (1): 145-168.

Kleineke, H. 'The Medicines of Katherine, Duchess of Norfolk, 1463–71', *Medical History*, 2015, 59 (4): 511-524.

Levy, Paul (ed.). *The Penguin Book of Food and Drink*, Penguin Books, 1997.

Leyel, Mrs C. F. *Herbal Delights; Tisanes, Syrups, Confections, Electuaries, Robs, Juleps, Vinegars, and Conserves*, Boston: Houghton Mifflin Co., 1938.

Liger, Louis. *The Compleat Florist; or, the universal culture of flowers, trees and shrubs, proper to imbellish gardens*, London: Tooke, 1706.

Lysons, Daniel. *Magna Britannia: Cambridgeshire, Volume II, Part I*, London: T. Cadell and W. Davies, 1808.

Mandeville, John. *The Travels of Sir John Mandeville*, London: Macmillan and Co, 1900.

Marshall, Agnes B. *Fancy Ices*, London: Marshall's School of Cookery, 1894.

Martin, R (ed.). 'The Autobiography of Grace, Lady Mildmay', *Renaissance and Reformation / Renaissance et Réforme*, 18, (1), 1994: 33–81.

Martyn, John, 'To the learned Mr. Batius', *Grub Street Journal*, 11, 19 March 1730.

McKenny Hughes, T. 'Dr Dale's Visits to Cambridge, 1722–1738', *Proceedings of the Cambridge Antiquarian Society*, 20, 1917.

Miller, James Innes. *The Spice Trade of the Roman Empire, 29 BC to AD 641*, Oxford: OUP, 1969.

Mills, Anthony David. *A Dictionary of English Place Names*, Oxford: Oxford University Press, 1991.

Milmo, Cahal. 'Saffron: How the lustre of Iran's 'red gold' is threatened by smuggling and counterfeit-ing as sanctions bite', *i-newspaper*, 22 January 2022 <https://inews.co.uk/news/long-reads/saffron-iran-red-gold-threatened-smuggling-counterfeiting-sanctions-1411979>

Morant, Philip. *The History and Antiquities of the County of Essex, Vol. II*, London: T. Osborne, 1748.

Moryson, Fynes. *An Itinerary Written by Fynes Moryson*, London: John Beale, 1617.

Nagy, Doreen. *Popular Medicine in Seventeenth-Century England*, Ohio: Bowling Green State University Popular Press, 1988.

Neale, Kenneth. 'Saffron Walden: 'Crocuses and Crokers'', in *Essex 'Full of Profitable Things'*, Oxford: Leopard's Head Press, 1996.

Norden, John, *Speculi Britanniae Pars: an Historical and Chronographical Description of the County of Essex*, edited by Sir Henry Ellis, London: Camden Society, 1840.

Ovid, *Metamorphoses*, translated by Dr Garth and others, London: Stanhope Press, 1812.

Page, William (ed.). *The Victoria History of the Counties of England: Norfolk: Volume II*, London: Constable, 1906.

Palmer, W. M. 'College Dons, Country Clergy, University Coachmen', *Proceedings of the Cambridge Antiquarian Society*, 16, 1912.

Panda, Himadri. Dr. *Herbal and Aromatic Plants: Saffron – Cultivation, Processing, Utilizations and Applications*, New Delhi: Discovery Publishing House, 2018.

Pelling, Margaret. 'Medicine: Trade or Profession?', in *Health, Disease and Society in Europe 1500–1800: A Source Book*, edited by Peter Elmer and Ole Peter Grell, Manchester: Manchester University Press, 2004.

Pepys, Samuel. *The Shorter Pepys*, selected and edited by Robert Latham, London: Guild, 1986.

Percival, John. *The English Travels of Sir John Percival and William Byrd II: the Percival Diary of 1701*, edited by Mark R. Wenger, Columbia: University of Missouri Press, 1989.

Bibliography

Pliny the Elder. *Natural History, Volume VI*, translated by W. H. S. Jones, London: William Heinemann, 1951.

Pliny the Elder. *Natural History, Volume VIII*, translated by W. H. S. Jones, London: William Heinemann, 1963.

Pollock, Linda. *With Faith and Physic: The Life of a Tudor Gentlewoman, Lady Grace Mildmay 1552–1620*, London: Collins & Brown, 1993.

Primrose, James. 'The place of women in learned medicine: James Primrose's Popular Erruors (1651)', in *Health, Disease and Society in Europe 1500-1800: A Source Book*, edited by Peter Elmer and Ole Peter Grell, Manchester: Manchester University Press, 2004.

Quiller Couch, Arthur. The Astonishing History of Troy Town, London: Dent, 1963.

Ridgard, J. M. *The Household Book of Dame Alice de Bryene of Acton Hall, Suffolk with Appendices*, translated by M. K. Dale and edited by Vincent B. Redstone, Bungay: Paradigm, 1984.

Ridgard, J. M. (ed.). *Medieval Framlingham*, Woodbridge, 1985.

Ridout, Honor. *Cambridge and Stourbridge Fair,* Cambridge: Blue Ocean Publishing, 2011.

Rosen, Adrienne B.; Keeling, Susan M. and Meekings, C. A. F. *A History of the County of Cambridge and the Isle of Ely*, Volume 6, edited by A. P. M. Wright, London: Victoria County History, 1978.

Schama, Simon. *A History of Britain: the British Wars 1603–1776*, London: BBC, 2001.

Schoff, W. H. *Periplus of the Erythraean Sea*, London: Longmans, Green & Co, 1912,

Shepro, R. W. 'The Geopolitics of Saffron and the Puzzles of Saffron Arithmetic', in *Herbs & Spices Proceedings of the Oxford Symposium on Food 2020*, Totnes: Prospect Books, 2021.

Skinner, C. M. *Myths and Legends of Flowers, Trees, Fruits, and Plants*, Philadelphia: J. B. Lippincott, 1911.

Souret, F. F. and Weathers, P. J. 'The Growth of Saffron (*Crocus sativus L*) in Aeroponics and Hydroponics', *Journal of Herbs, Spices and Medicinal Plants,* 7 (3), 2000: 25-35.

Sowan, Paul. 'Claimed Roman culture of the saffron crocus at Croydon', *Croydon Natural History and Scientific Society Bulletin*, 162/3, 2018.

Speed, John. *The Theatre of the Empire of Great Britaine, Presenting an Exact Geography of the Kingdomes of England, Scotland, Ireland,* London: William Hall, 1611.

Stacey, H. C. *Walden's Saffron – Crocus sativus: an historical study of the plant which gave Walden its prefix name 'Saffron',* Saffron Walden: H. C. Stacey, 1973.

Sumption, Jonathan. *The Age of Pilgrimage: the Medieval Journey to God*, London: Faber, 2003.

Theophrastus, '*De odoribus*', in Vol. II of *Enquiry into Plants*, Loeb Classical Library, 1926.

Thirsk, Joan. *Alternative Agriculture: A History from the Black Death to the Present Day,* Oxford: Oxford University Press, 1997.

Thompson, Hilary. *A History of Gerrans and Portscatho 1700-1830,* Truro: Thompson, 1991.

Thompson, Hilary. *A History of the Parish of Gerrans: Part 3, Village Life 1800–1914,* Porscatho: Hilary Thompson, 2005.

Thrush, Andrew; and Ferris, John P. (eds.). *The House of Commons 1604–1629,* Cambridge: Cambridge University Press, 2010.

Toussaint-Samat, M. *A History of Food,* translated by Anthea Bell, London: Blackwell Publishing, 2008.

Turner, Robert. *Botanologia: the British Physician or the Nature and Vertues of English Plants,* London: Obadiah Blagrave, 1687.

Wale, Henry John, *My Grandfather's Pocket-book, from A.D. 1701–1796,* London: Chapman

and Hall, 1883.
Webb, Andrew. 'This is what it's like to farm the world's most expensive spice', *Vice.com*, 15 October 2015 < https://www.vice.com/en/article/4xb7dd/this-is-what-its-like-to-farm-the-worlds-most-expensive-spice >
Webb, Diana. *Medieval European Pilgrimage, c.700–c.1500*, Basingstoke: Palgrave, 2002.
Wilson, C. Anne. 'I'll Take to Thee a Simnel Bring', *Petit Propos Culinaires*, 19, 1985.
Wilson, C. Anne. 'Ritual, From and Colour in the Medieval Food Tradition', in *Food and Society: The Appetite and the Eye*, edited by C. Anne Wilson, Edinburgh: Edinburgh University Press, 1991.
Wilson, C. Anne. *Water of Life. A History of Wine-Distilling and Spirits 500 BC to AD 2000*, Totnes: Prospect Books, 2006.
Woolgar, C. M. *Household Accounts from Medieval England*, Oxford: OUP, 1992.
Woolgar, C. M. 'Medieval Food & Colour', *Journal of Medieval History*, 2018, 44 (1): 1-20.
Worgan, George B. *General View of the Agriculture of the County of Cornwall*, London: G. & W. Nicol, 1811.

Culinary

Allen, Mary L. *Five O'Clock Tea*, London: Kegan, Paul, Trench & Co, 1887.
Anon. *The good Huswifes Handmaide for the Kitchin* (digital text and notes by Sam Wallace, 2006), London, 1594.
Anon. *The Indian Cookery Book*, Calcutta: Thacker, Spink & Co, 1880.
Anon. *The Lady's Companion: or, an infallible guide to the fair sex. Containing, rules, directions, and observations, for their conduct and behaviour*, London: T. Read, 1740.
Austin, Thomas (ed.). *Two Fifteenth Century Cookery Books*, London: N. Turner & Co, 1888.
Beeton, Isabella. *The Book of Household Management*, London: S. O. Beeton, 1861.
Blencowe, Ann. *The Receipt Book of Ann Blencowe AD 1694*, London: The Adelphi, 1925.
Brears, Peter. *Cooking and Dining in Medieval England*, Totnes: Prospect Books, 2012.
Brillat-Savarin, Jean Anthelme. *The Physiology of Taste (1825)*, translated by Anne Drayton, London: Penguin, 1994.
Byron, May. *May Byron's Cake Book*, London: Hodder and Stoughton, 1915.
Clutton, Angela. *The Vinegar Cupboard*, London: Bloomsbury, 2019.
Coulton, G.G. and Power, Eileen (eds). *The Goodman of Paris (Le Ménagier de Paris)*, London: Routledge & Sons, 1928.
David, Elizabeth. *Spices, Salt and Aromatics in the English Kitchen*, London: Penguin, 1975.
David, Elizabeth. *English Bread and Yeast Cookery*, London: Allen Lane/Penguin, 1977.
Dawson, Thomas. *The Good Housewife's Jewell*, London: John Wolfe, 1587.
Dey, I.R. *Indian Cookery and Confectionery (407 recipes)*, Calcutta: D.C. Dey, 1920.
Digby, Sir Kenelm. *The Closet of Sir Kenelm Digby Knight Opened*, edited by Anne McDonnell, London: Phillip Lee Warner, 1911.
Edwards, Jonathan. *The Roman Cookery of Apicius*, London: Random House, 1993.
Evelyn, John. *Acetaria : A Discourse of Sallets* (second edition), London: Rob Scot, 1706.
Francatelli, Charles Elmé. *The Modern Cook*, London: S. & J. Bentley, 1846.
Francatelli, Charles Elmé. *A Plain Cookery Book for the Working Classes (1852)*, Stroud: The History Press, 2010.
Glasse, Hannah. *The Art of Cookery Made Plain and Easy (1747)*, Totnes: Prospect Books, 2012.

Bibliography

Glasse, Hannah and Wilson, Maria. *The Complete Confectioner,* London: West and Hughes, 1800.

Heard, Vida. *Cornish Cookery, Recipes of Today and Yesteryear*, Trewolsta: Dyllansow Truan, 1984.

Hervey, Henrietta A. *Anglo-Indian Cookery at Home: A Short Treatise for Returned Exiles, London: Horace Cox, 1895.*

Jack, Florence B. *Cookery for Every Household,* London: Thomas Nelson, 1914.

Markham, Gervase. *The English Housewife,* edited by Michael R. Best, Montreal: McGill-Queen's University Press, 1998.

Martin, Edith. *Cornish Recipes: Ancient and Modern,* Truro: A. W. Jordan, 1930.

Merrick, Hettie. *Pasties and Cream: Memories and Recipes from a Cornish Childhood*, St Agnes: Truan, 2010.

Pegge, Samuel. *Forme of Cury (1390)*, edited by Samuel Pegge, Forgotten Books, 2008.

Raffald, Elizabeth. *The Experienced English Housekeeper*, London: W. Osborne and T. Griffin, 1794.

Riddell, Robert Flower. *Indian Domestic Economy and Receipt Book,* Madras: D. P. L. C. Connor, 1853.

Riley, Gillian. *The Oxford Companion to Italian Food*, Oxford: Oxford University Press, 2007.

Rose, Giles. *A Perfect School of Instructions for the Officers of the Mouth*, London: R. Bentley, 1683.

Sevilla, Maria Jose. *Delicioso: A History of Food in Spain*, London: Reaktion Books, 2019.

Smith, Eliza. *The Compleat Housewife: Or, Accomplish'd Gentlewoman's Companion*, Williamsburg: William Parks, 1742.

Toklas, Alice B. *The Alice B. Toklas Cookbook*, London: Serif, 2004.

Ude, Louis Eustache. *The French Cook*, London: John Ebers, 1822.

W. M. *The Queens Closet Opened Incomparable Secrets in Physick, Chyrurgery, Preserving, and Candying*, London: Nath. Brooke, 1659.

Webb, Diana. *Medieval European Pilgrimage, c.700-c.1500*, Basingstoke: Palgrave, 2002.

Wey, William. *The Itineraries of William Wey, fellow of Eton college. To Jerusalem, AD 1458 and AD 1462; and to Saint James of Compostella, AD 1456. From the original manuscript in the Bodleian library*, London: J. B. Nichols and sons, 1857.

Woods, Liz. *Cornish Feasts and Festivals*, Penzance: Alison Hodge, 2013.

Woolley, Hannah. *The Queen-Like Closet; or, Rich cabinet stored with all manner of rare receipts for preserving, candying & cookery*, London: R. Lowndes, 1670.

Woolley, Hannah. *The Gentlewoman's Companion or, a Guide to the Female Sex*, Totnes: Prospect Books, 2001.

Archives

Bedfordshire Archives (BA)
L5/1091. Lease: 21 yrs, 1567

Buckinghamshire County Archives (BCA)
D-CN/9/10/1/3. Lease for fourteen years, 1 Feb 1692

Cambridgeshire County Archives (CCA)
KP96/1/1. Ickleton Parish Church Register 1558-1693
71/T101. 'Copy of the probate of the will (13 December 1711) of Richard Tunwell of Great Shelford, wheelwright'

BIBLIOGRAPHY

Essex Records Office (ERO)
D/DBa T2/11. Will of John Bataill
D/ACR5/107/2. Registered copy of will of John Turnour, 1565
D/ACR4/183/4. Registered copy of will of Roger Newman, 7 January 1542
D/DGh T29. 'Deeds', 1595-1599
D/Dtu 164. 'Deed' 27 October 1627
Q/SR 103/18,19. Indictments' 11 November 1587
Q/SR 103/15. Indictments' 11 November 1587
Q/SR 76/22. Examinations, 15 September 1580

Gloucestershire Heritage Hub (GHH)
D760/9. Garden ground, between meadow of Edward Wilson, gent., and a lane. [Endorsed: Saffron Garden], 1668
D1957/T1. Properties in Church St., Mill St., the Bull Ring, "behind Avon nigh to Tewkesbury Mill", Wayte Lane and Walker's Lane (Geast Charity); Barton St. (Hicks Charity); Severn Ham (Porter & Kemble Charity); the Great Garden & Hopyard or Gt. Saffron Garden, and Severn Ham (Slaughter Charity), 1614–1864

Kresen Kernow Archives (KKA)
TF/567. Lease of Saffron Meadow, Fowey, 1 December 1653
TF/568. Lease of Saffron Meadow, Fowey, 9 December 1697
EN/472. Lease, Saffron Meadows, part of Nampity tenement, Church Town, Gerrans, 29 September 1711
CF/1/210. Lease, five fields in Tregorrick, St Austell, 25 Mar 1793
DCNEW/243/47. Letter dated 26 December 1917
DCNEWQ/243/79. Letter dated 3 January 1918
DCNEW/243/43. Letter dated 26 December 1917
AR/37/41/1. Account roll, receiver of John de Dynham junior
AR/37/44. Account roll, steward of John de Dynham, knight

Suffolk Archives (SA)
HB8/5/327. 'Bailey House/Lavenham Hall in Lavenham and ground called Saffron Pens in Lavenham and Acton'; C/3/10/2/10/4 'Annuity of 26 13s 4d [the 'Brooks Annuity'] out of messuage and land in Ipswich and Bramford'
HB8/5/101. 'Land called Saffron in Coddenham'

West Sussex Archives (WSA)
Add MSS 37193. 'A Particular of the Deeds, Writings and Papers of the Apuldram and Binderton Es-tates lately the jointure of Lady Milard, delivered to Joseph Cranmer'

Manuscripts

Sloane MS 4046, Sloane MS 4048, Sloane MS 4049: Sir Hans Sloane, Baronet: Original correspondence, chronologically arranged (British Library)
Tallamy, Rebecca. Wellcome, MS.4759, 1735–1739

Recipe Index

Recipe	Page
Almond Furmity	221-2
Almond Milk	275
Almond Pudding	222-4
Aloes of Lamb with Verde Sawse	115-6
Apricot Cake	138-40
Autumnal Tart	244
Baba au Rhum	224-7
Brie or Camembert Tart	250-1
Chicken Quorema	163-5
Chickpea & Saffron Dip	248
Courgette & Ginger Soup	247-8
Curd Pancakes	228-9
Daffodil Cocktail	266
Fennel Pollen Halibut & Fennel Broth	183-4
Fish & Spinach Pie with Saffron Seaweed Mash	184-6
Fragrant Egg Curry	170
Gilded Chicken with Hazelnut Bread Sauce	203-5
Gold Cup Cakes with Saffron Icing	137-8
Golden 'Apples' with Apple & Almond Sauce	118-20
Golden Bhoonee Kitcheeree	168-9
Grilled Gingery Oysters	187-9
Gyngerbrede (A Fairing of Sorts)	140-3
Ham Hock Terrine & Pickled Pears	121-4
Haricot Bean & Mackerel Salad	193
Herby Veal Stew with Almond Milk	116-7
Hypocras Cocktail	268
Hypocras Syrup	272
Lamb or Mutton 'Koftas'	165-8
Lamb Shanks in Spiced Ale	124-5
Marinated Pork Chops with Saffron Mustard Sauce	126-8
Marinated Sole Goujons	199-200
Milk Braised Chicken Thighs with Garlic & Saffron	206-7
Mussels with Leeks, Almond Milk & Saffron	189-93
Mutton or Lamb and Mango Curry	173-4
Onion & Almond Soup	254-7
Pasternak Fritters with Verde Sawse	251-3
Pea Tarts with a Parmesan Crust	257-9
Pheasant & Chorizo Stew	207-10
Pilchard Pasties	194-5
Pineapple Pilau	174-5
Pork & Fig Tart	128-30
Powder Douce	276
Powder Fort	275-6
Prawn and Cucumber Curry	179-80
Rhenish Cream	230
Rhubarb Syrup	271
Risshewes	143-4
Saffron & Orange Blossom Soufflé	233-5
Saffron & Seaweed Butter	279-80
Saffron Cinnamon Buns	152
Saffron Drizzle Seed Cake	145-7
Saffron Hot Cross Buns	160
Saffron Hot Water Crust Pastry	278-9
Saffron Macaroons	147-8
Saffron Rough Puff Pastry	277-8
Saffron Short Crust Pastry	276-7
Saffron Tea	268-71
Saffron Vinaigrette	280
Sarah Harrison's Saffron Cakes	151-2
Seared Pigeon Breast	217-8
Simnel Pudding	238-41
Simple Sugar Syrup	271-2
Skink with Kale & Barley	133-4
Spice Cake or Simnel Cake	155-7
Spiced Apple Fritters	237-8
Spiced Venison Stew & Dumplings	211-2
St Keverne Feast Cakes	157-8
Strawberry & Saffron Tarts	241-3
Tamarind Fish with Spicy Wedges	176-9
Traditional Saffron Buns	158-60
Trespassers Pie	213-7
Trout Fillets with Almonds & Currants	195-9
Usquebaugh	265-6
Vegetarian Toad in the Hole	260-2

General Index

A New Treatise of Husbandry (Trowell), 58
Accomplisht Cook, The (May), 76
Acetaria: A Discourse of Sallets (Evelyn), 280
adulteration (of saffron), 63-5
Alexander, William, 97
Apicius, Marcus Gavius, 29, 126, 272
Aragon, 27
Art of Cookery, The (Glasse), 85, 222
Art of Distillation, The (French), 70
Astonishing History of Troy Town, The (Quiller Couch), 82
Audley End House, 40-1
Avienus, 33

Beeton, Isabella, 98
Black Death, 33-4
Blencow, Ann, 70
Blith, Walter, 105
Bodey, Andrew, 102
Book of Dishes (*Kitāb al-Tabīkh*), 86-7
Bradley, Richard, 34, 35-8, 46, 54-5, 58-61, 64, 96, 103
Bradwell, Stephen, 69
Brillat-Savarin, Jean Anthelme, 86
British Medical Journal, 98
Brydges, James, 36-7
Bryene, Alice de, 88
Byron, May, 93

Cake Book (Byron), 93
Calendula officinalis, 63
Cambridge University, 35, 36, 89
Camden, William, 39, 43, 51
Canterbury Tales (Chaucer), 72
Carr, Robert, 43
Carter, Charles, 199
Carthamus tinctorius ('Bastard Saffron'), 23, 63, 64

Charles I, 41, 49
Charles II, 40, 73
Chaucer, Geoffrey, 72
Cheshire Saffron Company, 104
China, 34, 103
Chronicles of England, Scotland and Ireland (Holinshed), 13, 23
Clarke, Joseph, 96-7
Clarke, William, 53-4, 56, 57-9, 62, 64
Clerk, John, 69, 75
Codex Calixtinus, 27
Coke, Edward, 44
Compleat Florist, The (Liger), 12
Compleat Housewife, The (Smith), 72
Complete Confectioner, The, 228, 230
corm, 10, 14, 18, 31, 33, 34, 37-8, 48, 55-6, 61-2, 100, 101-3
Cornish Recipes: Ancient and Modern (Martin), 140, 194
Cornish Saffron Company, 48, 183
Cornwall, 32-4, 47-50, 80, 81-3, 89, 93, 99, 100, 102, 111, 140, 157, 158, 194
Country Housewife, The (Bradley), 58
Creighton, Oswin, 80
Crocologia (Hertodt), 56, 65, 70
Crocus sativus, 13, 14, 15, 18, 29, 48, 96
croker, 41, 55, 60, 61-2, 95-6, 100, 101-4
Cromarty, Dorothy, 22, 23, 39
Croydon, 28-9, 31
'Culex' (Virgil), 30
Culpeper, Nicholas, 20, 68
Cunliffe, Barry, 30

d'Ewes, Simonds, 44
Dale, Samuel, 61
David, Elizabeth, 65, 110, 145, 158, 159
Dawson, Thomas, 84, 121, 279
Description of England (Harrison), 23, 41
Devereux, Robert, 43

Index

Digby, Kenelm, 74
Diodorus Siculus, 33
Domesday Book, 22, 28
Douglass, James, 37, 38, 54, 56, 57, 59, 60, 61, 62, 96
Duffy's Elixir, 72

Edmonds, Richard, 33
Edward III, 23
Edward IV, 69, 75
Edward VI, 23
Ellis, William, 55, 56
English Improver Improved, The (Blith), 105
Essex, 13, 18, 22, 23, 25, 28, 39, 41-3, 46, 58, 60, 61, 96, 100, 105, 145
Evelyn, John, 39, 280
Eyers, Brian and Margaret, 48

Fancy Ices (Marshall), 94
Feate of Gardeninge, The (Gardener), 37
Fèvre, Nicolas le, 73
First World War, 79
Five Hundred Points of Good Husbandrie (Tusser), 38
Forme of Cury, 118, 121, 128, 183, 189, 195, 211, 244, 248, 250, 251
Francatelli, Charles Elmé, 76, 207, 268
Freke, Elizabeth, 71, 72, 74, 75, 76
French, John, 70

Galen, 11, 68, 69, 70
Gardener, John, 37-8
George I, 36, 41
George II, 36, 265
Gerard, John, 38, 67, 71
Glasse, Hannah, 85, 145, 222-3, 228, 230
Good Housewife's Jewell, The (Dawson), 84, 121
Great Cordial, 73-4

Hakluyt, Richard, 23-4, 28

Harrison, Sarah, 85, 151, 152, 238
Harrison, William, 13, 23, 24, 33, 41, 51, 54, 55, 56, 61-2, 63, 65, 95, 104
Hartman, George, 74
Hawkey, Charlotte, 48, 49
Heard, Vida, 47, 48, 99, 109-10
Henry II, 63
Henry IV, 92
Henry VIII, 22-3, 41, 45
Herbal (Gerard), 38, 71
Herbal Delights (Leyel), 98
Hertodt, Johann Ferdinand, 56, 65, 70
Hippocrates, 68, 272
Holy Land, 24, 25, 27, 34
Housekeeper's Pocket Book, The (Harrison), 85
Howard, Charles, 38-9, 54-5, 59
Howell, James, 43, 44

Indian Cookbook, The, 163, 169
Indian Cookery and Confectionery (Dey), 174
Indian Domestic Economy (Riddell), 93, 165, 170, 173
Inquiry into Plants (Theophrastus), 29
International Standards Organisation, 66

James I, 73
Jerusalem, 24, 25, 26-7, 86

Knott, John, 96

La Mancha, 27, 38, 99, 104
Land of Cockayne, 21
Larkin, William, 44
laudanum, 76-7
Leyel, Hilda, 14, 98
Liger, Louis, 12
Linton, 46

Mandeville, John, 24-5
Marshall, Agnes B., 94

Index

Martin, Edith, 81, 140, 194
materia medica, 68, 97
Maurier, Daphne du, 99
May, Robert, 76
Ménagier de Paris, Le, 91, 92
Metamophoses (Ovid), 12
Mildmay, Grace, 69, 76
Moryson, Fynes, 43

Natura exenterata (Philiatros), 70
Nature of Man, The (Hippocrates), 68
New Improvements of Planting and Gardening (Bradley), 37
Neale, Kenneth, 39, 55

'Of the kind of saffron' (Gardener), 38
Ora Maritima (Avienus), 33
Overbury, Thomas, 43-4
Ovid, 12

Panda, Himadri, 99
Pepys, Samuel, 75
Periplus of the Erythraean Sea, The, 31
Petronius, 39
Philiatros, 70
Philosophical Transactions, 38
Phoenicia, 31, 32-4
Physick for the Sicknesse, Commonly called the Plague (Bradwell), 69
Platina, Bartolomeo, 23
Pliny the Elder, 29, 31, 37, 61, 63, 65, 67, 76, 98
Principall Navigations, The (Hakluyt), 24

Queen Anne, 36
Queen Caroline, 265
Queen-Like Closet, The (Woolley), 133, 221
Queen's Closet Opened, The (W.M.), 76
Quiller Couch, Arthur, 82

Raleigh, Walter, 34, 72-4
Richard II, 23, 89

Richard III, 87
Riddell, Robert Flower, 93, 165, 170, 173
Royal Society, 35, 36, 37-8, 54,

Saffron Walden, 13, 18, 22-5, 28, 31, 32, 39-41, 42, 46, 51, 55, 58, 96, 97, 100
Saffronology, 99
Spices, Salt and Aromatics in the English Kitchen (David), 145
Satyricon (Petronius), 30
Shakespeare, William, 87
Simnel cake, 85-6, 155-7, 238-41
Sloane, Hans, 35-7, 60
Smale, David, 65, 100
Smith, Eliza, 72, 266
Spain, 18, 27, 32, 34, 38, 43, 50, 64, 86, 99

Theophrastus, 29
Thirsk, Joan, 34, 40, 96, 97, 98, 99, 101
Trowell, Samuel, 58
Turner, Anne, 42-4
Tusser, Thomas, 38
Two Fifteenth Century Cookery Books, 90, 115, 116, 118, 143, 187, 206, 211, 241, 254

Ude, Louis Eustache, 233
UNESCO, 26

Valencia, 27
Venice, 27
Virgil, 30

Wale, Henry John, 53-4, 101
Wales, 82, 97
Waller, William Chapman, 39
Wesley, John, 82-3
Wey, William, 27-8
William III, 41
Wilson, C. Anne, 34, 91,
Winter's Tale, The (Shakespeare), 87
Woolley, Hannah, 93, 133, 221